GW01270622

The Political Economy of Soviet Socialism: The Formative Years, 1918-1928

The Political Economy of Soviet Socialism: The Formative Years, 1918-1928

Peter J. Boettke

Foreword by
Yuri N. Maltsev
formerly of The Institute of Economics, Academy of Sciences of the USSR

Kluwer Academic Publishers
Boston/Dordrecht/London

Distributors for North America:
Kluwer Academic Publishers
101 Philip Drive
Assinippi Park
Norwell, MA 02061 USA

Distributors for all other countries:
Kluwer Academic Publishers Group
Distribution Centre
Post Office Box 322
3300 AH Dordrecht, THE NETHERLANDS

Library of Congress Cataloging-in-Publication Data

Boettke, Peter J.
The political economy of Soviet socialism: the formative years, 1918-1928 / Peter J. Boettke
p. cm.
Includes bibliographical references.
ISBN 0-7923-9100-4
1. Communism—Soviet Union—History—20th century. 2. Soviet Union—Economic policy—1917-1928. 3. Soviet Union-Politics and government—1917-1936. I. Title.
HX313.B58 1990
335.43'0947'09042-dc20 90-4172
CIP

Printed in the United States of America.

To Rosemary, with all my love.

Contents

About the Author

Peter J. Boettke, assistant professor of economics at New York University, received his Ph.D. in economics from George Mason University, where he was a Claude R. Lambe Research Fellow of the Center for the Study of Market Processes. He has held faculty positions at George Mason University and Oakland University. He is the former managing editor of *Market Process*, the academic publication of the Center for the Study of Market Processes. His research has been published in various journals and books, including *Research in the History of Economic Thought and Methodology*, *Critical Review*, *Journal of Economic Perspectives*, and *A Nation in Debt.*

Foreword

by Yuri N. Maltsev
formerly of the Institute of Economics,
Academy of Sciences of the USSR

The following study on the history of Soviet economic thought during the first years after the Bolshevik Revolution of 1917 is much more than the regular academic scribble on this turbulent period of modern history. It is a systematic treatise on economic theory. Interdisciplinary in nature, it discusses the central problems of political economy and provides the serious reader with deep insight and complete understanding of the greatest event of the twentieth century: the rise and fall of communism.

The foundations of the economic system that we see today in a state of full-fledged crisis were laid during the first ten years of the communist regime in the Soviet Union. The symptoms and manifestations of this crisis have been cogently described elsewhere. The author should be credited for his appraisal and illumination of the real causes, both economic and moral, of the great drama of our times. At the end of the treatise, it is absolutely clear that only by means of economic theory is it possible to organize and interpret seemingly chaotic historical and statistical data, isolated facts, and opinions that constitute the mass media's coverage of an overly complex array of events in the USSR.

A number of scholars whose views and positions are critically treated by the author have provided interesting analyses of the Soviet economic system, drawing on the history of past attempts to construct a "working model" of socialism, then to restructure and reform this system after it became obvious that the model was not working. Much less attention has been paid, however, to the theoretical and methodological problems involved in construction of the centrally planned economy and liquidation of the market system.

The response of the Soviet ruling class to the deteriorating economy and societal alienation was the program of reforms known as *perestroika*, which was initiated in 1985 and significantly amended in 1987 and 1989. In light of the stakes involved, it is urgent to accurately understand the nature of the declared reforms and the prospects for their success; such understanding is possible only on the basis of sound economic theory.

The spectacular failure to date of the "radical" economic reforms in the USSR has been due to the unwillingness or inability of Mikhail Gorbachev's administration to part with the obsolete and economically destructive Marxist-Leninist ideology and its economic doctrine. Mr. Gobachev and other spokesmen of the Communist Party do not make a secret that their commitment is not to abandon but to "better and improve" the current system. They view the socialist system as progressive and correct; its failures in practice result from a lack of discipline and a deviation from the Marxist-Leninist principles. The package of economic reforms adopted by the Central Committee of the party in June 1987 is aimed towards "perfection of the economic mechanism," and it included measures that at best can be considered inadequate to deal with the present situation. Designed by departmental bureaucrats and their academic assistants, with a complete disregard of economic theory, these measures were rubber-stamped by an inexperienced and economically incompetent government, which was easily deceived by the radical talk of the new ministry heads. The effect of these "reforms" on the economy has been disastrous. They have seriously undermined the vertical system of management of the economy, but have failed to replace it with horizontal linkages between enterprises. While the set of "negative" incentives for managers no longer works (discipline was maintained by fear of being relieved of one's duties or even of the party membership card), the positive incentives have failed to appear.

The real character of the so-called centrally planned economy is well illustrated by the fact that a fully balanced, checked, and detailed economic plan for the next year can theoretically be ready, with the help of computers, in about 30,000 years. There are tens of millions of product variants and hundreds of thousands of enterprises. It is necessary to make many billions of decisions in order to substitute for the market. The plans must relate both to outputs and inputs, involving billions of intermediate products; labor norms; wage rates; normatives for costs, prices, and profits; "planned return on investments"; and other things. Because next year's plan must be ready by next year, and not in 29,999 years, it is inevitably neither balanced nor disaggregated. It is not a plan in any meaningful sense of the term.[1]

But the large number of decisions and variables is not socialism's worst problem. There are two deeper problems: First, what actually thwarts the planner is not that the set of decisions and variables is large but that it is open-ended; it comprises knowledge and future discoveries that are (and will be) dispersed throughout society in incomplete and even inarticulate form. As such, it is unavailable to the planners. Second, even if this information were in principle knowable, the planners would be impotent anyway, because without real market prices, which provide a common, cardinal denominator for disparate things, they could not calculate the economic implications of the countless possible courses of action. Socialist planning, as Ludwig von Mises demonstrated in his classic *Socialism* (1922) and as Professor Boettke emphasizes, is *logically impossible* because the system cannot provide the knowledge required to determine which production projects are desirable and feasible and which are not. Only the market, with what Mises called its "intellectual division of labor," can generate that knowledge and put it in a usable form. The Soviets actually learned this early on. As is underlined by Professor Boettke in his conclusion,

> Not since war communism have the Soviets sought to realize the Marxian dream of a completely rational economic society so persistently, because that vision is a hopeless and unachievable utopia. The choice of development strategy was certainly shaped by ideology, but the consistent quest to abolish posthaste market methods of allocation was abandoned. Instead, a state capitalist system of economic management was instituted. Even at the height of the Stalin regime no attempt was made to achieve the Marxist utopia of a moneyless, comprehensively planned economic order. Thus, *perestroika* does not represent a move away from the ideal form of central planning—that move was made over 60 years ago.[2]

The so-called "political economy of socialism," formulated by Joseph Stalin after the bloody purge of his Marxist opponents, whose views are so clearly exposed in this book, is still considered to be the sacrosanct "theoretical" foundation of economic policy and applied economic analysis in the USSR. It is nothing, however, but a collection of political slogans discredited by harsh economic realities. For example, according to the "political economy of socialism," the main economic law is the "Law of the Complete Fulfillment of the Rising Needs and Requirements of the People." Other "basic laws" include the "Law of Remuneration According to the Quality and Quantity of the Work Performed," the "Law of Planned and Proportionate Development of the Socialist Economy," the "Law of Reproduction of the Population on the Basis of Rising Standards of Life and Constant Improvements of Living and Working Conditions," and so on.

It is a testimony to the strictures and rigidity of economic theory in the USSR that much of the ferment of *perestroika* has involved little more than heated discussions about these Orwellian "laws." Some Soviet scholars argue, for example, that these "laws" can implement themselves only through the rational conscious activities of the planners. Others oppose this view on the grounds that is is contrary to the Marxist-Leninist assumption of the independence of production relations (objective phenomena) from the will and mentality of the people (subjective phenomena). The absurdity of the current situation in Soviet economic science is manifested by the existence of the third "school," which insists that economic laws can exist but not operate.[3] None of these "scientific" discussions have helped increase the supply of goods on Soviet shelves. Instead, the obsolete theories are a significant part of the problem.

Another basic problem is that for the last seventy years, Western economics has been depicted in the USSR as "bourgeois vulgar political economy," and as a result, the vast majority of Soviet economists are unfamiliar with even its basic tenets. The old and discredited dogmas of Soviet economics are perpetuated by the system of higher education and academic training. The few Soviet economists who are acquainted with modern economics have no access to the decision-making process, which is still dominated by economists like Abel Aganbegyan, Leonid Abalkin, Boris Milner, and other economic advisers to the government who may pretend to be reformers, but still fall within the Marxist-Leninist mainstream.

All of these factors, as well as the opposition of hard-line *apparatchiks* to any kind of reforms (even the piecemeal ones) and widespread public confusion caused by the still-prevailing egalitarian thinking, have led to the serious deterioration of an already stagnant economy. The "command" economy was disrupted by 1987, while the market economy failed to appear because of the inconsistency of the reform package and complete disregard of economic theory.

The lack of sound economic theory is compounded by a complete absence of reliable economic and social statistics. Until recently, statistics were treated as a form of economic propaganda and as such, were used mostly to illustrate the "achievements" of economic and social policy. Even today, official statistics are based on often deliberately falsified reports of the ministries, republics, regions, districts, and enterprises, which are inclined to report economic indices in a way that is beneficial to them. The existing statistical methodology of the national accounts in the USSR is based on the simple adding up of the value of all material outputs at their stated prices. Services and other "nonmaterial" incomes are not included. This approach, based on the Marxist concept of "productive" and "nonproductive" labor, leads to some paradoxes. The dentist, for example, is a "nonproductive" individual, while the dental technician is a "productive" one.

Because of the complete absence of reliable economic statistics (DIA-CIA estimates, for example, are no more reliable when they are based on the official Soviet statistics[4]), it is impossible to quantify the depth of the economic and social crisis in the Soviet Union. Meanwhile, desperate economic adventurism based on a strange mixture of Marxism, Keynesianism, and "common sense" is assuming larger and larger proportions. The Council of Ministers of the USSR is issuing new, senseless economic decrees and regulations at an accelerated speed of 2,000 per year, compared to "only" 500 to 700 per year during the Brezhnev "stagnation" years of 1965 to 1982. As the Soviet economist O. Bogomolov recently admitted, "The final choice in favor of the market has not been made."[5] The time for such a decision is expiring.

When industries are monopolized by government ministries and enterprises, costs do not reflect final prices, nor do costs reflect anything except local or departmental bureaucratic interests. Centrally planned investment decisions, as well as the government campaigns against so-called "duplication and parallelism" of the 1960s and '70s, led the government ministries to assert nearly complete control over every industry. Moreover, Soviet prices are distorted by huge subsidies (104 billion rubles in 1989), on the one hand, and heavy indirect "turnover" taxes (105 billion rubles), on the other. These taxes sometimes contribute from 90 percent (cars) to 95 percent (alcoholic beverages) of the retail price. This situation completely disrupts normal functioning of the economy and distorts the picture to the point of complete irrationalism.

The eighteen million bureaucrats employed by the system still are "substituting for the market," determining everything in the sphere of production, distribution, and consumption. The results: 234 out of 277 basic consumer goods included by the USSR State Committee on Statistics in the "market basket" of the Soviet people are absent from the shelves, and the power of the bureaucrats has increased enormously. Given such a system, there is no room for hope that in the foreseeable future the needs of the consumer will influence what is to be produced.

The unique economic and political structures of the USSR and Eastern Europe, the level of their economic development, and the forms of the social organization there make them a separate and very different group in the world economy. So it is conventional wisdom today to observe that "thus far no society has yet made the transition from communism to capitalism" and "therefore there are no models" for what Eastern Europe and the Soviet Union wish to do. This may be a cliche, or a polemical point, but it does not rate as objective economic theory.

Although there are "no models" in the sense of absolute precedent, there certainly exists a body of empirical, hands-on experience in regard to political and economic reform that is both current and relevant: Spain, Taiwan, and Korea, for example, were single-party, authoritarian, statist regimes with centralized, directed economies that have undergone reform; as a result they are more democratic, pluralist, multiparty societies and market-oriented economies with proven track records of extraordinary development and growth. While Taiwan, Korean, and Spain have not transited from communism to capitalism, they can selectively provide pragmatic examples of a step-by-step successful transition to dynamic, productive, and influential societies increasingly integrated into the international economic system.

Many of the same people who see no models also counsel going slowly, "phasing in" freedom, rather than taking the always-reviled path of radical and comprehensive social change. Gradualism and piecemeal change are held up as the sober, practical, responsible, and compassionate path of reform, avoiding the sudden shocks, painful distortions, and unemployment brought by radical change. As is obvious from the Soviet experience, gradual reform provides a convenient excuse to the vested interests of the party and state bureaucrats to change nothing at all. Combine these interests with the standard resistance to change endemic under socialism, and meaningful change is reduced to mere rhetoric.

As well, it is necessary to differentiate among the diverse Eastern European states in regard to where each is going and how each is getting there. As long as the USSR maintains the primacy of the communist party and a single-party system and has not attempted serious steps toward introduction of genuine economic reform, there is even less comparability between Soviet and Eastern European reforms than there is within Eastern Europe or between it and Western Europe.

Finally, in addition to providing relevant experience in regard to the specific mechanics of economic reform, perhaps the most significant contribution that Taiwan, Korea, and Spain can make is their historical experience in regard to the interrelationship and timing of economic and political reforms. Economic reforms generate rising expectations, which inevitably surpass the pace of perceived change in the quality of life. There comes a point when those rapidly rising economic expectations cannot be met. It is then that political reforms become critical, for they can channel the energies of a dynamic society constructively into democratic, pluralistic political participation in the overall reform process and thereby relieve some of the unrealistic pressures on economic reformers to change the quality of life instantly. Further, they can provide the necessary consensus to sustain economic reform during difficult times. The failure of the Chinese leadership to understand this interdependence between economic and political reform, and its unwillingness to share power through democratic change, resulted in the setback we witnessed in the People's Republic in 1989.

It appears that the economic collapse experienced by the USSR and Eastern Europe can have the same effect on their societies as military defeat had on Germany, Italy, and Japan. The main problem of all the Eastern European countries and the USSR is to make the transition from a command economy to economic freedom, which implies private property, market allocation of resources, and democratic management of the transition within the rule of law.

One of the most important questions of the transition is that of the economic role of the state, particularly regarding the optimal quantity of "public goods," which today contribute from 62 percent (in Poland) to 81 percent (in the USSR) of the national income of the "Soviet bloc." The proper functions of government, and the desirable size and nature of government regulation, expenditure, and taxes, are matters of hot public debate in all of Eastern Europe and the USSR. The prevailing view shared by genuine reformers in Eastern Europe is that this role must be dramatically diminished, if not eliminated.

As a natural reaction to the statist practices and ideologies that dominated these countries for the last 40 to 70 years, the economic mentality of the reformers is more influenced by libertarian thinkers than it is in the West. Ideas originated by Ludwig von Mises and F.A. Hayek, whom Dr. Boettke draws on amply in his book, have greater appeal in the Soviet Union and Eastern Europe than those of Paul Samuelson and John Kenneth Galbraith. This can only be for the good.

It is obvious now even to the most staunch defenders of "socialism" in Eastern

Europe and the United States that it is absolutely hopeless to try to induce state enterprises to be efficient or to pay real attention to costs. Only genuine private companies can be truly responsive to profit-and-loss incentives. Moreover, the only genuine price system, reflecting costs and profit opportunities, consists of prices arising from real markets and not from bureaucratic "price calculations."

Many who have considered the problem of transition believe that the basis for the accumulation of capital has been undermined in Eastern Europe and the Soviet Union, that people don't have the money to purchase the mountain of state-held capital assets, and that it seems almost impossible for the state to price such assets correctly if we keep in mind that compared to the world market, most of the assets have negative value. A worthwhile idea for radically privatizing the means of production has been provided by Professor Murray N. Rothbard. He has noted that besides the lack of money to buy the assets, there is the moral question of why the Soviet subjects should have to pay the state anything after having suffered at its hands for so long. Rothbard proposes that the present users of assets be recognized as "homesteaders" and be granted pro-rata negotiable shares of ownership in the state enterprises. This would set off a market for ownership shares, the price of which would change according to the market's estimation of their productivity. This proposal contains many complex problems yet to be worked out, but it nonetheless merits close study. It has the virtue of removing the state's impediments in one shot and quickly channeling resourses and effort into productive activities. Professor Rothbard properly reminds us that the "miracle" of West German recovery after the devastation of World War II occurred because wage and price controls were abolished overnight.

An urgent discussion is now going on in the West about how to best assist the USSR in the effort to reform its crippled economy. The best form that Western assistance can take is a thorough, dispassionate economic analysis of the Soviets' situation and an economic theory of transition to a genuine free-market system. The book I have the honor to introduce is a very important and necessary step in this direction. The truism that "nothing is more practical than a good theory" is absolutely applicable to the present situation in the USSR, whose historical experience proved that without such a theory, to paraphrase Professor Boettke, political economy leads to arbitrary opinions about the causes of and solutions to social problems.

Here is the main problem of Soviet (and not only of Soviet) economics today: the failure to understand that the mere recognition of a crisis is not enough to deal with it. As Professor Boettke argues, the Soviet experience has lessons for those in mixed economies as well; they suffer from the same "pretence of knowledge." The lesson from the history of the Soviet Union, brilliantly delivered to us by the author, is a very convincing message in favor of freedom, both political and economic.

Notes

[1] See, for example, Alec Nove, "The Problems of Perestroika," *Dissent*, Vol. 2, no. 11 (Fall 1989), p. 463.

[2] Pp. 178-9.

[3] For an overview of this discussion, see A. Nekipelov, "*Iz plena mifov i dogm*," *Kommunist*, 1989, no. 7, pp. 21-29.

[4] See, for example, Franklyn D. Holzman, "Politics and Guesswork: CIA and DIA Estimates of Soviet Military Spending," *International Security*, Vol. 14, no. 2 (Fall 1989), pp. 101-131.

[5] *Moscow News*, 1989, no. 26, p. 12.

Acknowledgments

This book is a revised version of my doctoral thesis presented to the department of economics at George Mason University in the fall of 1988. In writing this book I have benefited greatly from the support of family, friends, and institutions. My mother and father, Elinor and Fred Boettke, have been a constant source of support and encouragement not only in my scholarly endeavors, but in life as well. They taught me both the value of family and the importance of independence of mind and courage of conviction. My Aunt, Eleanor Boettke Hotte, also provided emotional and intellectual support throughout the trials and tribulations of higher education. Her open mind and keen insight into the role of the public intellectual are a constant reminder to fight against the natural incentive to comfortably hide away within the walls of the academy. My in-laws, Ernest and Rosemary Ruberg, have also been supportive of my efforts and have provided family encouragement throughout.

I was extremely fortunate to have had excellent professors throughout my education. My interest in economics and social thought is the result of Dr. Hans F. Sennholz, chairman of the department of economics at Grove City College. Dr. Sennholz introduced me to the writings of Ludwig von Mises and the Austrian school of economics, and is more responsible than any other individual for my pursuit of an academic career. The department of economics at George Mason University provided me with more than a graduate education. The faculty, in the classroom, in seminars, at lunch, and in the halls, were a constant source of intellectual stimulus. I was extremely fortunate to have been exposed as a student at George Mason University to James Buchanan, Gordon Tullock, and Kenneth Boulding. Buchanan and Boulding, in particular, have influenced my approach to learning and research tremendously: Buchanan by challenging his students to "dare to be different" and get their ideas down on paper, and Boulding by reminding his students of the joy and urgency involved in intellectual pursuits.

The Institute for Humane Studies at George Mason University provided me with financial support in the form of a summer residential fellowship in 1987, when much of the original research for this project was begun, and later grants from the Hayek Fund for Scholars to present my research at professional meetings. I would like to thank, in particular, Walter E. Grinder, vice president of academic affairs at the institute, and Jeremy Shearmur, director of studies, for their encouragement and support. The Graduate School of George Mason University also provided me with a summer fellowship in 1988, and Professor Walter Williams of George Mason University provided me with financial support during the summer of 1988. My greatest debt, both financially and educationally, is to the Center for the Study of Market Processes and its director, Jack High. Professor High provided financial support throughout my graduate career and afforded the students at the Center an atmosphere of intellectual excitement and community of purpose. Colleen Morretta should also be mentioned for her vital role in maintaining the family atmosphere around the Center. I would like to thank my friends and colleagues at the Center—Deborah Walker, Matthew Kibbe, Roy Cordato, and Karen Palasek—for their constant encouragement and for teaching me so much about economics. I would especially like to thank my friends Steven Horwitz and David L. Prychitko for providing so much intellectual feedback on various research projects. These two individuals made graduate school enjoyable and rewarding, contributing to not only this project but all my thinking, in ways that remain inarticulate. I am proud to count them as my friends and intellectual comrades.

My dissertation committee was extremely helpful in seeing me through the thesis stage and in helping shape the present project. Professors Karen I. Vaughn, Viktor Vanberg, and Ronald Jensen gave me encouraging comments and sound criticisms, all of which improved this project. Professor Michael Alexeev was particularly helpful, with the thesis and throughout graduate school. His willingness to discuss ideas with a student who did not share his general approach to economics taught me as much about being a good person as it did about economics. My greatest intellectual debt, however, belongs to Don Lavoie. I went to George Mason University to study with Professor Lavoie, and working with him exceeded my greatest expectations. He is a constant source of intellectual inspiration and encouragement. I will be forever grateful to him for all he has taught me about interdisciplinary scholarship and critical thinking.

The transformation of my thesis into the present book was aided by several people. Zachary Rolnik, the editor at Kluwer Academic Publishers, provided encouragement throughout. Drafts of the chapters were presented at the meetings of the Eastern Economic Association (1987) and the American Economic Association (1988) and faculty seminars at: the University of Hartford (1987), George Mason University (1988), Oakland University (1988), and New York University (1989, 1990). In addition, I benefited greatly from the comments, criticisms, and encouragement of several readers: Gordon Tullock (University of Arizona), Ralph Raico (State University College at Buffalo), Israel Kirzner (New York University), Sherman Folland (Oakland University), James Ozinga (Oakland University), Silvana Malle (Universita degli Studi di Verona), Gertrude Schroeder (University of Virginia), and three anonymous readers. I would also like to thank Jeffrey

Friedman of *Critical Review* for his comments and our various discussions concerning my work on the war-communism period, and for giving me permission to use material I published in his journal. The usual caveat applies.

I owe a great debt to Sheldon L. Richman of the Institute for Humane Studies for his perceptive questions and editorial suggestions. Whatever degree of clarity and readability this book possesses is due in large part to his work. I would also like to thank the following individuals at the Institute for Humane Studies for proofreading the manuscript: Kurt Weber, David Fitzsimons, Tom W. Bell, Andrea Jardine, and Snow P. Simpson. I am thankful to Margo Reeves, who handled the technical transformation of a typed manuscript into a book. In addition, I am grateful to Leah Jackson Kennedy, my copy editor at Kluwer, and Lieselotte Hofmann, who constructed the index.

Oakland University provided a congenial atmosphere for the revisions and final writing of the book. I would also like to thank my research assistants during the past two years, Jai Rao, John Caronis, Eileen Mullin, and Katherine Keefer, for all their help in preparing this book.

My deepest gratitude, though, belongs to my wife, Rosemary. She has supported me in all my endeavors and put up with my obsessions. It is with all my love that I dedicate this project to her.

Rochester, Michigan
February 1990

It must be admitted that the idea of Socialism is at once grandiose and simple....We may say, in fact, that it is one of the most ambitious creations of the human spirit. The attempt to erect society on a new basis while breaking with all traditional forms of social organization, to conceive a new world plan and foresee the form which all human affairs must assume in the future—that is so magnificent, so daring, that it has rightly aroused the greatest admiration. If we wish to save the world from barbarism we have to refute Socialism, but we cannot thrust it carelessly aside.

—Ludwig von Mises, *Socialism* (1922)

Was there an alternative to the economic system that was established at the end of the 1920s? We believe there was. But history cannot be relived, and today we must deal with what *is*, not with what might be theoretically possible. The study of our past is not an aim in itself; it is a way of understanding the real defects and difficulties facing our economy today and of finding realistic ways to overcome them.

—Nikolai Shmelev and Vladimir Popov, *The Turning Point: Revitalizing the Soviet Economy* (1989)

1

INTRODUCTION

Ideas have consequences. World history has been, and continues to be, shaped by various religious dogmas, secular utopias, and demands for pragmatic reforms. Indeed it is ideas and not vested interests that govern the path of human history in the long run. John Maynard Keynes perhaps articulated this point best:

> The ideas of economists and political philosophers, both when they are right and when they are wrong, are more powerful than is commonly understood. Indeed the world is ruled by little else. Practical men, who believe themselves to be quite exempt from any intellectual influences, are usually the slaves of some defunct economist. Madmen in authority, who hear voices in the air, are distilling their frenzy from some academic scribbler of a few years back.[1]

Other social scientists often accuse the discipline of economics,of denying the role of ideas, and, instead, concentrating exclusively on the material interests of the economic agents under investigation.[2] Criticism of the "new" political economy and public choice theory, in particular, is leveled at this apparent failure to account for ideological factors.[3]

Although it may be excusable for economists to concentrate on the material incentives (or private interests) economic actors face within certain confines (rule structures), however, it is inexcusable to ignore the role of ideas in history, especially when the rules themselves come under scrutiny during a revolutionary period.[4] As Ludwig von Mises wrote:

> There is for history nothing beyond people's ideas and the ends they were aiming at motivated by these ideas. If the historian

> refers to the meaning of a fact, he always refers either to the interpretation acting men gave to the situation in which they had to live and to act, and to the outcome of their ensuing actions, or to the interpretation which other people gave to the result of these actions.[5]

Ironically, it is not the theoretical economists per se who are guilty of denying the role of ideas in human history, but rather many economic historians. By denying or downplaying Karl Marx's influence on the Soviet experience, for example, many political and economic historians reduce the Soviet experience to a mere compilation of facts and political maneuvers, neither of which does justice to the grand tale of Soviet political and economic history.

Both friend and foe do a great disservice to Marx. While foes merely equate Marx with Stalin, friends distort Marx's project to absolve him of responsibility. Neither interpretation treats Marx seriously enough; nor does either recognize unintended consequences in human interaction. Moreover, economic historians, such Alec Nove, see no connection between Soviet reality and Marx's economic project because Marx's economic analysis was confined to a critique of capitalism; they fail to see the picture implied in the negative. On the other hand, political historians, such as Stephen Cohen, see no direct connection between Soviet reality and Marx's political project because Marx expressed radical democratic values, and Soviet society under Stalin was the renunciation of those values. As I hope to demonstrate, both the economic and the political interpretation distort our understanding of the significance of the Soviet experience with socialism.

The goals, aspirations, and dreams about a better future world, all the things that motivate revolutions, are lost or hidden in the traditional narrative. Pragmatic concerns of political survival take the center stage; yet it is never asked why Lenin, Trotsky, or Bukharin so passionately believed the Bolsheviks needed to maintain state power. This denial of the force of ideas, caused by the failure to understand the content of Marx's proposal for a better world, let alone the economic problem that this proposal must confront, results in a fundamental misunderstanding of Soviet political and economic history.

Moreover, by denying the historical force of ideas, social theorists inadvertently deny social science perhaps its greatest role in the discussion of practical policy. As F.A. Hayek states:

> Utopia, like ideology, is a bad word today; and it is true that most utopias aim at radically redesigning society and suffer from internal contradictions which make their realization impossible. But an ideal picture of a society which may not be wholly achievable, or a guiding conception of the overall order to be aimed at, is nevertheless not only the indispensable precondition of any rational policy, but also the chief contribution that science

> can make to the solution of the problems of practical policy.[6]

The social scientist, according to Hayek, should take on the role of a social critic willing to question any of society's values or moral principles, though not all at the same time.[7] The social critic, therefore, confronts his or her subject as a critical utopian, an intellectual radical who wants to get at the root cause of social ills. He or she examines utopian proposals for self-contradictions, and confronts these proposals with the difficulties they would have to face in reality. Utopia is not a bad ideal, but certain utopias can represent bad ideas.

Purpose and Methodology

This study presents a narrative of one of the more interesting utopian experiments in comparative political and economic history: the first decade of the Soviet experience with socialism (1918-1928). My goal is to render this experience intelligible, to get at the meaning of the Soviet experience with socialism for comparative political economy today.

My format of investigation is a simple one, although one that is sometimes undervalued among my peers in economics: textual examination and intellectual history. To understand the Soviet experience with socialism, I believe it is necessary to understand what the actors who made the history thought they were doing. As Emma Goldman correctly observed: "[F]uture historians of the Great Russian Revolution—if they are to write real history and not a mere compilation of facts—[will] draw from the impressions and reactions of those who lived through the Russian Revolution, who have shared the misery and travail of the people, and who actually participated in or witnessed the tragic panorama in its daily unfoldment."[8] My task, however, is not to merely record what Lenin or Trotsky or Bukharin thought they were doing, but also to examine—with the aid of historical distance—what this historical episode has meant (and means today) to comparative political economists in terms of theory, empirical research, and policy espousal.

In the 1990s, with full knowledge of the effects of Stalinism and the problems that continue to plague so-called socialist economies throughout the world, we can perhaps come to a better understanding of the true meaning of the critical decade following the Russian Revolution. As philosopher Hans-Georg Gadamer states in reference to effective historical understanding in general:

> Time is no longer primarily a gulf to be bridged, because it separates, but is actually the supportive ground of process in which the present is rooted. Hence temporal distance is not something that must be overcome. This was, rather, the naive assumption of historicism, namely that we must set ourselves within the spirit of the age, and think with its ideas and its

> thoughts, not with our own, and thus advance towards historical objectivity. In fact the important thing is to recognize the distance in time as a positive and productive possibility of understanding....It lets the true meaning of the object emerge fully....Not only are fresh sources of error constantly excluded, so that the true meaning has filtered out of it all kinds of things that obscure it, but there emerge continually new sources of understanding, which reveal unsuspected elements of meaning....It not only lets those prejudices that are of a particular and limited nature die away, but causes those that bring genuine understanding to emerge clearly as such. It is only this temporal distance that can solve the really critical question of hermeneutics, namely of distinguishing the true prejudices, by which we understand, from the false ones by which we misunderstand.[9]

With the aid of historical distance and a renewed appreciation of the force of ideas in human history, I have attempted in the current study of Soviet history to provide a more coherent account of its meaning for political economy: to discover, as Gadamer put it, those true prejudices that enable us to understand, and to separate them from those false prejudices that only lead to misunderstanding.

My exclusive focus on textual evidence is warranted by the apparent consensus that surrounds the historical facts of the first decade of Soviet socialism.[10] No one disputes that the Bolsheviks came to power in November of 1917 (new calendar). Nor is there any disagreement that Lenin and his associates followed extreme policies of centralization from the summer of 1918 to the spring of 1921, and that the economic performance during these years was disastrous, reducing every area of economic life to far below pre-war levels. Nor does one doubt that the New Economic Policy (NEP) was introduced through the "The Tax in Kind," and that during this and later policies the Soviet economy produced an economic recovery. Nor does anyone disagree that following the death of Lenin in January 1924, a great political economic debate was waged among the Bolsheviks as to the future direction of socialist construction which Stalin eventually won by 1928. No one disputes the compilation of mere historical facts. But what these facts mean is another story.

The resolution of disputes over the meaning of the first decade of Soviet socialism does not primarily turn on better fact finding or statistical manipulations. It requires a richer understanding of the intellectual history of the period.

By weaving the economic facts into a more coherent narrative than the currently dominant view within comparative political economy, I hope to advance our understanding of this critical moment in human history. In fact, I plan to make sense out the "enigma wrapped up in a contradiction" that represents the Soviet economic system. Evidence compiled on the Soviet system appears as a puzzling paradox. As Alain Besançon writes:

> The Soviet economy is the subject of a considerable volume of scholarly work which occupies numerous study centres in Europe and the United States and which provides material for a vast literature and various academic journals. But those born in the Soviet Union or those who approach Soviet society through history, literature, travel or through listening to what the emigres have to say, find that they cannot recognize what the economists describe. There seems to be an unbridgeable gap between this system, conceived through measurements and figures, and the other system, without measurements or figures, which they have come to know through intuition and their own actual experience. It is an astonishing feature of the world of Soviet affairs that a certain kind of economic approach to Soviet reality, no matter how well-informed, honest and sophisticated, is met with such absolute scepticism and total disbelief by those who have a different approach that they do not even want to offer any criticism—it being impossible to know where to begin.[11]

Standard economic analysis, as Besançon points out, with its preoccupation with aggregate measurements, such as gross national product (GNP) or statistical correlation, does not do justice to the facts. Economists who merely focus on growth rates, output figures, or some measure of economic efficiency simply cannot understand the system or its history. The standard comparative political economist faced with this apparent paradox in the evidence is left declaring that "The Soviet Union is an absolute puzzle...capable of putting men into space to perform cutting edge experiments outside of this world, but [unable to] make a decent two-slice toaster in Moscow."[12]

This observation is not limited to macroeconomists, but includes much of the microanalysis being done on the Soviet system. Moreover, it is not unique to the Soviet system but is a systemic problem of much of formal economic analysis. As Michael Polanyi argues: "If the scientific virtues of exact observation and strict correlation of data are given absolute preference for the treatment of a subject matter which disintegrates when represented in such terms, the result will be irrelevant to the subject matter and probably of no interest at all." Moreover, with regard to all the sciences, Polanyi argues that the search for "objective knowledge" embodied within the formalist/empiricist framework not only hinders understanding but threatens the very basis of science itself. As he states:

> This is how a philosophic movement guided by aspirations of scientific severity has come to threaten the position of science itself. This self-contradiction stems from a misguided intellectual passion—a passion for achieving absolutely impersonal knowledge which, being unable to recognize any persons, pres-

> ents us with a picture of the universe in which we ourselves are absent. In such a universe there is no one capable of creating and upholding scientific values; hence there is no science....
>
> Only by accrediting the exercise of our intellectual passions in the act of observing man, can we form conceptions of man and society which both endorse this accrediting and uphold the freedom of culture in society. Such self-accrediting, or self-confirmatory, progression will prove an effective guide to all knowledge of living beings.[13]

By incorporating insights from historians and political philosophers along with economic analysis, I hope to shed some light on the puzzlement. I do not intend, however, to "merely" produce a "better" economic history, but to tell the "grand tale" of the Soviet experience with socialism.

"Academics," writes Paul Craig Roberts, "have amassed much detailed information about the Soviet system, but they lack a paradigm for interpreting it....Consequently," he concludes, "they can never tell a grand tale. Their books contain interesting details and perceptive observations but are nevertheless boring."[14] But there is a grand tale to be told—a story of no small significance to both human understanding and social cooperation. As Roberts argues:

> The grand tale is the utter superiority of private property. Revolutions that attempted to achieve socialist economic organization that would be superior productively and morally to private property have now demonstrated that no such outcome is possible....[T]he Soviet story is one of the interaction of speculative excess or utopian aspirations with refractory reality. But scholars cannot see this as long as they believe that Soviet central planning originated not in an effort to eliminate the market but in a decision to squeeze agriculture in order to rapidly industrialize.[15]

In my attempt to render the history of the Soviet economic system intelligible and to glean from this historical episode the grand tale for humane social organization, my argument will be greatly influenced by the "liberal" social philosophers and scientists Ludwig von Mises, F.A. Hayek, and Michael Polanyi.

My historical interpretation rests crucially on two theoretical criticisms of the standard literature. First, the standard economic history literature does not treat Marxism seriously enough as a system of thought. Second, the standard literature does not recognize fully the economic coordination problem that any society, let alone a Marxian economic system, would have to confront.[16] Both my understanding of Marxian political economy and the economic coordination problem society confronts represent "subsidiary arguments" within my investigations. Within the bounds of the current study, I will not examine these subsidiary arguments in detail; I grant authority to certain authors for them.[17]

My contention that the Soviet experience has been fundamentally misunderstood, however, will not rest solely upon argument from authority. Rather, it emerges from my examination of the texts of Lenin, Bukharin, and the other actors who wrote their purposes and plans upon the pages of human history during that first decade of the Soviet experience. In addition, I will examine the interpretations of contemporary historians of the revolution and the writings of more recent interpreters of Soviet political and economic history.

My argument is twofold. First, I strive to demonstrate that the first three years of the Bolshevik regime (1918-1921) constitute an attempt to carry out the Marxian ideal of comprehensive central planning, and that the disastrous results, which all commentators agree occurred, were the inevitable outcome of this Marxian ideal coming into conflict with the economic reality of the coordination problem that all economic systems face. Second, I hope to demonstrate that, by understanding the Soviet experience in this manner, much of the confusion that surrounds the Soviet system and its history will disappear. Events that seem to be either aberrations or mysteries will become intelligible.

Chapter 2 serves to set the stage by dealing with the dominant secondary literature on the first decade of the Soviet experience with socialism. Chapters 3 and 4 represent examinations of the economic history of Bolshevik policies from 1918 to 1921 and 1921 to 1928, respectively, paying particular attention to the point of view of the actors who created and instituted these economic policies. Chapter 5 discusses the Soviet Industrialization Debate that took place from 1924 to 1928, when the Stalinist forces emerged victorious and began to institute forced collectivization and industrialization. In conclusion, I maintain that if this analysis is found to be convincing, then it offers a radical challenge to contemporary comparative political economy at the level of high theory, applied research, and public policy.

Notes

[1] J.M. Keynes, *The General Theory of Employment, Interest and Money* (New York: Harcourt, Brace and Jovanovich, 1964[1936]), 383.

[2] See Mark A. Lutz and Kenneth Lux, *Humanistic Economics: The New Challenge* (New York: The Bootstrap Press, 1988), for a recent criticism of standard economics along these lines.

[3] See Joseph Kalt and Mark Zupan, "Capture and Ideology in the Economic Theory of Politics," *American Economic Review*, Vol. 74, n. 3 (1984), 279-300. However, see Dwight Lee, "Politics, Ideology, and the Power of Public Choice," *Virginia Law Review*, Vol. 74, n. 2 (March 1988), 191-198, for a discussion of the role of ideology within public choice analysis of the voting process and political decision making.

[4] James M. Buchanan, for example, argues that economists must adopt a "constitutional perspective." This perspective demands that the theorist examine both pre- and postconstitutional choice. Postconstitutional analysis focuses upon choice within rules, that is, the strategies of economizing actors, while preconstitutional analysis concerns itself with the normative discussion of appropriate rules. The task of the political economist is to weave back and forth between these two very different set of questions. Public-choice analysis of vote-seeking and rent-seeking behavior is an analysis of economic behavior within a set of established rules. Ideology is about the rules themselves. Preconstitutional analysis is the realm of social theory, postconstitutional analysis is the realm of technical economics.

[5] L. von Mises, *Theory and History: An Interpretation of Social and Economic Evolution* (Auburn, AL: The Ludwig von Mises Institute, 1985), 161.

[6] F.A. Hayek, *Law, Legislation and Liberty*, 3 vols. (Chicago: University of Chicago Press, 1973-79), I: 65.

[7] See Hayek, "The Errors of Constructivism," *New Studies in Philosophy, Politics, Economics, and the History of Ideas*, (Chicago: University of Chicago, 1978), 19 .

[8] Emma Goldman, *My Disillusionment in Russia* (New York: Doubleday, Page and Company, 1923), vii.

[9] Gadamer, *Truth and Method* (New York: Crossroads, 1985[1960]), 264-266.

[10] Debates over Soviet statistics, which are well known, are usually over the growth rates achieved in the post-1928 era, that is, during the collectivization and industri-

alization under Stalin and after. Little or no debate centers around the economic statistics of the first decade of Soviet socialism. In fact, most statistical studies of the Soviet economy do not even concern themselves with the first decade. As G. Warren Nutter commented: "Most specialists on the Soviet economy start their studies with the year 1928, when comprehensive centralized planning was introduced." From *The Growth of Industrial Production in the Soviet Union* (Princeton: Princeton University Press, 1962), 5.

[11] Besançon, "Anatomy of a Spectre," *Survey*, Vol. 25, n. 4 (Autumn 1980), 143.

[12] Susan Linz, "Reorganization and Reform in the Soviet Economy," *Comparative Economic Studies*, Vol. XXIX, n. 4 (Winter 1987), 1.

[13] Polanyi, *Personal Knowledge: Towards a Post-Critical Philosophy* (Chicago: University of Chicago Press, 1962[1958]), 139, 142. Edmund Husserl, in *The Crisis of European Sciences and Transcendental Phenomenology* (Evanston: Northwestern University Press, 1970), 6, raises a similar concern when he argues that positivistic restriction on the idea of science "excludes in principle the questions which man...finds most burning: questions of the meaning or meaninglessness of the whole of this human existence." Also see Donald McCloskey, *The Rhetoric of Economics* (Madison: University of Wisconsin Press, 1985), 30, where he argues, following Rorty, that the search for objective knowledge resulted in the "triumph of the quest for certainty over the quest for wisdom." One goal of my analysis is to obtain a broader wisdom of social cooperation than is possible under more formalist modes of analysis.

[14] Paul Craig Roberts, "The Soviet Economy: A Hopeless Cause?" *Reason* (July 1988), 57.

[15] Roberts, "The Soviet Economy," 57.

[16] This coordination problem is not something external to the Marxian system and imposed on it—Marx understood the problem and addressed it. He did not argue that the problem would disappear under communism, but rather that planning would solve the problem to such an extent that man would eventually be able to advance from the realm of necessity to the realm of freedom. As he argued in the third volume of *Capital*:

> The realm of freedom really begins only where labour determined by necessity and external expediency ends; it lies by its very nature beyond the sphere of material production proper. Just as the savage must wrestle with nature to satisfy his needs, to maintain and reproduce his life, so must civilized man, and *he*

> *must do so in all forms of society and under all possible modes of production.* This realm of natural necessity expands with his development, because his needs do too; but the productive forces to satisfy these expand at the same time. Freedom, in this sphere, can consist only in this, that socialized man, the associated producers, *govern the human metabolism with nature in a rational way, bringing it under their collective control instead of being dominated by it as a blind power*; accomplishing it with the least expenditure of energy and in conditions most worthy and appropriate for their human nature. But this always remains a realm of necessity. *The true realm of freedom, the development of human powers as an end in itself, begins beyond it, though it can only flourish with this realm of necessity as its basis.*

See Marx, *Capital: A Critique of Political Economy*, Vol. 3 (New York: Vintage Books, 1981[1894]), 958-959, emphasis added.

[17] On Marxian theory of socialism I defer to Paul Craig Roberts, *Alienation and the Soviet Economy* (Albuquerque: University of New Mexico Press, 1971); Paul Craig Roberts and Matthew A. Stephenson, *Marx's Theory of Exchange, Alienation and Crisis* (New York: Praeger, 1983[1973]); and David Reese, *Alienation, Exchange and Economic Calculation: An Inquiry into the Nature and Possibility of Marxian Socialism* (unpublished PhD thesis, Virginia Polytechnic Institute, Blacksburg, VA, 1980, revised edition, 1985).

On the nature of economic theory I defer to the Austrian tradition of economic analysis, and, in particular, the emphasis of that tradition on viewing the economic problem as an outgrowth of the *division of knowledge* within society. Relevant works, though certainly not exhaustive, include: Ludwig von Mises, *Socialism: An Economic and Sociological Investigation* (Indianapolis: Liberty Press, 1980[1922]); *Human Action: A Treatise on Economics* (Chicago: Henry Regnery, 3rd rev. ed., 1966[1949]); F.A. Hayek, *Individualism and Economic Order* (Chicago: University of Chicago Press, 1980[1948]); *The Counter-Revolution of Science* (Indianapolis: Liberty Press, 1979[1955]); Israel Kirzner, *Competition and Entrepreneurship* (Chicago: University of Chicago Press, 1973); *Perception, Opportunity and Profit* (Chicago: University of Chicago Press, 1979); Gerald O'Driscoll and Mario Rizzo, *The Economics of Time and Ignorance* (New York: Basil Blackwell, 1986); Don Lavoie, *Rivalry and Central Planning* (New York: Cambridge University Press, 1985a); and *National Economic Planning: What Is Left?* (Cambridge, MA: Ballinger Press, 1985b).

On the rehabilitation of the legitimate use of authority within scholarly discussion, see Hans-Georg Gadamer, *Truth and Method* (New York: Crossroad, 1985[1960]), 245 ff. For an interesting discussion of the connection between the philosophy of Polanyi and that of Gadamer, see Joel Weinsheimer, *Gadamer's Hermeneutics* (New Haven: Yale University Press, 1985), 1-59.

2

THE MEANING OF THE FIRST DECADE OF SOVIET SOCIALISM

Introduction

Following the October Revolution in 1917, the Bolsheviks embarked upon a series of economic policies in the attempt to establish a socialist economic order. Commenting on the consequences of the economic policies enacted in the wake of the October Revolution, Maurice Dobb doubted "whether in any previous age so profound a change, affecting so large an area of the world's surface, has ever occurred within such a narrow span of time."[1] The influence of these radical changes in the political and economic structure of the Soviet Union, however, carried far beyond the border of Russia. Whether one looks at the early intellectual excitement embodied in Sidney and Beatrice Webb's prediction of a "new civilization" and the heralding of "true democracy" by E.H. Carr, or the later revelation of the totalitarian reality of the Soviet system, the force of this Soviet experiment in socioeconomic reorganization on intellectual discourse is undeniable.[2]

Reflection on the impact of the economic and social changes that took place during the decade following the Bolshevik rise to power on both Western and Eastern European countries testifies to the awesome and unique significance of this historical event. As two recent commentators put it: "On the date of October 25, 1917, under the old Russian calendar (November 7 by the Western calendar), a new era began. The history of Russia ended on that day. It was replaced by the history of the Soviet Union. The new era affected the entire human race, because the whole world felt, and still feels, the consequences of the October revolution."[3]

The way social theorists have understood the Russian experience has conditioned attitudes and policies toward economic development, microeconomic efficiency, and macroeconomic stability ever since. Many political economists regard the Russian Revolution as the single most important event of the twentieth century.

Yet traditional accounts of the economic consequences of the revolution seem deficient, for two reasons. First, economic historians have failed to take seriously the policy prescriptions of early twentieth century European and Russian Marxism.[4] Leading economic historians, such as Alexander Gerschenkron and Alec Nove, argue that little or nothing in the Soviet experience needs to be explained or understood in terms of Marxism. Gerschenkron summarizes his position by arguing that "the economic order (or disorder) as was developed in Soviet Russia was created, not in obedience to any theoretical tenets, but as a pragmatic response to the exigencies of the practice with the power mechanics of the dictatorship well in mind....[H]ardly anything in the momentous story of Soviet economic policies needs, or suffers, explanations in terms of its derivation from Marx's economic theories."[5] Nove, who is recognized as perhaps the foremost authority on Soviet economic history, argues with regard to the early policies of the Bolsheviks that Marxian ideology was used only as an ex post rationalization for policies introduced as practical responses to emergency situations. "Actions taken in abnormal situations for practical reasons," Nove states, "are often clothed in ideological garb and are justified by reference to high principles. It is all too easy then to conclude, with documentary evidence to prove it, that the action was due to a principle."[6] Gerschenkron and Nove, I believe, both misunderstand the policy prescriptions suggested by Marxian political economy and underestimate the ideological commitment of the Bolshevik leadership.

The second reason standard accounts fail is that they do not account for the economic coordination problems the Bolsheviks faced in implementing their policies. The theoretical debate, which first took place within the German-language economics and sociology literature during the 1920s and then later within the technical economics literature in English-speaking countries during the 1930s and 1940s, over the feasibility of economic calculation under socialism seems to be irrelevant to the standard economic historian.[7] The typical attitude appears to be that while the theoretical debate might be interesting in itself, it has nothing to add to our analysis of the practice of socialism.[8] This kind of theory/practice split suggests an unhealthy state—either implying that theory has gone off in an esoteric direction and become irrelevant for solving practical problems, or economic historians are failing to use theoretical developments to aid them in interpreting reality. While historical research on the Soviet experience and theoretical discussion about socialist economic organization continue to accumulate, a healthy cross-fertilization is not evident. As a result, both the historical interpretation of this period and the theoretical discussion of socialism seem to misunderstand the *significance* of the economic policies of war communism (1918-1921), the new economic policy (1921-1927), and the first five-year plan (1928).

Recent Interest in the Soviets

The seventieth anniversary of the Russian Revolution brought renewed interest in understanding the impact of this event. Historical understanding is further enhanced by Mikhail Gorbachev, who seems to encourage historical consciousness. He told the Central Committee in November 1987: "It is essential to assess the past with a sense of historical responsibility and on the basis of historical truth."[9] Gorbachev's twin policies of *glasnost* (public openness or frankness) and *perestroika* (restructuring) have captured the imagination of American intellectuals.

In his recent book, *Perestroika*, Gorbachev explains the necessity of the economic restructuring he is seeking. "Our rockets can find Halley's comet and fly to Venus with amazing accuracy," he argues, "but side by side with these scientific and technological triumphs is an obvious lack of efficiency in using scientific achievements for economic needs, and many Soviet household appliances are of poor quality."[10] Gorbachev justifies *perestroika*, as well as *glasnost*, by reference to the past: "The essence of perestroika lies in the fact that it unites socialism with democracy and revives the Leninist concept of socialist construction both in theory and in practice." He describes these policies as "the comprehensive development of democracy, socialist self-government," and argues that they require "more *glasnost*, criticism, and self-criticism." *Perestroika* calls for a revival and development, Gorbachev claims, "of the principles of democratic centralism in running the national economy." These policies, according to Gorbachev, represent "the most important and most radical program for economic reform our country has had since Lenin introduced his New Economic Policy [NEP] in 1921."[11]

These constant references to Lenin suggest that an understanding of the first decade of Soviet rule might provide important insights for social reform today. Open examination of the past is perfectly understandable and desirable, Gorbachev told the Central Committee in his speech celebrating the anniversary of the revolution. "For decades, we have been returning to that time [the first decade of Soviet socialism] again and again. This is natural. Because that was when the world's first socialist society had its beginnings, when it was being built....And if, at times, we scrutinize our history with a critical eye, we do so only because we want to obtain a better and fuller idea of the ways that lead to the future."[12]

Although much of the interest is due to the profound nature of the Russian experience, much is also due, I believe, to the Gorbachev ascendancy and the promise of reform. As Theodore Draper states: "This return to a NEP-type reform is particularly characteristic of the unfolding Gorbachev period; Gorbachev himself has invoked the precedent of the NEP, as if it gave him a license to do what he wants to do. Thus, we are not straying too far from the present in paying special attention to the NEP period. NEP-thinking is imbedded in the present."[13] Of particular importance for us today is understanding NEP's lack of staying power as a reform measure—it lasted a mere seven years, while the Stalinist period that followed lasted for 25 (1928-1953). Is this what we can expect from Gorbachev's new NEP?

The Soviets, perhaps more than any other rulers in human history, understand the importance of the past. History is politics applied to the past, wrote Mikhail Pokrovsky—one of the first Soviet Marxist historians—anticipating George Orwell's famous dictum, "Whoever controls the past controls the future." I too think that historical interpretation rules the path of the future. My concern is with understanding the economic thought and policies of the first decade of Soviet rule and what that experience means for us today. Economic theory and policy do not exist in a vacuum, however. Economic factors interact with, and are intertwined with political concerns, institutional make-up, and historical conditions. And, in the Soviet case, political interests and interaction cannot be underestimated. As Mikhail Heller and Aleksandr Nekrich state: "In studying the history of the Soviet state it is insufficient to consider such factors [as urbanization, industrialization, and demographic cycles alone]. One particular characteristic—the total influence of the ruling party on all spheres of existence on a scale never before known—acts as a determining force in all Soviet institutions and on the typical Soviet citizen, Homo Sovieticus."[14]

Despite all the recent interest, it is not apparent that we are getting any closer to understanding the origin of the Soviet state and the significance of the economic policies that were implemented during its early years. A subject that should evoke nothing but controversy seems to have settled into an unhealthy state of consensus. Among political historians, as Stephen Cohen has pointed out, the profession is dominated by the totalitarian school which sees a logical continuity between Lenin and Stalin. Cohen challenges the dominant view, and suggests that there was a nontotalitarian and decentralized alternative to Stalinism, namely the path proposed by Nikolai Bukharin.[15] While Cohen has some cogent points against the totalitarian school, he is weakest in his understanding of the nature and incentives of the political/economic institutions during the crucial first decade, and on the economic ideas of Bukharin and the significance of Bukharin's change of mind during the period in question.[16] He accepts unreservedly the standard interpretation of economic historians. This standard interpretation is what has produced the failure among economists to understand the lessons of the origin of the Soviet economic system.

The Standard View

A voluminous collection of economic history has accumulated because of the interest in the Russian Revolution. One would expect varied and competing reports. Yet the interpretation of the origin of the Soviet economic system among economic historians and comparative systems specialists is almost unanimous. Interpretations differ only in terms of the relative value individual scholars attach to the establishment of socialism. Few question that socialism was, in fact, established by the Soviets.[17] The major division lies between economic historians who see the events following the revolution as leading to totalitarianism, and those who see them as unprecedented and necessary moves toward the "new social order."

Though these two positions may differ in regard to their ethical assessment of, or economic efficiency attributed to, socialism, the historical description of the policies of the first decade are the same. Thus, despite the apparent dichotomy, most scholars on both sides agree with the following rough narrative of events: In October of 1917 (November on a Western calendar) the Bolsheviks came to power because the provisional government was unable to maintain power. Because of the civil war between Red and White forces, and because of foreign interventionism, the Bolsheviks had to engage in emergency measures ("war communism") beginning in June 1918, and they increased and continued these emergency policies until April 1921. After the detour necessitated by war, the Bolsheviks returned to the economic policies of the victorious proletariat in the transition period from 1921 to 1928 (the New Economic Policy), at which time the Stalinist regime began its "revolution from above." Policies of collectivization and industrialization were followed as the Soviet Union established the first advanced centrally planned economy. Economic historians of the Soviet Union as diverse as Alec Nove and G. Warren Nutter endorse and promote this standard view.[18]

Economics textbooks reinforce this image of Soviet economic history and its theoretical implications. Robert Ekelund and Robert Tollison, for example, ask in retrospect whether "the socialist calculation debate [was even] relevant." Their answer seems ambiguous: neither Lange's nor Lerner's model of market socialism has had much impact on existing socialist economies. And the mere existence of socialist economies seems to "imply that Mises and Hayek were wrong; socialism is indeed possible." Moreover, they accept the dominant historical interpretation:

> The Bolsheviks, influenced by the writings of Karl Marx and Friedrich Engels and the leadership of Vladimir Ilyich Lenin, sought to implement pure socialism—an economy in which all the means of production were owned and operated by the state and in which all economic activity would be centrally planned and controlled by the central government. *Although Lenin, the revolutionary leader, did not live to see these goals accomplished, Joseph Stalin, his successor, was responsible for implementing them to a very great extent in the 1930s.*[19]

The discounting of the calculation debate, and the interpretation of the Soviet economy represented by Ekelund and Tollison, are symptomatic of the dual failure that dominates economic analysis of the Soviet system in particular and the theory of socialism in general—a failure to understand (1) the policy prescriptions of early twentieth century Marxism, and (2) the nature of the Austrian challenge in the socialist calculation debate.

Standard economic textbooks in Soviet studies accept this interpretation of history and trace the beginning of the Soviet planned economy to Stalin's collectivization drive and the establishment of the five-year planning system.[20] The latest research in comparative economic history continues to reinforce the standard interpretation. Gur Ofer, for example, argues:

> The Soviet model of development was introduced in the late 1920s, when it was heralded as superior, as promising to become the wave of the future, and as a model for other underdeveloped countries. At the same time counterclaims were being voiced: that modernization cannot be achieved without basic economic freedoms and that central planning is inherently inefficient and bound to fail. *So far, history has proved both extreme claims wrong.*[21]

The standard interpretation is reiterated by even some of the most important proponents of Marxian social theory, such as Tom Bottomore. Bottomore contends that "it is a considerable exaggeration to argue...that the period of 'War Communism' in the USSR reflected a deliberate policy to abolish the market and the price system, rather than being in large measure an *unavoidable practical response to the conditions produced by the war, the civil war and foreign intervention.*"[22] Bottomore defends this claim by relying on the "more balanced view" of Alec Nove.

Two points are apparent. First, how one from an economic point of view assesses the Soviet experience with socialism depends on the interpretation of war communism one holds. Second, those economists who stress the emergency nature of the policies of war communism have been greatly influenced by economic historians of the Soviet Union such as Alec Nove. In fact, it appears that the dominance of the "emergency" interpretation in the economics literature is due to the historical work of three authors, Maurice Dobb, E. H. Carr, and Alec Nove.[23]

Maurice Dobb

Maurice Dobb argues that although there was some ideological justification for the policies from 1918 to 1921, the notion of establishing an immediate socialist economic order was "no more than flights of leftist fancy."[24] We must consider the policies of war communism within the context in which they were introduced, Dobb argues. If we remember that these centralization policies fall between the more decentralized periods of the first eight months of Bolshevik rule and the New Economic Policy, then war communism "emerges clearly as an empirical creation, not as the a priori product of theory: as an improvisation in the face of economic scarcity and military urgency in conditions of exhausting civil war."[25]

The Bolsheviks had to increase centralized direction and the use of coercive measures in order to obtain and manage the resources necessary for the war effort. Lenin's regime originally tried to obtain the necessary resources for the civil war by following inflationary policies, according to Dobb. By issuing new currency the Bolsheviks were temporarily able to procure command over the necessary resources. Inflation "acts as a forced levy or tax upon the community, forcing other people to go without, in order that the government as consumer may command a larger share of the available resources."[26] In keeping with socialist principles, though, this tax would be levied upon the "moneyed class, who were extensively expropriated by the fall in the value of money, and the peasantry," not the industrial worker, who was the backbone of the revolution, since it became the practice for workers to receive an increasingly larger part of their wages in kind.[27]

But these inflationary policies so devalued the currency that it was impossible for the Bolsheviks to procure enough grain from the peasants. While the issuance of new rubles only increased 119 percent in 1918, 1919 and 1920 saw increases of 300 percent and 400 percent, respectively. By October 1920 "the purchasing power of the rouble was no more than 1 percent of what it had been in October 1917."[28] But Dobb argues that this was all in the name of raising funds for the war effort, and had nothing to do with the Marxian desire to eliminate the monetary economy and substitute for it a comprehensive central plan.[29]

Since the Soviet government could no longer obtain resources through the normal process of market exchange, even with the aid of the printing press, it became necessary to "obtain these resources only by measures of coercion, and by centralized control and distribution of supplies." Peasants were required to forfeit any surplus beyond "essential needs of subsistence and seed corn" to the Commissariat of Supply for allocation among the army and industrial workers. The centralization of the "collection and distribution of supplies was the keystone of the system."[30]

These policies of compulsory requisitioning and centralized economic control could only have been intended as expedient measures, Dobb argues, because they threatened the alliance between the peasantry and the industrial working class which was the basis of the revolution. The Kronstadt rebellion of March 1921 brought home this point with an ever-growing sense of urgency.[31] The three-year reign of war communism had left the economy in ruins and threatened the Bolsheviks' ability to maintain political power. The decision to abandon the policies of war communism in April 1921 is seen by Dobb, however, as a "reversion to the road which was being travelled during the early months, before the onset of the civil war....NEP," Dobb argues, "is the normal economic policy of the proletariat after the revolution."[32]

Dobb suggests that his historical interpretation of war communism and NEP directly contrasts with the predominant Western idea of that time (1940s) that war communism "was a product of an attempt to realise an ideal Communism, which, coming into inevitable conflict with realities, had to be scrapped in favour of a retreat in the direction of Capitalism, as represented by the New Economic Policy."[33] In a twist of scholarly fashion, however, Dobb's historical and economic interpretation went from outlier to mainstream within a matter of years.

E. H. Carr

The famous historian of the Soviet Union E. H. Carr reiterated Dobb's interpretation of the war-emergency nature of war communism. Even though Carr's narrative is ambivalent toward the ideology versus emergency explanation of war communism, he is probably more responsible than anyone else for promoting the "war communism as expedient" view. The Bolsheviks found themselves in a theoretical and practical paradox, Carr argues. They rose to political power smoothly because of the economic backwardness of Russia; opposition came solely from the remnants of feudalism and from elements of underdeveloped capitalism. This backwardness, however, also made the task of socialist construction that much more difficult. The Bolsheviks wished to construct a socialist economic order without the advanced political (bourgeois democratic) or economic (capitalistic) development that Marxian theory had treated as essential for social change. The situation dictated slow and cautious going. The revolutionary cadre, according to Carr, knew it was necessary in theory and in practice to complete the bourgeois revolution before moving forward to the socialist revolution.

The outbreak of civil war in the summer of 1918, though, no longer afforded the Bolsheviks the luxury of slow and cautious policies. It "removed all hesitations by driving the regime forward willy-nilly at break-neck speed along the socialist road."[34] But Carr argues that the policies of war communism were "artificial and unstable," similar to the period known as "War Socialism" in Germany.[35] "It was the product of a special emergency and lacked a sufficiently solid social and economic basis to ensure its full survival (even though some of its legacies were likely to remain) when the emergency was over."[36]

War communism consisted of two major policy objectives: centralization of economic decision-making and concentration of industry, on the one hand, and the substitution of a "natural" economy for the market economy, on the other. Carr argues that the objective of centralization and concentration can be clearly traced to the first period of the revolution. "Lenin had long ago insisted," Carr points out, "that socialism was the logical next step forward from state capitalism, and that forms of organization inherent in the one were equally indispensable for the other....Here war communism," Carr continues, "was building on a foundation of what had gone before, and many of its achievements stood the test; only in their detailed application, and in the extended scope given to them were its policies afterwards subject to criticism and reversal."[37]

Policies intended to eliminate market relations, however, are not seen as products of theory by Carr. "The second element of war communism, the substitution of a 'natural' for a 'market' economy, had no such foundations." This policy objective, far from following the original path of the victorious proletariat, was the exact opposite, according to Carr. It "was a direct abandonment" of the policies of the first eight months, an "unprepared plunge into the unknown." This is how Carr describes the attempt to substitute "production for direct use rather than for a hypothetical market" that characterized the economic policies from 1918 to 1921.[38]

But at other places in his narrative, Carr seems to suggest that the polices of war communism were not just emergency measures, but also seemed to be "an authentic advance into socialist order."[39] At one point he even refers to war communism as "the attempt to implant socialism by shock tactics." [40] In another instance, Carr states: "The real issue in the period of war communism was not the nationalization of industry,...but the attempt of the state to administer industry on socialist lines.[41]... But the civil war," he is always quick to add, "dwarfed every other issue."[42]

Forced requisitioning was introduced because the "needs of the Red Army and the urban population could not be met in a devastated, mutilated and disorganized country by anything short of the total surplus of agricultural population."[43] War emergency, in the final analysis, dictated policy objectives, not adherence to any socialist principles.

The crisis situation demonstrated the need to militarize the economy. Small-scale peasant agriculture was inconsistent with the objective of feeding the industrial workers. Large-scale, collective farming was necessary. Arguments in favor of "collective cultivation" are described by Carr as irrefutable "from the standpoint of theoretical socialism or of practical efficiency."[44] Unfortunately, collective farming was not implemented; only grain requisitioning occurred. The mistake committed during war communism, with regard to agriculture, was treating the food shortage as a problem of "collection and distribution" and "not of production."[45]

Industry also needed to be mobilized for the war effort. All major industry had to be transformed into "a supply organization for the Red Army." Industrial policy became "an item of military strategy" where "every decision was dictated by emergency and taken without regard to long-term prospects and principles." The civil war drove home the necessity, according to Carr, for industry to come under "centralized control, direction, and planning."[46] Mobilization of labor was necessary to insure that "every man and every machine" were allocated in the "interests of military victory over the 'white' armies." Labor policy "became a matter of recruiting workers for the war effort and of sending them where they were most urgently required."[47]

This drive toward planning, Carr argues, had everything to do with the emergency situation, and nothing to do with Marxist principles.[48] In fact, Carr describes declarations of principles and theoretical explanations of the transition phase by leading theoreticians, such as Bukharin or Kritsman, as "ex post facto justifications of something which had not been expected but which it had not been possible to prevent."[49]

Carr even ascribes the motive of wartime expediency to passages that seem to suggest the socialist aspirations of the decision-makers. A passage from the party program at the Eighth Party Congress in March 1919, for example, states that the "maximum utilization" of the labor force for the purpose of the "planned development of the national economy" must be the "immediate task of the economic policy of the Soviet power." The program further states that the "socialist method of production" can only be made possible by such mobilization efforts.[50] But Carr argues that these passages demonstrate merely the key function of the trade unions in the civil war emergency.[51] Furthermore, he argues that "The argument for the permanent and unlimited conscription of labor by the state, like the contemporary argument for the abolition of money, reads like an attempt to provide theoretical justification for a harsh necessity which it had been impossible to avoid."[52]

So while the harsh necessity of war communism, which demanded securing resources for the Red Army and the urban population, could be described at one point as "a foretaste of the future communist society" where "methods of exchange" were substituted for by "the principles of taking from each according to his capacity and giving to each according to his need," Carr opts to interpret the policy of forced requisitioning as being "rendered imperative by the civil war" and justifies it "on grounds of military necessity."[53] It is clear that war communism was brought on by military emergency, Carr argues, because such "hand-to-mouth policies" could only be tolerated as long as the war lasted. Grain requisitioning, in particular, "whose raison d'être lay in the continuous and inexorable need to meet today's emergency," could not last beyond the emergency situation. The peasants' loyalty to the Bolshevik regime and "reluctant submission to the requisitions" were based on the "fear of a 'white' restoration"; once that fear passed, continued adherence to "oppressive exactions" produced peasant resentment and unrest. This culminated in peasant uprisings beginning in 1920 and continuing through the spring of 1921.[54]

The financial burden of the civil war and industrialization, moreover, called for the nationalization of the banks and the later devaluing of the currency. "The printing of notes," Carr argues, "remained the sole serious available source of funds to meet current public expenditure and to make advances to industry." So although the financial policies of war communism produced the "virtual elimination of money from the economy," it would be quite mistaken to view this result as the product of any theory. The destruction of the rouble, according to Carr, was "in no sense the product either of doctrine or of deliberate design."[55] The collapse of the currency had originally "been treated by every responsible Soviet leader as an unmixed evil against which all possible remedies should be invoked." It was only after no remedy could be found that Soviet leaders began to make a virtue out of the elimination of money and "the view became popular that the destruction of the currency had been a deliberate act of policy."[56]

The crisis atmosphere of March 1921 led to the substitution of the New Economic Policy for the "more extreme policies of war communism." Carr acknowledges that Lenin and the other Bolshevik leaders gave mixed accounts of the significance of the decision to change course, but claims that it was "unanimously accepted as a welcome and necessary relief."[57] This contention simply ignores the subsequent debate over NEP within the Bolshevik cadre.[58] Carr, however, finds it convenient to view NEP as an uncontroversial move away from the pragmatic, emergency-induced, but problem-plagued policies of war communism. "NEP was a retracing of steps from a regrettable, though no doubt enforced, digression and a return to the safe path which was being followed before June 1918."[59]

While pointing out that traces of both the emergency interpretation and the ideological interpretation can be found in Lenin's writings in the postwar-communism era, Carr relies on Lenin's description of NEP "as a resumption of the true line laid down by him in the spring of 1918 and interrupted only by the civil war emergency."[60] It was military concerns not economic theory, that dictated the policies of war communism. NEP was the path back to the road of economic development on the way to socialism.

Alec Nove

Perhaps the most well-known economic historian of the Soviet economy is Alec Nove, whose classic *An Economic History of the U.S.S.R.* is regarded by many as the most important book on the subject. Nove reinforces the Dobb-Carr interpretation of the origins of the Soviet economic system, though his treatment is more sensitive to the ideological aspirations of the Bolsheviks. In his final analysis of war communism, for example, Nove argues that there were probably both ideological and practical reasons behind the economic policies of 1918-1921, though he is quick to point out that "all the events of 1917-21, were, naturally, dominated by war and civil war...[and] the policies of the Soviet government in these years cannot, of course, be considered in isolation from these conditions."[61] Moreover, Nove suggests that the rationale for war communism might constitute an "ideology of necessity" and not an adherence to Marxian principles. The cause was obviously the war, even though ideological trappings were added as justification.[62]

In addition, Nove denies that this period should be viewed as an attempt at centralized economic planning. "It would be somewhat over-simple to conclude that the war communism period represented a model of full-fledged quantitative planning, or that the communists only later on came to blame war conditions for actions which they had all along intended."[63] But no one ever argued that the Soviet experience was a case study of the material balances approach, or Leontief's input-output model, or the planometric models of Hurwicz.[64] The argument for the planning interpretation of the events relies solely on the logic of the policies in the minds of the decision-makers at the moment of the decision to pursue one path and forgo another.

Nove arrives at his conclusion, just as Dobb and Carr did before him, by discounting the political economy of socialism that existed at the turn of the century. This point will be more fully addressed later. But by discounting Marxian aspirations to supersede market relations by eliminating money and exchange relations, these authors misread the historical significance of the policy changes that characterized the first decade of Soviet socialism. In particular, they cannot determine the nature and significance of NEP. Nove argues that "if the economic system of 1918-21 was either a forced reaction to an emergency situation or an error, then a return to the status quo ante June 1918 was a return to the *correct road, and not a withdrawal* in the face of the superior forces of the army."[65] But the existence of commodity production, profit seeking, and markets clearly ran in contrast to the Bolsheviks' values. As Nove himself points out, "Lenin and all his comrades must have believed that the advance [toward socialism] would be resumed, otherwise they had no raison d'être as Bolsheviks at all....*They were bound to regard the ultimate achievement of socialism as the one possible justification for their being in power.*"[66]

Stephen Cohen

Besides Nove, perhaps today's most important Soviet historian is Stephen Cohen. Cohen, a political historian, fully endorses the Dobb-Carr-Nove economic history interpretation of the beginning of Soviet socialism. "These spectacular policies," Cohen argues, "originated not in the party's ideology, but in response to the perilous military situation that suddenly confronted the Bolsheviks with the outbreak of civil war in the summer of 1918." War communism, then, "was born and took shape in the crucible of military expediency and the Bolsheviks' desperate efforts to survive as the government of Soviet Russia."[67]

It is indeed ironic that the biographer of Bukharin would hold such a position. Bukharin himself was very explicit on his understanding of war communism and the meaning of NEP. "We conceived War Communism," Bukharin points out, "as the universal, so to say 'normal' form of the economic policy of the victorious proletariat and *not as being related to the war, that is, conforming to a definite stage of the civil war.*"[68] Bukharin understood NEP as an admission of, and retreat from, the failure of war communism. It was "not only a strategic retreat, but the solution to a large social, organizational problem." The Bolsheviks had tried to take on the organization of everything, and Bukharin readily admits that "from the viewpoint of economic rationality this was madness."[69]

Socialism, in its Marxian sense, had been tried and had failed. Bukharin and other Bolsheviks searched for a "feasible socialism." The search continues today. But we cannot hide from the historical lesson and its theoretical significance: the search for "socialism with a human face" may well be inconsistent with the socialist dream of overcoming the "anarchy of production." Perhaps Bukharin understood this. Perhaps he even understood the nature of the problem and its significance better than all but a few have since.

Theoretical Issues of Socialism

The economic policies advocated by socialist thinkers in the first decades of this century (for example, those of the German Social Democrats and especially the economic program followed during the first decade of Soviet rule) led many economists to debate fundamental issues in comparative economic systems. Ludwig von Mises launched the debate over the feasibility of economic calculation under socialism with his famous 1920 article, "Economic Calculation in the Socialist Commonwealth." In 1922, Mises's argument was refined and extended in *Socialism: An Economic and Sociological Analysis*. The Misesian argument was that under conditions of a complex industrial economy, private ownership of the means of production was necessary for rational economic calculation.

The logic of Mises's argument was that without private ownership in the means of production there could not be any market for the means of production. Without a market for these higher-order producer goods there could not be any money prices for them. And without money prices reflecting the relative scarcities of the means of production, there could not be rational economic calculation.

Implicit in Mises's logical chain of reasoning is the recognition that no one mind or group of minds could possess the necessary knowledge to plan the economic system. Without the use of monetary calculation, which Mises referred to as "the guide amid the bewildering throng of economic possibilities," complex industrial production could not be rational.[70] Mises states this knowledge problem in his original challenge as follows: "No single man can ever master all the possibilities of production, innumerable as they are, as to be in a position to make straightway evident judgments of value without the aid of some system of computation."[71]

Since, as Mises notes, market exchange and production within a monetary economy provide for the discovery and dissemination of the knowledge necessary to make such computations systematically, attempts to eliminate market rivalry would meet insurmountable coordination problems.[72] Mises understood socialism in terms of its original Marxian aspiration of eliminating commodity production by substituting "production for direct use" through conscious design for "production for exchange" which was dictated by the "blind forces of the market." The elimination of the rivalry among competing plans of market participants, which characterizes commodity production, would result, argued Mises, in the elimination of the only computational device available to human beings for rational economic calculation. The problem confronting socialism, in its original Marxian version, was and is its technical impossibility. Rational economic calculation is rendered logically impossible. Without monetary prices and calculation, which serve as "an aid to the human mind," there is no way for the central planning board to *know* which production projects are economically feasible and which ones are not.

F.A. Hayek developed the Misesian argument against central planning even further by clarifying the role of knowledge in society. Hayek's work can best be understood as the continued attempt to make explicit what Mises left implicit, to refine what Mises had stated explicitly, and to answer questions Mises left unanswered.[73] Hayek pointed out that because of the vast division of knowledge in society, economic actors are capable of possessing only local bits of knowledge. Not only is market knowledge dispersed among many market participants, Hayek argued, but much of it is also inarticulate or tacit.[74] This epistemological perspective precludes either the theorist or planner from treating market knowledge as data.[75]

The economic problem that society confronts, therefore, cannot be fully characterized by the static allocational problem of arranging means to obtain the appropriate end. Standard welfare economics concerns itself with finding the best use of available resources under the assumption that all the relevant information concerning preferences and production techniques is known and given. But this is emphatically *not* the main economic problem that society confronts. The economic problem, Austrians argue, is a problem of "the utilization of knowledge which is not given to anyone in its totality."[76] Thus, while standard welfare economists view the market in a mechanistic fashion, Austrians view the market "as a social instrument for mobilizing all the bits of knowledge scattered throughout the economy."[77]

Don Lavoie has recently restated the Austrian arguments against centralized economic planning.[78] Lavoie integrates the insights of Mises and Hayek with the research on epistemology and the philosophy of science by Michael Polanyi.[79] Polanyi himself endorsed the Mises position on the impossibility of socialist economic calculation, and developed an analogy with the failure of centralized scientific planning.[80] In fact, Polanyi differs with Mises and Hayek only to the extent that they use the term *socialism* too lightly—attributing to certain regimes the appellation of *socialist* when in reality these regimes achieved little more than becoming vast bureaucratic-interventionist states. I will return to Polanyi's interpretation of the Soviet experience later, but first we will examine some of his theoretical arguments against centralized economic planning and their connection to the Austrians.

Because of the complexity of industrial production it is impossible for central direction to achieve the same results as the "spontaneously ordered systems in which persons mutually adjust their full-time activities over a prolonged period, resulting in a complex and yet highly adaptable coordination of these actions."[81] Attempts to replace the mutual adjustment processes of the market with central direction will result, Polanyi argues, in an "overwhelming reduction, amounting to a standstill in the possible rate of production."[82] A "centrally directed industrial system," Polanyi forcefully states, "is administratively impossible—impossible in the same sense in which it is impossible for a cat to swim the Atlantic."[83]

Polanyi's arguments against economic planning, much like his arguments against scientific planning, stem from his research on the nature of scientific progress and the growth of knowledge in society. Polanyi has demonstrated that much of the knowledge with which we live and work is inarticulate. We know how to do certain things even though we may not know enough to state objectively how we do them. The fact that we cannot represent this knowledge explicitly does not mean it is not knowledge, or that such knowledge is not fundamental to society or scientific progress.

Much of our day-to-day knowledge (practical knowledge) is embodied within skills and can be transmitted or acquired only through learning-by-doing.[84] Lavoie, integrating the Mises-Hayek understanding of the market process with Polanyi's contributions to epistemology, states: "The practical use of cost accounting by an entrepreneur to guide production activity can be usefully viewed as the kind of skillful knowing that Polanyi describes....Only in the context of practicing within a competitive price system are 'costs' meaningful keys that serve as 'aids to the mind' in the entrepreneur's skilled direction of production toward more profitable undertakings."[85] The skillful pursuit of profit by an entrepreneur is based on his knowledge of the relevant trade-offs and the subsidiary awareness of at least some of the procedures to be followed in this pursuit.

Only within the context of the competitive market will entrepreneurial alertness be translated into meaningful and effective knowledge to other market participants. Effective economic knowledge, in other words, is contextual knowledge. As Mises wrote:

> The attributes of the business man cannot be divorced from the position of the entrepreneur in the capitalist order....An entrepreneur deprived of his characteristic role in economic life ceases to be a business man. However much experience and routine he may bring to his new task he will still only be an official in it.[86]

The competitive flux of market activity serves to disseminate the economic knowledge necessary to bring into coordination the various and diverse plans of economic actors. It is this very process of spontaneous mutual adjustment that Marxian political economy aspired to dispense with. This was the anarchy of production that must be overcome by scientific economic planning and conscious design.

The argument that the complex interrelationship of market exchanges produces an order beyond the ability of any one mind, or group of minds, to comprehend in detail is one of the fundamental insights of the Austrian tradition of economic analysis. The argument is intimately connected to the Austrian understanding of capitalist production processes and the knowledge that is conveyed within this process that directs and redirects the allocation of scarce capital resources. Carl Menger explained this relationship in terms of the connection between "lower order" and "higher order" goods within the production process, and the notion that the value of higher order goods is imputed from the value of the lower order goods they are used to produce.[87] In this manner capital goods (goods of the higher order) are shuffled and reshuffled within the production process to meet individual demands for consumer goods (goods of the lower order).

This process of valuation and production takes place *within time*. The current market value of goods of the lower order does not determine the value of higher order goods. Higher order goods are attributed value by way of the expected value of the future lower order goods they help to produce. The importance of the passage of time and the generation of fresh knowledge in economic activity has been a major tenet of the Austrian tradition throughout its history. Menger explicitly connected the passage of time, the role of error, and the progress of human knowledge to explain economic processes.[88] In developing and defending his approach to the human sciences, Mises was concerned with the implication for economic understanding of treating seriously the passage of time in processes of human interaction.[89] Gerald O'Driscoll and Mario Rizzo recently gave the Austrian conception of time within economic processes a modern restatement.[90]

Mises's emphasis throughout his life-work was on viewing the market as a dynamic process of human valuation and interaction. He argued that understanding the problem of the utilization of dispersed knowledge within society was made possible only with the further developments of economic understanding made possible by the subjectivist revolution. "To understand the problem of economic calculation," Mises wrote, "it was necessary to recognize the true character of the exchange relations expressed in the prices of the market. The existence of this important problem could be revealed only by the methods of the modern subjective theory of value."[91] The exchange ratios established on the market, according to Mises, were the result of a process that was "anchored deep in the human mind."[92] Monetary calculation based upon these freely established exchange ratios, despite its imperfect character, allows us to separate out from among all those technologically possible projects ones that are economically feasible. Monetary calculation provides all that practical life demands. "Without it, all production by lengthy and roundabout processes of production would be so many steps in the dark."[93] With the growing division of labor and the lengthening of the process of production, monetary calculation has become "an aid that the human mind is no longer able to dispense with."[94]

Mises was explicit from the beginning on the central role of knowledge dispersion in both his positive case for the liberal economic order and his negative case against central planning. As he states in *Liberalism*: "[T]he *decisive objection* that economics raises against the possibility of a socialist society [is that] it must forgo the intellectual division of labor that consists in the cooperation of all entrepreneurs, landowners, and workers as producers and consumers in the formation of market prices."[95] Hayek, in addition, has emphasized that the intellectual division of labor that is utilized in market interaction is "knowledge of particular time and place."[96]

The importance placed on knowledge in the Austrian literature is unique among economists, and it led even the early Austrians, including those not predisposed toward classical liberal values, such as the Fabian socialist Friedrich Wieser, to raise doubts about the possibility of comprehensive central planning. Social economic activity will be more productive and successful, Wieser argued, if conducted by "thousands and millions of human beings, seeing with thousands and millions of eyes, exerting as many wills: they will be balanced, one against the other, far more accurately than if all these actions...had to be guided and directed by some superior control....A central prompter of this sort," Wieser concluded, "could never be informed of the countless possibilities, to be met with in every individual case, as regards the utmost utility to be derived from given circumstances or the best steps to be taken for future advancement and progress."[97]

Lavoie has argued that this emphasis on the market as a user and conveyor of knowledge is a particular instance of a general philosophical position on the nature and growth of knowledge in society that pervades the Austrian tradition and that has received increased philosophical attention in the past few years.[98] I have argued, moreover, that this emphasis on "knowing" in the Austrian literature can be rendered intelligible by recognizing that the central tenets of Austrian theory are the result of the peculiar interaction between continental philosophy and classical economics.[99] Whatever the reason, the most consistent theme running throughout the history of the Austrian school, from Menger to Mises and Hayek, all the way to Kirzner, Lachmann, and Lavoie, is the subjective nature of economic activity—the view of the market as a dynamic interaction of human minds. Or, as Ludwig Lachmann has most recently expressed it, the subjectivist economist views "the market as a pattern of meaningful utterances of the human mind."[100]

Theoretical Confusion

These theoretical insights into the market process, however, were overlooked in the debate over the feasibility of socialist economic calculation. The debate was diverted into statics by the counterargument put forth by Oskar Lange.[101] Although the theoretical discussion proceeded at a very abstract level, it was implicitly influenced to a great degree by the socialist experiment in Russia. "The subsequent developments of the discussion were," Polanyi argued, "largely determined by events in Russia," including what was meant by socialism. "At the time of L. v. Mises's first writing, the meanings of Socialism and central planning were unquestioningly identified with the elimination of the market as a means of allocating resources and its replacement by a system of direct central allocations."[102]

The market-socialist response to Mises, however, did not advocate the elimination of the market. But it went "unnoticed," Polanyi pointed out, that "modern Socialist theory, by adopting the principles of commerce, has quietly abandoned the cardinal claim of Socialism: the central direction of industrial production."[103] Two reasons might explain this oversight. First, the existence of the five-year planning system, which was interpreted by everyone as central planning, suggested that socialism was indeed possible and not devoid of economic rationality. Thus, Mises was thought to be proven wrong by the Soviet facts. Second, it became commonplace to view the market in the perfectly competitive framework and to read this framework onto Mises. Thus, Mises was also thought to be proven wrong by the mathematical model of general competitive equilibrium. The first reason revealed a failure to understand the original meaning of socialism, which is what Mises had challenged; it also revealed an implicit belief that a system was socialist if it was called socialist, regardless of its actual organizational form. The second reason was a result of the confusion between the respective debaters over what they considered theory. The misunderstanding over what constituted theory did not allow either the Austrians or the market socialists to understand what the other was saying.[104]

While Lange considered theory to imply the pure, institutionless logic of choice, Mises considered socialism to be a problem of the appropriate choice of institutions and organizational forms in a dynamic setting. The problem of socialist calculation was (is) a theoretical and practical problem in the world of continuous change. As Mises states: "The problem of economic calculation is of economic dynamics; it is no problem of economic statics."[105] So while there is a "formal similarity" in the choice-making problem between capitalism and socialism, the institutional differences are of utmost importance in economic calculation.

The problem is obtaining the necessary *economic* knowledge. Even if the technological knowledge were given to the planner, Mises argued, the socialist planner would lack the knowledge necessary to allocate capital goods in an economically rational manner. Only the knowledge embedded within money prices can aid economic calculation. Economic knowledge cannot be simply derived from given technological knowledge. It can only be revealed within the competitive market process. Because Mises sees the market process as the interaction of human minds, a price is not a mere number or measurement of value. "Numbers applied by acting man in economic calculation," according to Mises, "do not refer to quantities measured but to exchange ratios as they are expected—on the basis of understanding—to be realized on the markets of the future to which alone all acting is directed and which alone counts for acting man."[106] Technological knowledge conveys "mere information" and ignores the economic problem, according to Mises.

Despite popular perception, Mises was not concerned with generating pure, deductive, a priori proofs of the competitive economy. This has been more or less the research program most opposite the Austrian tradition—namely, general equilibrium theory.[107] The Misesian research program is not limited to the "pure logic of choice," but instead emphasizes the phenomenology of human action.[108] Institutional factors concerning the rule of law, ownership rights, and political interests are all involved within economic theory. Misesian a priority aids us in developing the basic principles of economics, which are necessary interpretative tools.[109] Beyond these basic concepts and principles, the economist is in the realm of applied economic theory.[110]

This misunderstanding over what constitutes theory had profound implications within the debate. Abram Bergson, for example, argued that it was generally recognized that "once tastes and techniques are given, the values of the means of production can be determined unambiguously by imputation without the intervention of a market process"—and, therefore, that the arguments advanced by Mises were "without much force."[111] But consider Mises's own statements on this point: "Under stationary conditions there no longer exists a problem for economic calculation to solve....*The essential function of economic calculation has by hypothesis already been performed.*"[112]

The whole point of the original challenge to the socialists by Mises, and later developments of the Austrian understanding of the market, is precisely that production projects cannot be treated as essentially known and given. They must be discovered by real-world entrepreneurs within the context of market competition.

The market process allows us to exploit, use, and discover knowledge that had previously been unknown to market participants. Economic actors do not choose the optimal production project from an array of known projects, subject to a constraint. Economic actors must discover opportunities for profitable ventures. They must be alert to opportunities and exercise keen entrepreneurial judgment in pursuing those opportunities. As Lavoie states: "[T]he key point of the calculation argument is that the required knowledge of objective production possibilities would be unavailable without the competitive market process."[113]

This discussion about theory has a purpose. The confusion in the theoretical debate led to the esoteric direction that much of modern comparative-systems economics has gone. "By equating the achievement of competitive equilibrium with the goal of socialism," Paul Craig Roberts argues, "the Lange-type model takes the problem of socialist planning out of its historical context and obscures it."[114] Fundamentally, then, the theoretical confusion produced historical misinterpretation of the Soviet experience. "Even the most careful study of the Russian facts," Hayek has argued, "cannot lead very far if it is not guided by a clear conception of what the problem is; i.e., if it is not undertaken by a person who, before he embarks on the investigations of the special problems of Russia, has arrived at a clear idea of the fundamental task that economic planning involves."[115]

Socialism does not face the task of allocating scarce resources among competing ends within a static framework any more than it is concerned with the choice of good production projects out of known portfolios. Socialism, in its original intent, faces the problem of substituting for the "blind forces of the market" a conscious and deliberate plan that can maintain advanced material standards of living and promote the flourishing of human potential. The Russian experience can provide some important insights into the feasibility of this quest.

Denying Marx's Influence

Before I criticize the standard account, one more theoretical point must be made. The role of Marxism is often denied as an important component in understanding the Soviet experience. Joseph Berliner, for example, argues that Marxism has had little impact on Soviet socialism, and that economists writing about Soviet economic policy and institutions should not find it necessary to consider Marxian theory.[116] Gerschenkron and Nove, as pointed out above, argue that Marxism is of little importance in studying the Soviet system.

Nove has most recently reiterated this point in *The Economics of Feasible Socialism*. He argues that Marx's economic analysis is confined to capitalism and does not extend to the economic problems facing a socialist economy. "Marxist economics," he concludes, "is either irrelevant or misleading, in respect of the problems that must be faced by any socialist economy which could exist."[117] While this statement contains a degree of truth, the failure to understand the policies of war communism, NEP, and the first five-year plan in light of the Marxian theory of socialism distorts the significance of the Soviet experience.[118] It allows Nove to search for a "feasible socialism" without paying credence to the idea that combining market and plan is incompatible with the original aspirations of Marxian socialism. It also distorts what we can learn about socioeconomic organization from the Soviet system. As Paul Craig Roberts and Matthew Stephenson have stated: "If scholars do not understand that Marx was out to abolish exchange and institute production for direct use, little wonder they do not recognize this Marxian endeavor in the momentous story of Soviet economic policies."[119] The policies of the first decade of Soviet socialism have to be interpreted through the purposes and plans of the agents seeking to implement them. The consequences of the policies can be understood by reference to the fundamental problem that socialist economic organization must overcome, but the original purposes and plans of the economic decisionmakers must be given full force in any narrative if we want to present a meaningful discussion of the events.

The Critique of the Standard Account

Boris Brutzkus, Michael Polanyi, and Paul Craig Roberts have presented arguments for viewing the Soviet experience in almost the complete reverse of the standard account. They did not find any new facts or uncover any hidden documents; rather, the narrative they put forward is the product of the different interpretative framework they adopt. As Polanyi states: "Mr. Dobb's account of the events does not materially differ from that given in my text, which was completed before his book came out. Yet he rejects as superficial the view that the Soviet government actually tried to establish Communism at that time and met with disaster in consequence."[120] The difference, then, is fundamentally over which theoretical framework better aids our understanding of the events. There are no facts independent of how we arrange and look at them. And the arranging of facts in order of importance is a product of theoretical framework.[121]

Brutzkus-Polanyi-Roberts explicitly state the framework from which they view the events of the Soviet experience. They treat Marxism seriously as a system of thought, and they understand fully the fundamental tasks that socialist planning involves. Contrary to the perspective that views war communism as an expedient, NEP as the necessary organizational form during the transition period, and the first five-year plan as the fulfillment of centralized economic planning, Brutzkus-Polanyi-Roberts argue that war communism was derived from the Marxian aspiration to abolish the market, NEP was a retreat to capitalist economic relations so the Bolsheviks could regroup and retain political power, and the five-year-planning system was the solidification of that power.

Brutzkus first made his argument in the 1920s that what was being experienced in Soviet Russia after the revolution was a derivative of the economic ideas of Karl Marx. "The Doctrines of Marxism in Light of the Russian Revolution," which constitutes the first part of *Economic Planning in Soviet Russia*, was first published in August 1920 in Russia. "The ideas set forth in these pages," Brutzkus states, "matured in my mind during the early years of constructive communism in Petrograd." The Bolsheviks, intoxicated by their defeat of the counterrevolutionaries, promised to deal promptly with existing economic problems. "It was at this moment of its greatest triumphs that [Brutzkus] put forward [his] contention that the system of Marxian communism, as then conceived, was—quite apart from conditions produced by the war—intrinsically unsound and must inevitably break down."[122]

Brutzkus readily admits, as Nove pointed out, that Marx's analysis was confined to capitalism, and therefore that there was a lack of any systematically elaborated socialist economic theory. He nevertheless argues that a definite Marxian outline follows the criticism of capitalism. "Although Marxism had produced no systematic theory for a socialist economy, it has nevertheless determined its outline."[123] "Marxian socialism," he continues, "rejects in principle the market and market prices as regulating factors of production....In comparison with capitalism, socialism appears as the most perfect form of economic organization. *Socialism directs the economic life according to a unitary state plan, which is founded upon statistics.*"[124]

The attempt to substitute a central plan for the "spontaneous process" of market evaluation leads to the "atrophy of economic calculation," argues Brutzkus. He suggests that the economic difficulties confronting the attempt to direct the economic life according to a unitary plan could be overcome by restoring the free market. But such a method "does not lie within the framework of socialism as Marx conceived it."[125] Therefore, the introduction of NEP, according to Brutzkus, "forsakes the framework of socialism as Marxism conceives it."[126]

This helps us understand the Brutzkus-Polanyi-Roberts view that even the five-year planning system cannot be considered a centrally planned economy, for as Brutzkus later points out: "The fundamental difference between this second scheme [the five-year plans] and the first [war communism] lay in the fact that it was planned on the lines of a money economy and not on natural socialism."[127] Labelling oneself a socialist, without admitting that the original goals have been abandoned—namely, the elimination of the monetary exchange economy—does not make one a socialist.

The reason that economic calculation atrophies under the unitary plan, according to Brutzkus, is the same as the knowledge problem discussed above. The attempt to bring complex industrial production under the control of a single decision-making entity overwhelms the ability of the human mind. While one could imagine a small firm or peasant farm being organized and managed by a reasonably intelligent person, the task becomes increasingly difficult as the complexity of the organization to be centrally directed increases.[128] "Is there any analogous *intelligence* capable of supervising intuitively the economic life of a small country, let along that of Russia in all its immensity?" asks Brutzkus. "The central organ of the socialist system—say the Supreme Economic Council—no longer possesses the sensitive barometer provided by the market prices."[129] So how is it going to gather the information necessary for economic coordination? And even more important than the technical problems of statistical gathering is the impossible task required of the Supreme Economic Council—determining the people's needs for economic goods a priori.

Demands for economic goods are only revealed within the actual choice-making process of market exchange. Without the spontaneous market process, which brings into coordination the most willing suppliers with the most willing demanders, the Supreme Economic Council "is unable to put together a minimum ration, and to direct production accordingly."[130] The point Brutzkus is attempting to make is simply this: what the Supreme Council is unable to achieve, even with all of science at its disposal, *is accomplished* every day through the interaction of ordinary citizens in the market. The reason the simple citizen accomplishes what the most advanced tools of science fail to produce is simply that the knowledge generated by the spontaneous adjustments of market interaction exceeds the ability of any one mind or group of minds to comprehend in detail.

"The truth is," Brutzkus argued, "that socialism lacks any mechanism for coordinating the separate processes of production....Socialism," he concluded, "overcomes the 'anarchy of capitalist production' by substituting a condition of super anarchy; and in comparison with this 'super anarchy' capitalism presents a picture of the utmost harmony."[131] It is this reason, and not the stronghold of world capitalism that erected a blockade or the strain of civil war, that led to the economic collapse from 1918 to 1921. "No single branch of economic life can be mentioned as having blossomed and borne fruit under the new economic regime, and it was just this complete evidence of failure that compelled even convinced communists to put their hopes henceforth in a partial return to a free exchange of goods and to capitalism."[132] The "renunciation of socialism" led to recovery during the NEP period, argued Brutzkus. He concluded that the "Russian experience bears out in the clearest manner our basic conclusion—namely, that the principle of socialism is not creative; that it leads the economic life of society not to fruition but to ruin."[133]

Polanyi argued that the Soviet experience confirms Mises's original contention that socialism, in its original Marxian sense, is technically impossible. "The only full-scale attempt to [direct all the resources of an industrial system from one center] was the one undertaken in Soviet Russia during the last six or eight months of 1920; and the results were disastrous." Even Trotsky, Polanyi pointed out, admitted the impossibility of socialism as Marxists originally envisioned it. Only a "Universal Mind as conceived by Laplace," Trotsky argued, "could successfully conduct a centrally-directed economy."[134] Mises was proven right.

The program of Marxian central planning died in March 1921, but the ideology of socialism was not buried. The Soviet economy, Polanyi argued, was turned into a military state-capitalist system. "The Five-Year Plans with all their sound and fury are but the parading of a dummy dressed up in the likeness of the original purpose of socialism."[135] Later he argued, "We have forgotten what the Russian Revolution was about; that it set out to establish a moneyless industrial system, free from the chaotic and sordid automation of the market and directed instead scientifically by one single comprehensive plan."[136]

Roberts, following up on Brutzkus and Polanyi, demonstrates that war communism was not conceived as a set of emergency measures by the Bolshevik leaders at the time. Rather, it was an outright attempt to abolish market relations. He argues that the prevalent Western interpretation that the Soviet experience between 1918 and 1921 represents an economic system brought on by the emergency of civil war is a result of the work of Dobb and Carr. Roberts points out that in the standard account, such as Dobb's, only quotes from Lenin after the establishment of the New Economic Policy are used as evidence.[137] In addition, the accounts of others, such as Carr, even though they may allow some ideological influence, blend ideology and emergency so that ideology quickly falls into the background, and the conditions of the time become the motive behind Soviet economic policy.[138]

To combat the emergency interpretation, Roberts goes to the evidence from Marx's and Lenin's writings. He demonstrates that Lenin understood that in Marx's negative view of capitalism there existed the positive view of socialism. The Marxian theory of alienation and its relation to commodity exchange and production play a crucial role in understanding the motivation behind the attempt to abolish all market relations during war communism.[139] Lenin and his associates sought to abolish the anarchy of capitalist production and substitute a comprehensive planning system. In a world where market forces continue to operate, alienation persists and the Marxian dream is unfulfilled.

The utter collapse that occurred because of the attempt to implement Marxian socialism forced Lenin to choose between putting an end to ideological aspirations, at least for the time being, or losing control of the government. Lenin chose to maintain political power at the expense of strict adherence to ideological principles. "Lenin thought," argues Roberts, "that the reintroduction of market exchange was necessary to retain power and he understood the practical need to sacrifice doctrine to power rather than the other way around." Thus, "it is clear that the program of eliminating commodity production was abandoned *not because it was a wartime measure unsuited to peacetime but because it had caused economic disruption and dissatisfaction that were threats to the political power of the Bolsheviks.*"[140]

Roberts concludes by issuing a challenge to those who interpret war communism as a set of expedient measures:

> Those who maintain that the policies of war communism were temporary measures to cope with war and inflation rather than an effort to establish a socialist organization should explain why Lenin repeatedly described the policies as efforts to establish socialism. If they were wartime policies, why should Lenin not have said so? If in fact the measures were meant to be temporary and were a response to war and inflation, Lenin's admission that he and the R.C.P.(B.) had made mistakes in their efforts to introduce socialism was not only needless and erroneous but also a fabrication.[141]

NEP, therefore, is seen as a retreat to market methods of economic organization, according to Brutzkus-Polanyi-Roberts. The revolutionary government, however, needed to be justified ideologically, otherwise the Bolsheviks had no reason to maintain power. The economic policies of NEP contained a political dynamic of their own, and they could not be maintained indefinitely. Emerging out of the controversy of the mid-1920s, the bureaucratic state comes to full power. The five-year plans, the policies of collectivization, and forced industrialization are not an application of Marxian economics as much as they are a product of an ideal that was unrealizable.

The Stalin era produced "unfortunate excesses," argues Gorbachev. Yet he maintains that collectivization and industrialization were necessary for Soviet development. We are told that *perestroika* represents the new NEP. But why did the old NEP fail? And what of NEP? The evidence seems to suggest that in its economic form it betrays the values of Marxian socialism. How about its political form? And what about Stalin? Was it the political form of NEP that enabled Stalin to establish his "cult of personality"?

Radoslav Selucky argues convincingly that the problem with Marxian central planning is that its necessary political form betrays the fundamental values of socialism. Marx wanted a centralized economic system, but a decentralized political system. Selucky argues that these two systems are incompatible. The base, according to Marxian theory, must determine the superstructure. The centralized economic system must result in centralized politics, that is, totalitarianism.[142]

Logical Continuity or Historical Determinism?

Michael Polanyi charged Mises and Hayek with being too pessimistic toward the original claim of the impossibility of socialist economic organization in the face of the existence of the Soviet regime. Although they endorsed Brutzkus's interpretation of the events, neither Mises nor Hayek extended or reiterated Brutzkus's analysis during the 1940s when both the theoretical and historical literature moved away from their position. Polanyi charged Mises with denouncing "the Soviet Government for wickedly doing precisely that which in 1920 he had proved to be impossible."[143] Instead of clarifying the theoretical issues, Polanyi argued, Mises and Hayek "retreated" to the issue of economic freedom versus totalitarianism. "Of all the intellectual triumphs of the Communist regime," Polanyi stated, "it seems to me the greatest is to have made these eminent and influential writers [Mises and Hayek] so completely lose their heads.... Could anything please that regime better," he asked, "than to hear itself proclaimed by its leading opponents as an omnipotent, omniscient, omnipresent socialist planner?" That is exactly the picture they so desperately want to draw themselves. "Such accusations supply the Soviet government with an incontestable 'testimony' of having achieved the impossible aspirations of socialism, when in fact it has simply set up a system of state capitalism—a goal which leaves the regime next door to where it started."[144]

Abram Bergson also charged that Mises and Hayek retreated to the totalitarian argument against planning, but for a different reason from that offered by Polanyi. "The emphasis that critics of socialism have lately placed on this issue [i.e., human freedom]," Bergson stated, "sometimes has the appearance of a tactical maneuver, to bolster a cause which Mises' theories have been found inadequate to sustain."[145]

The problem arises, in the first place, from the fact that both Mises and Hayek were diverted into a debate over the equilibrium conditions of perfect competition and alternative models of market socialism. Concern was not with understanding and analyzing the actual practice of real-world "socialist" economies. The interrelationship between theory and history has depreciated in comparative economic systems ever since.

Second, the argument by Mises and Hayek that the loss of human freedom logically results from attempts to establish a socialist economic order has been misunderstood by its critics. It is not simply an empirical argument that "bad" people have tended to achieve leadership positions in these command economies.[146] Rather, it is a logical argument that relies on understanding the nature of the planning institutions required to accomplish the goals of socialism. It is not merely a matter of a better selection of persons. As Mises put it: "It has not been realized that even exceptionally gifted men of high character cannot solve the problems created by the socialist control of industry....[T]he problems with which we are concerned do not arise from the moral shortcomings of humanity. They are problems of logic of will and action which must arise at all times and in all places."[147] The argument, in this regard, is very similar to the argument offered by modern public-choice theory and the economics of bureaucracy.

The bureaucratic structure that fell into the hands of Stalin was a logical development of the failure of planning and the retreat from Marxian goals. Stephen Cohen has argued that anyone postulating a logical continuity between the policies of war communism and the Stalinist collectivization period is guilty of historical determinism that results from viewing the Soviet experience through totalitarian lenses, a legacy of the cold war era.[148] Cohen, on the other hand, is interested in arguing that there is a fundamental discontinuity in the Soviet experience. The "reign of terror" was not a logical outcome of socialist construction. The alternative to Stalin was real: it was Nikolai Bukharin.[149]

But the totalitarianism of Stalin need not be the theoretical conception through which a theorist views the origin of the Soviet political economy, though it would be irresponsible to ignore it.[150] The logical continuity between Lenin and Stalin, which in the final analysis can render intelligible the rise of Stalinism, can be understood from a different theoretical perspective—the Austrian argument against planning, combined with insights from modern public-choice theory.[151]

The problems with planning consist of four (conceptually separate, but logically connected) arguments: (1) property-rights and incentive problems, (2) problems of informational complexity, (3) epistemological (tacit knowledge) problems, and (4) the totalitarian problem. Each leads logically to the next one. Socialist managers do not face the same incentives as capitalist managers do to insure efficient allocation of resources. Even if we assume that the incentive problem is overcome, the task of collecting and processing the necessary information for coordination plans is too complex. If the socialist planner could gather the information required to insure efficient allocation and distribution of resources, the amount of information necessary to complete the task in a reasonably efficient manner would be too vast. But beyond the problem of informational complexity lies the epistemological problem that planners must overcome. Much of the knowledge necessary to accomplish the task required of the socialist planner cannot be treated as "data" since it largely consists of the tacit, or inarticulate, knowledge generated within the competitive market. Moreover, relevant economic knowledge is contextual knowledge and not abstract. Economic circumstances change daily, and information gathered yesterday may not be relevant for tomorrow. Fourth, the totalitarian problem arises because of the nature of planning as such. To engage in centralized economic planning, certain institutional structures have to be established. Discretionary power has to be turned over to someone or some group.[152]

Public-choice economics has informed us that we cannot model policy makers as benevolent despots.[153] Rather, economists must view political actors in the same manner as they view economic actors—as self-interested individuals. In planning situations this argument is intensified, for now the very institutions under discussion require concentrating power in the hands of a few. We should expect those with a comparative advantage in exercising discretionary power to rise to the top of the planning apparatus.[154]

The economic-planning institutions of war communism were left in place after the abandonment of war communism. During NEP the Bolshevik regime, while allowing market relations to exist, maintained power over the "commanding height" industries. More important, however, were the political institutions established during this time. The Bolsheviks declared themselves the monopolist political party, and this institutional order persists today.[155]

If one considers the arguments advanced by Austrian, as well as other, economists concerning the connection between political and economic freedom, the move to declare a political monopoly by Lenin and his associates is intelligible.[156] The voluntary organizations of a market society put pressure on political institutions that seek to control human interaction. But the whole point of planning is to overcome the haphazard and chaotic fashion in which people interact and coordinate with each other in a market environment.

The existence of a liberal political order and central planning are incompatible. As F.A. Hayek states:

> The authority directing all economic activity would control not merely the part of our lives which is concerned with inferior things; it would control the allocation of the limited means for all our ends. And whoever controls all economic activity controls the means for all our ends and must therefore decide which are to be satisfied and which not. This is really the crux of the matter. Economic control is not merely control of a sector of human life which can be separated from the rest; it is the control of the means for all our ends. And whoever has sole control of the means must also determine which ends are to be served, which values are to be rated higher and which lower—in short, what men should believe and strive for. Central planning means that the economic problem is to be solved by the community instead of by the individual; but this involves that it must also be the community, or rather its representatives, who must decide the relative importance of the different needs.[157]

NEP was an admission that the task of centrally planning an economy was beyond the ability of the Bolsheviks (at least at the stage of development in which they found themselves in 1921). But, by moving to market methods of economic organization, Lenin inadvertently threatened the political survival of the Communist Party. The logic of this statement is presented by Thomas Sowell in an abstract discussion of reform within the Soviet system. As he says:

> The incumbent leader of the Soviet Union at any given time could make himself more popular by liberalizing government restrictions or by reducing military spending and allowing the people's standard of living to rise accordingly. The immediate dangers to his own regime during his own term of office could be minimal, and yet the larger dangers to the internal and external goals of the Communist party could well be sufficiently serious to cause that party to depose the leader for even trying to initiate such reforms.

> A party with a longer time horizon requires more pervasive control than an individual with only his own term of office to consider.[158]

Moreover, as Alain Besançon argues, the Soviet leader "has been chosen for his ability to uphold the fiction that the fictional reality is not fictitious and therefore to promote it." He must balance the "principle that capitalism has to be destroyed" with the principle that "enough capitalism must be preserved so that the power is not threatened in its material and political base.... The whole economic art of the Soviet government," Besançon concludes, "consists in combining these two principles so that the socialist design of destroying capitalism is achieved while the strength and vitality of the Party-State on which depends the achievement of this task are preserved....Lenin was, and still is, the master of the strictly Bolshevik art of the Soviet economy. It was he who had Trotsky's plans rejected in 1921, *plans which would have resulted in the absolute ruin of capitalism, but also the end of Soviet power.*"[159]

Survival could be insured, however, if political competition were eliminated, and that was accomplished by decree at the same time that NEP was introduced. "The monolithic party," Theodore Draper points out, "was officially ordained in March 1921 at the same time as the NEP—and both at the behest of Lenin." The resolution declared party unity and made "official a policy of banning opposition." Though the debates of the 1920s were not inhibited by this outlawing of "factional struggles," the ultimate beneficiary of this political set-up was Stalin, "who succeeded in imposing his own type of 'party unity' prescribed by Lenin."[160]

Stalin's victory and the failure of NEP are due in large part to the political system Lenin had established.[161] Lenin declared the party a monopoly; Stalin merely took the next step and declared himself the monopolist within the party. The abandonment of NEP does not reflect "the needs of a state committed to rapid, large-scale industrialization to reduce the commitment of resources to agriculture and to enforce reduced living standards on both town and country," as Mark Harrison argues.[162] The failure of NEP to persist does not represent the failure of market forms of organization to promote economic development. Collectivization did not possess an "economic logic." It possessed a political, military, and bureaucratic logic.[163] But as for economic logic, the policies of collectivization and forced industrialization were devoid of it.[164]

Conclusion

History is the story of the human condition. It has its lessons, and we would be foolish not to learn them. The history of the Soviet Union appears to be a lesson not yet learned. The confusion surrounding the fundamental task of socialist economic organization has produced a voluminous collection of work that has little relevance to the nature of the problem under discussion. The historical interpretation, influenced as it is by the theoretical confusion, has blinded scholars to the meaning of this rich experience. The failure to appreciate both the original aspirations of Marxian political economy and the economic coordination problem that the Marxist system confronts has led to a lack of appreciation for this decade in economic history. As Michael Polanyi argued: "Volume upon volume of excellent scholarship is rapidly accumulating on the history of the Russian Revolution, but as I read these books I find my own recollection of this event dissolving bit by bit." He concluded, "The Revolution *is about to be quietly enshrined under a pyramid of monographs*."[165]

We must understand the problem under consideration. This is not a matter of antiquarian interest, but one of fundamental concern for us today if we want to understand the human condition as it exists in the Soviet Union, both in its historical context 70 years ago and now.[166]

Gorbachev faces similar problems today. He wants to reform the economic system by introducing new incentives and allowing market relations to come above ground. Yet real economic reform is slow in coming. Moreover, the connection between economic freedom and the demand for political freedom is clearly demonstrated in the drive to catch up with the West. Even Gorbachev admits this. "Today," he told the delegates to the 19th Party Conference (June 28—July 1, 1988), "we must have the courage to admit that if the political system remains immobile and unchanged, we will not cope with the tasks of reform."[167] Or, as Gorbachev put it just a few days later, "It is the logic of economic reform [that] has led us to be conscious of the need for political reform."[168]

Political demands and protest go with *glasnost* and *perestroika*, but toleration of dissent goes only so far. The fundamental problem Gorbachev faces is not so much reforming the system, it *is* the system. The political-economic institutions of Soviet society are responsible, and unless Gorbachev moves toward fundamental change—change that admits the problems of bureaucratic power—real reform will have to wait.

In the meantime, it is crucial to continue examination of the past with a critical eye. Understanding the Soviet experience should produce a fundamental rethinking of the political economy of the socialist order and structure. In the chapters that follow, I hope to provide historical evidence and produce a coherent narrative that continue the criticism of the standard account I have presented here. In so doing, I plan not just to defend the revisionist thesis but also to advance our understanding of the first decade of the Soviet experience beyond the level of Brutzkus, Polanyi, or Roberts.

Notes

[1] M. Dobb, *Soviet Economic Development Since 1917* (New York: International Publishers, 1948), 1.

[2] See Sidney and Beatrice Webb, *Soviet Communism: A New Civilisation?* (New York: Scribner's, 1938); E.H. Carr, *The Soviet Impact on the Western World* (New York: Macmillan, 1947); Aleksandr I. Solzhenitsyn, *The Gulag Archipelago*, 3 vols. (New York: Harper and Row, 1974).

[3] Mikhail Heller and Aleksandr Nekrich, *Utopia in Power: The History of the Soviet Union from 1917 to the Present* (New York: Summit Books, 1986), 11.

[4] My concern is not so much with what Marx meant by socialism, though this is obviously a point of importance, but rather what leading European and Russian Marxist thinkers thought Marx meant by socialism, and what policies they should follow. In particular, with regard to Russia, what did Lenin, Bukharin, Trotsky, and others, think a Marxian world should look like?

[5] Alexander Gerschenkron, "History of Economic Doctrines and Economic History," *American Economic Review*, Vol. 59, n. 2 (May 1969), 16.

[6] Nove, *An Economic History of the U.S.S.R.* (New York: Penguin Books, 1984[1969]), 47.

[7] Ludwig von Mises sparked the debate in 1920 with his challenging article "Economic Calculation in the Socialist Commonwealth," which was later translated and reprinted in ed. F.A. Hayek, *Collectivist Economic Planning* (New York: Augustus M. Kelley, 1975[1935]). Mises refined his argument in *Socialism: An Economic and Sociological Analysis* (Indianapolis: Liberty Press, 1981[1922]). Mises's conclusion that rational economic calculation is impossible under socialism was reinforced by Max Weber, *Economy and Society*, 2 vols., edited by Guenther Roth and Claus Wittich (Berkeley: University of California Press, 1978[1922]), I: 63-211, especially 100-113. This triggered responses from German socialist writers such as Karl Polanyi and Eduard Heimann, see Mises, *Socialism*, 473-478. Also see William Keizèr, "Two Forgotten Articles by Ludwig von Mises on the Rationality of Socialist Economic Calculation," *Review of Austrian Economics*, Vol. 1 (1987), 109-122, for a more extensive discussion of the central European debate of the 1920s.

Mises's contention was later challenged in the English-language journals during the 1930s and 1940s. The counter argument was made by Oskar Lange, *On the Economic Theory of Socialism*, ed. Benjamin Lippincott (New York: Augustus M. Kelley, 1970[1939]); and Abba Lerner, *The Economics of Control* (New York: Macmillan, 1944) among others. Mises's student and associate, F. A. Hayek, was an active participant in the debate with the market socialist writers. See Hayek's essays in *Collectivist Economic Planning* and *Individualism and Economic Order* (Chicago: University of Chicago Press, 1980[1948]). The debate has been a subject of growing attention among economists, and useful summaries can be found in Trygve J.B. Hoff, *Economic Calculation in the Socialist Society* (Indianapolis: Liberty Press, 1981[1949]); Murray Rothbard, "Ludwig von Mises and Economic Calculation Under Socialism," *The Economics of Ludwig von Mises*, ed. Lawrence Moss, (Kansas City: Sheed and Ward, Inc., 1976), 67-77; Karen Vaughn, "Economic Calculation Under Socialism: the Austrian Contribution," *Economic Inquiry*, Vol. 18 (1980), 535-554; Peter Murrell, "Did the Theory of Market Socialism Answer the Challenge of Ludwig von Mises?" *History of Political Economy*, Vol. 15, n. 1 (Spring 1983), 92-105. The most extensive treatment of the debate, however, is provided by Don Lavoie in *Rivalry and Central Planning: The Socialist Calculation Debate Reconsidered* (New York: Cambridge University Press, 1985).

[8] Ironically, Hayek might be partially responsible in creating this theory-history split. *Collectivist Economic Planning* was published as a companion volume to Boris Brutzkus, *Economic Planning in Soviet Russia* (Westport, CT: Hyperion Press, 1981[1935]), which Hayek also edited, and introduced. The subsequent discussion, however, cared little about what Brutzkus, or anyone for that matter, had to say about the Soviet experience. Rather, the debate was diverted into the realm of pure theory. By conveying the idea that theory and history could be neatly separated in two separate volumes, Hayek might have inadvertently promoted the theory-history split that dominates comparative political economy to this day.

[9] Mikhail Gorbachev, "Revolution's Road From 1917 to Now," *The New York Times* (Tuesday, November 3, 1987), A11.

[10] Gorbachev, *Perestroika: New Thinking for Our Country and the World* (New York: Harper and Row, 1987), 21.

[11] Gorbachev, *Perestroika*, 35, 34, 33.

[12] Gorbachev, "Revolution's Road from 1917 to Now," A11.

[13] Theodore Draper, "Soviet Reformers: From Lenin to Gorbachev," *Dissent* (Summer 1987), 287.

[14] Heller and Nekrich, *Utopia in Power*, 11.

[15] S. Cohen, *Rethinking the Soviet Experience* (New York: Oxford University Press, 1985), 71-92; and Cohen's classic treatment, *Bukharin and the Bolshevik Revolution: A Political Biography, 1988-1938* (New York: Oxford University Press, 1980[1973]).

[16] At a crucial point in his narrative on Bukharin's switch from extreme left to the extreme right of the Bolshevik party, Cohen relies upon Oskar Lange's model of market socialism to answer Bukharin's (in his leftist days) own characterization of the socialist economy as an economy where "relations between people are not expressed in relations between things, and social economy is regulated not by blind forces of the market and competition, but consciously by a plan" and Bukharin's further claim that with the introduction of socialist economic relations political economy ceases as a subject of study: "there can be no place for a science studying the 'blind laws of the market' since there will be no market." Cohen cites Lange as providing in the 1930s the scientific search for "the political economy of socialism." See *Bukharin and the Bolshevik Revolution*, 93, and fn. 133. Lange argues that economics is a universal science, applying to socialist as well as capitalist economies, and I can agree with him here. But the Lange framework transforms economics into the study of the static allocation problem and, in fact, assumes away the importance of institutions in economic interaction. I do not want to suggest that Cohen follows Lange here, but rather, that Lange is irrelevant for the problem at hand. He did not provide any foundation for the scientific search for a political economy of socialism; Lange merely provided a proof that if one assumes everything is known and given, then there is no economic problem to solve. Needless to say this had *nothing* to do with the problems with which Bukharin was coping.

[17] The notable exceptions are Boris Brutzkus, *Economic Planning in Russia* (Westport, CT.: Hyperion Press, 1982[1935]); Trygve Hoff, *Economic Calculation in the Socialist Society* (Indianapolis: Liberty Press, 1981[1949]); Michael Polanyi, *The Contempt of Freedom: The Russian Experiment and After* (London: Watts & Co., 1940); *The Logic of Liberty* (Chicago: University of Chicago Press, 1980[1951]); Elisabeth Tamedly, *Socialism and International Economic Order* (Caldwell, ID: Caxton Printers, 1969); Paul Craig Roberts, *Alienation and the Soviet Economy* (Albuquerque: University of New Mexico Press, 1971); Paul Craig Roberts and Matthew Stephenson, *Marx's Theory of Exchange, Alienation, and Crisis* (New York: Praeger, 1983[1973]); Don Lavoie, *Rivalry and Central Planning* (New York: Cambridge University Press, 1985a); *National Economic Planning: What Is Left?* (Cambridge, MA: Ballinger Press, 1985b); and Peter Rutland, *The Myth of the Plan* (LaSalle, IL: Open Court, 1985). These writers all view comprehensive central planning as impossible. Polanyi, Roberts, and Lavoie refer to the Soviet system as a polycentric bureaucratic economic system. Some recent theorists of the Soviet system have also begun to realize the difficulty of viewing the Soviet system as a

centrally planned economy, and prefer to classify the system as a centrally managed economic system, cf. Eugene Zaleski, *Planning for Economic Growth in the Soviet Union, 1918-1932* (Chapel Hill: University of North Carolina Press, 1971); *Stalinist Planning for Economic Growth* (London: Macmillan, 1980). Also see Alec Nove, *The Economics of Feasible Socialism* (London: George Allen & Unwin, 1983), 79-81.

[18] See Alec Nove, *An Economic History of the U.S.S.R.*, 46-187 and G. Warren Nutter, *The Growth of Industrial Production in the Soviet Union* (Princeton: Princeton University Press, 1962), 3-10. As Nutter points out, "Most specialists on the Soviet economy start their studies with the year 1928, when comprehensive centralized planning was introduced" (5). The fact that most studies within comparative political economy begin their analysis of central planning with the five-year planning system represents the fundamental misunderstanding of the Soviet experience which I am trying to correct in my study.

[19] Robert Ekelund and Robert Tollison, *Economics*, 2nd ed. (Boston: Scott, Foresman and Co., 1988), 914-915; emphasis added. It should be emphasized that this interpretation, that is, the standard interpretation, is greatly influenced by what the authors consider to be socialism, which in turn is influenced by the theoretical debate. As will be argued throughout, the theoretical debate had the consequence of obscuring the meaning of socialism and tearing it from its historical context.

[20] See Paul Gregory and Robert Stuart, *Soviet Economic Structure and Performance*, 2nd ed. (New York: Harper and Row, 1981), 15-110.

[21] Ofer, "Soviet Economic Growth: 1928-1985," *Journal of Economic Literature*, Vol. 25 (December 1987), 1768; emphasis added.

[22] Bottomore, "Is Rivalry Rational?" *Critical Review*, Vol. 1, n. 1 (Winter 1986-87), 45; emphasis added.

[23] Dobb, *Soviet Economic Development Since 1917*; Carr, *The Bolshevik Revolution*, 3 vols. (New York: Norton, 1980[1952]); and Nove, *An Economic History of the U.S.S.R.*.

[24] Dobb, *Soviet Economic Development Since 1917*, 122.

[25] Dobb, 122.

[26] Dobb, 101.

[27] Dobb, 101.

[28] Dobb, 100.

[29] Although it is not my purpose here to outline a Marxian theory of alienation and exploitation, it is necessary to realize that the decision-making cadre of the Soviet government were revolutionary Marxists who sought to rid Russian society of the evils of capitalism. The Marxian theory of alienation is intimately connected to commodity production and, in particular, the monetary exchange economy. Alienation to Marx was an objective condition coexistent with commodity production,that is, the separation of production from use. It is *not* a psychological or subjective condition felt by frustrated man. The transcendence of alienation means to Marx the transcendence of market relations. Viewing Marx as an organizational theorist enables the student of Marx to see a tremendous unity in Marx's life-work that is denied by those who want to split Marx into a young Marx and a mature Marx. The young Marx, just as the mature Marx, was concerned with transcending the organizational form of alienation, that is, the commodity production of capitalist social relations. As Marx argued himself in the *Economic and Philosophical Manuscripts of 1844* (Moscow: Progress Press, 1977), 78-79: "Just as we have derived the concept of private property from the concept of estranged, alienated labor by analysis, so we can develop every category of political economy with the help of these two factors; and we shall find again in each category, e.g., trade, competition, capital, money, only a particular and developed expression of these first elements." Also see Marx's discussion of the power of money as the "alienated ability of mankind" (127-132). On Marx's theory of alienation and central planning, see Paul Craig Roberts, *Alienation and the Soviet Economy*; Roberts and Stephenson, *Marx's Theory of Exchange, Alienation and Crisis*; and Lavoie, *Rivalry and Central Planning*, 28-47.

[30] Dobb, 102-103.

[31] For an excellent discussion of these events, see Paul Avrich, *Kronstadt 1921* (New York: W. W. Norton & Co., 1974). Also see Robert Vincent Daniels, *The Conscience of the Revolution* (Cambridge: Harvard University Press, 1960), 137-153 and Israel Getzler, *Kronstadt, 1917-1921* (New York: Cambridge University Press, 1983).

[32] Dobb, 123. However, Richard Sakwa argues contrary to Dobb that:

> In the chaotic conditions of late 1917, however, the development of direct democracy and decentralization in both political and economic spheres, was not so much a policy implemented by the Bolshevik party as one that emerged largely regardless of its wishes and out of circumstances. The institutions of the dictator-

> ship of the proletariat were only consolidated by June 1918. The practical implementation of commune ideas before then has given rise to a highly idealized if barely credible vision of a golden age of Bolshevism that came to end in spring 1918.

See Sakwa, "The Commune State in Moscow in 1918," *Slavic Review* (Fall/Winter, 1987), 431. Also notice the use of the term *New Economic Policy*; if these policies did constitute the policies that were followed directly after the revolution and represent the "normal economic policy of the proletariat," then why refer to the policies as "New"?

[33] Dobb, 120.

[34] Carr, *The Bolshevik Revolution*, 2: 270.

[35] Ironically, many other commentators point out the same connection between war communism and war socialism as evidencing the theoretical nature of war communism as an experiment with Marxian central planning. See Laszlo Szamuely, *First Models of the Socialist Economic Systems: Principles and Theories*, (Budapest: Akademiai Kiado, 1974); Vladimir Treml, "Interaction of Economic Thought and Economic Policy in the Soviet Union," *History of Political Economy*, Vol. 1, n. 1 (Spring 1969), 187-216. For a discussion of the German ideas of planning that had a direct influence upon the Bolshevik's see Judith Merkle, *Management and Ideology* (Berkeley: University of California Press, 1980), 172-207; Walter Rathenau, *In Days to Come* (New York: Alfred A. Knopf, 1921), 63-128; Nicholas Balabkins, "*Der Zukunftsstaat*: Carl Ballod's vision of a leisure-oriented socialism," *History of Political Economy*, Vol. 10, n. 2 (Summer 1978), 213-32. Also see Mises's discussion of war socialism in *Nation, State and Economy*, translated by Leland B. Yeager (New York: New York University Press, 1983[1919]), 141-147.

[36] Carr, 2: 271.

[37] Carr, 2: 273.

[38] Carr, 2: 273.

[39] Carr, 2: 207.

[40] Carr, 2: 162.

[41] Carr, 2: 175.

[42] Carr, 2: 157.

[43] Carr, 2: 151.

[44] Carr, 2: 157.

[45] Carr, 2: 172.

[46] Carr, 2: 173.

[47] Carr, 2: 198.

[48] Compare this with the recent twist on the standard interpretation by Thomas Remington, *Building Socialism* (Pittsburgh: University of Pittsburgh Press, 1984), who, in discussing the nationalization and central control of cottage industries, states that "*after* military emergencies declined to the point where *they no longer interfered with the Bolshevik preference for centralization*," new attempts to nationalize craftsmen were undertaken in late 1920 (170; emphasis added).

[49] Carr, 2: 197. But see Carr's discussion of the beginnings of planning on 2: 360 ff., which seems to state that both ideology and emergency played a role. Carr, however, argues that planning was not possible until 1920 because of the demands of civil war. The institutions of planning were established in 1918 and 1919, but they took on an ad hoc character because of the emergencies of civil war. Thus, centralized economic planning could not be properly instituted until 1920, according to Carr. He gives a rather strange argument, however, for the planning policy. "The experience of civil war," Carr states, "revealed the *practical necessity* of a central department strong enough to impose its authority on the existing economic organs of government and to *direct economic policy in light of a single plan of campaign* (2: 368; emphasis added). But wasn't this the policy objective, that is, centralized economic planning, which the standard account argues did not receive attention until 1928? Yet Carr, at least here, admits explicitly that the economic policy of central planning was instituted in 1920. The collapse occurs in 1921, during the regime of economic planning and *not* civil war.

[50] Carr, 2: 205-206.

[51] Carr, 2: 205.

[52] Carr, 2: 216.

[53] Carr, 2: 228.

[54] Carr, 2: 271.

[55] Carr, 2: 246.

[56] Carr, 2: 260-261.

[57] Carr, 2: 275.

[58] See Szamuely, *First Models*, 84-91, for a discussion of the debate among Bolshevik decision-makers over the introduction of NEP and the defense of war communism by Yuri Larin.

[59] Carr, 2: 275.

[60] Carr, 2: 276. Here again Carr does not maintain a consistent position. The confusion over war communism was even represented within official Soviet publications. Consider the following statement from an article in *Bol'shaya Sovetskaya Entsiklopediya*, XII, 1928:

> It would be a great error not to see, behind the obvious economic utopianism of the attempt of war communism to *realize an immediate marketless-centralized reorganization of our economy*, the fact that fundamentally the economic policy of the period of war communism was imposed by the embittered struggle for victory....The historical sense of war communism consisted in the need to take possession of the economic base by relying on military and political force. But it would be *incorrect* to see in war communism only measures of mobilization imposed by war conditions. In working to adapt the whole economy to the needs of the civil war, in building a consistent system of war communism, the working class was at the same time laying the foundation for further socialist reconstruction (as quoted in Carr, 2: 275, fn. 1, emphasis added).

One is left wondering what was the purpose of war communism. Was it an attempt to realize a Marxian utopia or was it mobilization for war? While Carr can argue that Marxian language was an ex post justification for policies that were unavoidable, it seems just as possible that war emergency language is an *ex-post* excuse for a dream that was left unfulfilled.

[61] Nove, *An Economic History of the U.S.S.R.*, 47.

[62] Nove, 47.

[63] Nove, 81.

[64] These techniques of planning cannot even be considered part of the Marxian aspiration to transcend the market—they have nothing in common with Marxism. These models are not representations of the "association of producers" developing a general plan, but rather are theoretical attempts to develop technical mechanisms to gather the data deemed necessary for planning. They represent technocratic attempts to provide a theoretical vision of how it might be possible to establish a network of information within the planning bureaucracy to achieve *ex-ante* coordination of economic activity. Not much of the emancipatory aspect of Marxism is left. See David L. Prychitko, "The Political Economy of Workers' Self-Management: A Market Process Critique" (unpublished Ph.D. thesis, Department of Economics, George Mason University, 1989), for the essential tension between Marx's praxis philosophy and models of economic planning.

[65] Nove, 120; emphasis added.

[66] Nove, 120; emphasis added.

[67] Cohen, "In Praise of War Communism," in *Revolution and Politics in Russia*, ed. Alexander and Janet Rabinowitch, (Bloomington: Indiana University Press, 1972), 193. For a more recent statement of Cohen's views on war communism see Cohen, *Rethinking the Soviet Experience*, 38-70.

[68] Bukharin, *The Path to Socialism in Russia* (New York: Omicron Books, 1967[1924]), 178, as quoted in Szamuely, *First Models*, 108, fn. 57; emphasis added. Also see Nove, "Some Observations on Bukharin and His Ideas," in *Political Economy and Soviet Socialism* (London: Allen and Unwin, 1979), 81-99.

[69] Bukharin, *Pravda* (December 3, 1922), 3, as quoted in Cohen, *Bukharin and the Bolshevik Revolution*, 146.

[70] Mises, *Socialism*, 101.

[71] Mises, "Economic Calculation," 102.

[72] This is the view of the market process that is characteristic of Austrian economics. Lavoie has argued that the failure on the part of the neoclassical market socialists to understand, let alone appreciate, this aspect of the Mises-Hayek argument led to the confusion in the debate. See *Rivalry and Central Planning*, 78-116.

[73] See Hayek, *Individualism and Economic Order* and *The Counter-Revolution of Science: Studies on the Abuse of Reason* (Indianapolis: Liberty Press, 1979[1952]).

[74] In contrast, Joseph Farrell argues that Hayek ignored the problem of how to get people, when private information is important, to reveal their true preferences. If the central authority, therefore, can insure that people will reveal their true preferences through an appropriate mechanism design, then Hayek's argument may not be as strong as it first appears. The point is that in regard to certain goods, that is, public goods, the market is a "poor" mechanism to give people an incentive to reveal their private information. In such an instance the market will produce suboptimal results, while even a "stumbling bureaucrat" might produce "better" results. See Farrell, "Information and the Coase Theorem," *Journal of Economic Perspectives*, Vol. 1, n. 2 (Fall 1987), 113-129. For a critique of standard public goods theory see Tyler Cowen, "A Public Goods Definition and Their Institutional Context: A Critique of Public Goods Theory," *Review of Social Economy*, Vol. 43, n. 1 (April 1985), 53-63. Also see Roy Cordato, "An Analysis of Externalities in Austrian Economics" (unpublished PhD thesis, Department of Economics, George Mason University, 1986).

Beyond the point about market problems when goods possess certain "publicness" aspects to them, Farrell misunderstands Hayek's argument against planning and the use of knowledge in society. Hayek never ignored the demand revealing processes of the market. In fact, that is essentially Hayek's point of criticism. The competitive market process serves as a vehicle for the discovery and conveyance of "private information." In the absence of the competitive process, according to Hayek, there is no practical way to insure that individuals will reveal their preferences for goods and services. See Hayek, "The Meaning of Competition," *Individualism and Economic Order*, 92-106; and "Competition as a Discovery Procedure," *New Studies in Philosophy, Politics, Economics and the History of Ideas* (Chicago: University of Chicago, 1978), 179-190. Also see Boettke, "Comment on 'Information and the Coase Theorem,'" *Journal of Economic Perspectives*, Vol. 3, n. 2 (Spring 1989), 195-197.

[75] For a recent statement of this point see Israel M. Kirzner, *Perception, Opportunity and Profit* (Chicago: University of Chicago Press, 1979), 137-153. Also see Lavoie, *National Economic Planning*, 52-65.

[76] Hayek, "The Use of Knowledge in Society," *Individualism and Economic Order*, 78.

[77] Kirzner, *Competition and Entrepreneurship* (Chicago: University of Chicago Press, 1973), 214.

[78] Lavoie, *Rivalry and Central Planning; National Economic Planning*; "The Market as a Procedure for Discovery and Conveyance of Inarticulate Knowledge," *Comparative Economic Studies* (Spring 1986), 1-19; "Political and Economic

Illusions of Socialism," *Critical Review*, Vol. 1, n. 1 (Winter 1986-87), 1-35; and "The Accounting of Interpretations and the Interpretation of Accounts: The Communicative Function of 'The Language of Business,'" *Accounting, Organizations, and Society*, Vol. 12, n. 6 (1987), 579-604.

[79] See Polanyi, *The Logic of Liberty* (Chicago: University of Chicago Press, 1980[1951]); *The Study of Man* (Chicago: University of Chicago Press, 1959); *Personal Knowledge: Toward a Post-Critical Philosophy* (Chicago: University of Chicago Press, 1962[1958]); *Knowing and Being: Essays by Michael Polanyi*, ed. Marjorie Green, (Chicago: University of Chicago Press, 1969).

[80] See Polanyi, *The Logic of Liberty*; *The Contempt of Freedom*; and *Science, Faith and Society* (Chicago: University of Chicago Press, 1964[1946]); *Knowing and Being*; "The Foolishness of History," *Encounter* (November 1957); and "Toward a Theory of Conspicuous Production," *Soviet Survey* (October/December 1960). Also see John Baker, *Science and the Planned State* (New York: Macmillan, 1945).

[81] Polanyi, *The Logic of Liberty*, 115.

[82] Polanyi, *The Logic of Liberty*, 111. Polanyi is here directly challenging the claim made by traditional Marxists that the Marxian system would, because it did away with the irrationalities of capitalist production, lead to great increases in material well-being. If one assumes the end or goal of his opponent, and demonstrates that the means employed are inconsistent with the end sought, the opponent's argument can said to be wanting or, at least, incomplete. Of course, there is no a priori reason why material well-being should be the highest of all social values, and the fact that most economists accept efficiency and wealth as their standards reveals the utilitarian bias of most modern economics, which represents a hidden value judgment within their analysis of "social welfare." For a discussion of these issues see Murray N. Rothbard, "Value Implications of Economic Theory," *The American Economist*, Vol. 17 (Spring 1973), 35-39, and Jack High, "Is Economics Independent of Ethics?," *Reason Papers*, No. 10 (Spring 1985), 3-16.

[83] Polanyi, *The Logic of Liberty*, 126.

[84] See Polanyi, *Personal Knowledge*, 49-65. For a contemporary application of Polanyi's arguments to organization within the firm, see Richard Nelson and Sidney Winter, *An Evolutionary Theory of Economic Change* (Cambridge: Harvard University Press, 1982), 72-95.

[85] Lavoie, *Rivalry and Central Planning*, 102.

[86] Mises, *Socialism*, 190-191.

[87] See Menger, *Principles of Economics* (New York: New York University Press, 1981[1871]), 63-67; 149-152.

[88] See Menger, *Principles*, 67-71.

[89] See Mises, *Human Action: A Treatise on Economics*, 3rd rev. ed. (Chicago: Henry Regnery, 1966[1949]), 99-104.

[90] O'Driscoll and Rizzo, *The Economics of Time and Ignorance* (New York: Basil Blackwell, 1985), 52-70. Also see Roger Garrison, "Time and Money: The Universals of Macroeconomic Theorizing," *Journal of Macroeconomics*, Vol. 6, n. 2 (Spring 1984), 197-213.

[91] Mises, *Socialism*, 186.

[92] Mises, *The Theory of Money and Credit* (Indianapolis: Liberty Classics, 1980[1912]), 153.

[93] Mises, *Socialism*, 101.

[94] Mises, *The Theory of Money and Credit*, 62.

[95] Mises, *Liberalism* (San Francisco: Cobden Press, 1985[1927]), 75; emphasis added.

[96] Hayek, "The Use of Knowledge in Society," 80.

[97] Wieser, *Social Economics* (New York: Augustus M. Kelley, 1967[1927]), 396-397.

[98] See Lavoie, *National Economic Planning*, 51-92; 247-265.

[99] See Boettke, "Understanding Market Processes: An Austrian View of 'Knowing,'" *Marketing Theory* (Chicago: American Marketing Association, 1987), 195-199, and "Austrian Institutionalism: A Reply," *Research in the History of Economic Thought and Methodology*, Vol. 6 (1989), 181-202. The central tenets of Austrian economics can be summarized as follows. The task of an economist is twofold: (1) he must render economic events intelligible in terms of the purposes and plans of the actors involved; and (2) he must trace out the unintended consequences, both desirable and undesirable, of those actions. To accomplish this task, Austrian economists rely on three methodological tenets: (1) methodological individualism, (2) methodological subjectivism, and (3) recognition of spontaneous order. In other

words, market phenomena are best understood as the result of the interaction of purposeful human beings.

[100] Lachmann, *The Market as an Economic Process* (New York: Basil Blackwell, 1986), 165.

[101] See Lange, *On the Economic Theory of Socialism*; and Lavoie, *Rivalry and Central Planning*, 78-116.

[102] Polanyi, *The Logic of Liberty*, 123.

[103] Polanyi, *The Logic of Liberty*, 125. That this abandonment of the cardinal claim of socialism continues to go unnoticed is borne out in current events within the Soviet Union. Compare the analysis of two of the Soviet Union's leading economists on this subject of market and plan; see Abel Aganbegyan, *The Economic Challenge of Perestroika* (Bloomington: University of Indiana Press, 1988), 125-139, and Leonid Abalkin, *The Strategy of Economic Development in the USSR* (Moscow: Progress Publishers, 1987), 145 ff. Aganbegyan argues that commodity production and market relations are consistent with socialism, both in theory and practice. Abalkin, on the other hand, points out that the goal of socialist planning is to eliminate the contradictions in the capitalist mode of production by eliminating private ownership in the means of production and substituting a settled plan for the anarchy of the market, that is, production for direct use as opposed to production for exchange. "Socialism," Abalkin writes, "eliminates this contradiction due to the public ownership of the means of production. It promotes unity between the final and direct goal of production....Hence the need to develop planning and the system of economic links so that the producer knows what the consumer wants" (154-155). Organizationally, Abalkin's proposal requires the elimination of the social relations of production associated with capitalism. Aganbegyan's, on the other hand, maintains the social relations of production of capitalism but calls for a high degree of government regulation of the market—in fact, he defines a socialist market as "a government-regulated market" (127). To Abalkin, *perestroika* means more efficient central planning; to Aganbegyan, it means a more efficient economy. Needless to say, there is a world of difference between these economic proposals in terms of the organizational form of the social relations of production, even disregarding the more interesting issue of Karl Marx's possible opinion of mixing market with plan.

[104] See Lavoie, "Between Institutionalism and Formalism," Center for the Study of Market Processes, Working Paper #21, 1986; Israel M. Kirzner, "The Economic Calculation Debate: Lessons for Austrians," *Review of Austrian Economics*, Vol. 2 (1988); and Bruce Caldwell, "Austrians and Institutionalists: The Historical Origins of their Shared Characteristics," *Research in the History of Economic Thought and Methodology*, Vol. 6 (1989).

[105] *Socialism, op. cit.*, p. 121.

[106] See Mises, *Human Action*, 210. Also see 206-211 and 689 ff.

[107] See Boettke, Steve Horwitz, and David Prychitko, "Beyond Equilibrium Economics: Reflections on the Uniqueness of the Austrian Tradition," *Market Process*, Vol. 4, n. 2 (Fall 1986), 6-9, 20-25, for a discussion of these issues.

[108] Contrary to the positivistic and formalistic philosophical foundation of modern neoclassical economics, familiarity with the Austrian tradition of economic analysis reveals philosophical roots in the continental philosophies of phenomenology and hermeneutics. The philosophical grounds for theory (conception) is the phenomenological tradition of Franz Brentano, Edmund Husserl and Alfred Schutz. See Barry Smith and Wolfgang Grassl, edited, *Austrian Economics: Historical and Philosophical Background* (New York: New York University Press, 1986); Richard Ebeling, "A Phenomenological Foundation for Dynamic Subjectivism," paper presented at a Liberty Fund Conference on *The Economics of Time and Ignorance*, November 3-6, 1984; "Cooperation in Anonymity," *Critical Review*, Vol. 1, n. 4 (Fall 1987), 50-61; "The Roots of Austrian Economics," *Market Process*, Vol. 5, n. 2 (Fall 1987), 20-22; "Expectations and Expectations Formation in Mises's Theory of the Market Process," *Market Process*, Vol. 6, n. 1 (Spring 1988), 12-18; Christopher Prendergast, "Alfred Schutz and the Austrian School of Economics," *American Journal of Sociology*, Vol. 92, n. 1 (July 1986), 1-26; and Ludwig von Mises, "The Treatment of 'Irrationality' in the Social Sciences," *Philosophy and Phenomenological Research*, Vol. 4 (June 1944), 527-545, where he states: "The importance of phenomenology for the solution of the epistemological problems of praxeology has not been noticed at all" (530).

The philosophical grounds for economic history, and historical study (understanding) in general, within the Austrian school is the hermeneutics of Dilthey, Weber, and Collingwood, see Mises, *Theory and History: An Interpretation of Social and Economic Evolution* (Auburn, AL: Ludwig von Mises Institute, 1985[1957]), 303-320. Once these philosophical roots are understood, it is quite understandable why some modern Austrians have paid particular attention to the work of Hans-Georg Gadamer. Gadamer sees his work as an attempt to understand human understanding and provide a "phenomenological hermeneutics." In this regard, he has made some of the most articulate statements concerning the philosophical underpinning of the Austrian school, see Don Lavoie, "The Interpretive Dimension of Economics: Science, Hermeneutics, and Praxeology," Center for the Study of Market Processes Working Paper No. 15, 1985. Also see G. B. Madison, "Hermeneutical Integrity: A Guide for the Perplexed," *Market Process*, Vol. 6, n. 1 (Spring 1988), 2-8, and "Hayek and the Interpretive Turn," *Critical Review*, Vol. 3, n. 2 (Spring 1989), 169-185.

[109] As Don Lavoie argues: "The fact that the point of departure for praxeology is reflection upon the essence of action recalls Dilthey's, Weber's and Schutz's points of departure for their 'interpretative sociology' far more than Russell's or Hildreth's formalizations of mathematics or, for that matter, Debreu's of economics. And Mises' intertwining of theory with history in such a way as to view theory not as an elegant construction of formal, intellectual beauty, like mathematics, but as a practical device through which the facts of history are to be interpreted, sounds much more like the hermeneutical than the Euclidean variety of a priorism." See Lavoie, "Euclideanism versus Hermeneutics: A Reinterpretation of Misesian A Priorism," *Subjectivism, Intelligibility, and Economic Understanding*, ed. Israel M. Kirzner (New York: New York University Press, 1986), 205-206.

[110] See Menger, *Investigations into the Methods of the Social Sciences with Special Reference to Economics* (New York: New York University Press, 1985[1883]). According to Menger, the discipline of economics can be subdivided into pure or exact theory, applied theory, and economic history and public policy.

[111] Bergson, "Socialist Economics," *A Survey of Contemporary Economics*, ed. Howard Ellis (Philadelphia: Blakiston Company, 1948), 446, 412.

[112] Mises, *Socialism*, 120; emphasis added. Also see Mises, "Economic Calculation," 109, where he states: "The static state can dispense with economic calculation. For here the same events in economic life are ever recurring; and if we assume that the first disposition of the static socialist economy follows on the basis of the final state of the competitive economy, we might at all events conceive of a socialist production system which rationally controlled from an economic point of view. But this is only conceptually possible."

[113] Lavoie, *Rivalry and Central Planning*, 102.

[114] Roberts, *Alienation and the Soviet Economy*, 90.

[115] Hayek, "Foreword," in Boris Brutzkus, *Economic Planning in Soviet Russia*, ix.

[116] Berliner, "Marxism and the Soviet Economy," *Problems of Communism*, Vol. 12, n. 5 (September/October, 1964), 1-11.

[117] Nove, *The Economics of Feasible Socialism*, 58.

[118] Many modern proponents of Marxism realize that they cannot escape the Soviet experience, but instead must face it head on. As Svetozar Stojanovic argues: "We no longer have the right to judge Marx in utter isolation from the many miscarried

attempts to achieve his ideas, no matter how unacceptable these attempts may be to humanist marxists." See Stojanovic, "Marx and the Bolshevization of Marxism," *Praxis International*, Vol. 6, n. 4 (January 1987), 450. Stojanovic goes further and argues that Marxists need to come to grips with the repression of the proletariat by the dictatorship in its name. "A theory which deliberately takes upon itself the responsibility for changing the world, must not in principle avoid the (co-) responsibility for its own fate in the world" (451). Certainly if Marxian social theorists recognize the influence of Marx on the Soviet experience, even in those aspects that no one wants to take credit for, then economists should recognize the influence that Marx had on the positive formulation of policy within the Bolshevik regime.

[119] Roberts and Stephenson, *Marx's Theory of Exchange, Alienation and Crisis*, xv.

[120] Polanyi, *The Logic of Liberty*, 132, fn. 1.

[121] Thus, the importance placed throughout this study on the history of ideas (doctrines). Doctrines not only guide human actions, but allow us, as social theorists, to interpret these actions in a manner that renders them intelligible.

[122] Brutzkus, *Economic Planning in Soviet Russia*, xv.

[123] Brutzkus, *Economic Planning in Soviet Russia*, 6.

[124] Brutzkus, *Economic Planning in Soviet Russia*, 7; emphasis added.

[125] Brutzkus, *Economic Planning in Soviet Russia*, 14. This problem persists today in Gorbachev's reforms. Gorbachev insists that *perestroika* "is fully based on the principle of more socialism and more democracy." See Gorbachev, *Perestroika*, 36. But see Nikolay Shmelyov, "Advances and Debts," *Novy Mir*, n. 6 (1987), reprinted in *Problems of Economics* (February 1988), 7-43, for an excellent discussion of the "free-market" socialism necessary for reforming the Soviet economy. In addition, see Vasil Selyunin, "Sources," *Novy Mir*, n. 5 (May 1988), reprinted in *The Current Digest of the Soviet Press*, Vol. 40, n. 40 (1988), 14-17. Selyunin argues that Lenin was mistaken when he attempted to abolish private property in the period following the revolution [war communism], and that NEP represents a proper change of mind.

[126] Brutzkus, *Economic Planning in Soviet Russia*, 31.

[127] Brutzkus, *Economic Planning in Soviet Russia*, 97.

[128] A confusion results if this analogy is taken too literally. During the calculation debate, for example, it became common practice to view Mises and Hayek as

arguing that there was no planning within a market system, and therefore that the existence of firms (islands of planning) was an anomaly to the market system. See Ronald Coase, "The Nature of the Firm," *Economica* (November 1937), 386-405. Also see Oliver E. Williamson, *Markets and Hierarchies* (New York: The Free Press, 1975) for a further discussion of the organizational contrast between market mechanisms of price adjustment and resource allocation by planning within a firm. For the confusion that can result from this artificial dichotomy between market and hierarchy, see P. T. Wanless, "The Efficiency of Central Planning: A Perspective from 'Markets vs. Hierarchies,'" *Scottish Journal of Political Economy* (February 1987), 52-68, and Ralph Rector, "Has Market Coordination Been Replaced?" *Critical Review*, Vol. 1, n. 4 (Fall 1987), 40-49, for a clarification of some of the issues involved.

[129] Brutzkus, *Economic Planning in Soviet Russia*, 37.

[130] Brutzkus, *Economic Planning in Soviet Russia*, 41.

[131] Brutzkus, *Economic Planning in Soviet Russia,* 48-49.

[132] Brutzkus, *Economic Planning in Soviet Russia*, 93.

[133] Brutzkus, *Economic Planning in Soviet Russia*, 94.

[134] Polanyi, "The Foolishness of History," 35.

[135] Polanyi, "The Foolishness of History," 35.

[136] Polanyi, "The Foolishness of History," 36.

[137] Roberts, *Alienation and the Soviet Economy*, 23.

[138] Roberts, *Alienation and the Soviet Economy*, 24. This policy of introducing ideological justification only to discount it has recently been reiterated in two otherwise extremely informative and important works: see Malle, *The Economic Organization of War Communism*, and Remington, *Building Socialism.*

[139] See Roberts and Stephenson, *Marx's Theory of Exchange, Alienation and Crisis* for a further discussion of the oneness of central planning and Marxism. Also see Lavoie, *Rivalry and Central Planning*, 28-47, and N. Scott Arnold, "Marx and Disequilibrium in Market Socialist Relations of Production," *Economics and Philosophy*, Vol. 3 (1987), 23-47.

[140] Roberts, *Alienation and the Soviet Economy*, 37; emphasis added.

[141] Roberts, *Alienation and the Soviet Economy*, 39.

[142] Selucky, *Marxism, Socialism, Freedom* (New York: St. Martin's Press, 1979).

[143] Polanyi, "The Foolishness of History," 36. Mises does at times recognize the importance of the shift of policies within the Soviet Union. In *Critique of Interventionism*, for example, Mises argues that since the shift to NEP all countries followed interventionist policies: "We call such an economic policy *interventionism*, the system itself the *hampered market order*." See Mises *Critique of Interventionism* (New York: Arlington House, 1977[1929]), 13; emphasis in original). At other times, however, Mises misclassifies the Soviet system. He argues in *Omnipotent Government* (Spring Mills, PA: Libertarian Press, 1985[1944]), 55 ff., that the Stalinist planning system is socialism, but that its operation depends upon the international price system—under such conditions socialism is not impossible just inefficient. But really the Soviet system under Stalin is more similar to the *Zwangswirtschaft* pattern of planning Mises ascribes to Nazi Germany—the highest form of Etatism. Market relations of production are not eliminated, just dominated by political arbitrariness.

[144] Polanyi, "The Foolishness of History," 36.

[145] Bergson, "Socialist Economics," 412-13.

[146] This is the argument raised against Hayek's *The Road to Serfdom* (Chicago: University of Chicago Press, 1976[1944]), for example by Barbara Wooton, *Freedom under Planning* (Chapel Hill: University of North Carolina Press, 1945); Herman Finer, *Road to Reaction* (Chicago: Quadrangle Books, 1963[1945]); and John M. Keynes, *Collected Works*, Vol. XXVII (New York: Cambridge University Press, 1980). Keynes, for example, in a letter to Hayek dated June 28, 1944, states:

> I should say that what we want is not no planning, or even less planning, indeed I should say that we almost certainly want more. *But the planning should take place in a community in which as many people as possible, both leaders and followers, wholly share your own moral position.* Moderate planning will be safe *if those carrying it out are rightly orientated in their own minds and hearts to the moral issue* (387, emphasis added).

For a collection of various essays in defense of Hayek's thesis see *Hayek's "Serfdom" Revisited* (London: Institute for Economic Affairs, 1984).

[147] Mises, *Socialism*, 187, 191.

[148] But as Remington, *Building Socialism*, 202, fn. 6, shows, a survey of the current literature clearly counters Cohen's claim; the military explanation reigns dominant.

[149] See Cohen, *Bukharin and the Bolshevik Revolution*, xv-xxiv; and *Rethinking the Soviet Experience*, 3-92. Others—for example, Isaac Deutscher and E.H. Carr—have tried to suggest that it could have been Trotsky.

[150] It would be hard to imagine any serious treatment of the Soviet experience not at least accounting for or dealing with the work of Robert Conquest, *The Harvest of Sorrow* (New York: Oxford University Press, 1986), Miron Dolot, *Execution by Hunger* (New York: W. W. Norton & Co., 1985), and Roy Medvedev, *Let History Judge*, revised and expanded ed. (New York: Columbia University Press, 1989).

[151] Gordon Tullock in *The Politics of Bureaucracy* (Lantham, MD: University Publications of America, 1987[1965]) states that he is in virtual agreement with Polanyi and Hayek on the very point of knowledge dispersion and the critique of socialist modes of production (124, fn. 3).

[152] Although I am concentrating on the economic arguments against planning, it is interesting to note that the Russian revolutionary anarchist Michael Bakunin raised a similar theoretical criticism to Marx during their battles at the First International and after. Bakunin basically argued that a "dictatorship of the proletariat" would amount to a dictatorship nevertheless. See Bakunin, *Bakunin on Anarchism*, edited by Sam Dolgoff (Montreal: Black Rose Books, 1980), 286-320, 323-350. In this regard, Emma Goldman reports that on her disillusionment with the Bolsheviks by 1920 she questioned the Russian anarchist Peter Kropotkin on the Bolshevik's totalitarianism. Kropotkin's reply is a simple one: "We have always pointed out the effects of Marxism in action. Why be surprised now?" See Goldman, *My Disillusionment in Russia* (New York: Doubleday, Page and Co., 1923), 55.

[153] See James Buchanan and Gordon Tullock, *The Calculus of Consent* (Ann Arbor: University of Michigan Press, 1962) and Tullock, *The Politics of Bureaucracy*. Also see Geoffrey Brennan and James Buchanan, *The Reason of Rules* (New York: Cambridge University Press, 1985), especially 33-45.

[154] This is essentially Hayek's argument in *The Road to Serfdom*, 134-153.

[155] The result of this political monopolization is described by Isaac Deutscher, *Stalin* (New York: Oxford University Press, 1970[1949]).

> The sensitiveness of the party had to be blunted, its sight dimmed, and its hearing dulled in order to make its mind immune from

> undesirable influences. The need for all this seemed to become even more urgent in connexion with the reforms of the N.E.P. Capitalist groups and interests were allowed new scope in the economic domain; but no party was left to represent them in the political field. It was only natural that they should seek channels of expression, and that they should seek them amid the only political party left in existence....To save the revolution's conquests it [the party] had to suppress the spontaneous rhythm of the country's political life. But in doing so, *the party was mutilating its own body and mind*. From now on its members would fear to express opinions which might, on analysis, be found to reflect "the pressure of alien classes" (226; emphasis added).

[156] The best works on the relationship between political and economic freedom are: Mises, *Liberalism*, *Human Action*; Hayek, *The Road to Serfdom*, *The Constitution of Liberty* (Chicago: University of Chicago Press, 1960) and *Law, Legislation and Liberty*, 3 vols. (Chicago: University of Chicago Press, 1973-1979); and Milton Friedman, *Capitalism and Freedom* (Chicago: University of Chicago Press, 1982[1962]). Also see Murray Rothbard, *Man, Economy and State*, 2 vols. (Los Angeles: Nash Publishing, 1970[1962]); *Power and Market* (Kansas City: Sheed, Andrews and McMeel, 1977[1970]); *For a New Liberty* (New York: Collier, 1978[1973]); and *The Ethics of Liberty* (Atlantic Highlands, NJ: Humanities Press, 1982).

[157] Hayek, *The Road to Serfdom*, 91-92. Hayek's argument, it should be pointed out, is not that economic freedom ensures political freedom, but rather that the loss of economic freedom entails the loss of political freedom. Also Hayek's use of the word *control* may be misleading, but in the passage quoted he is only tracing out the logical relationship that evolves under central planning and is making no real world empirical claim as to the existence of actual control over the economy. The Mises-Hayek argument implies that *control* over the economic system is impossible. Planning bureaus can (and do), however, exercise *power* over the economic system and its citizens.

[158] Sowell, *Knowledge and Decisions* (New York: Basic Books, 1980), 132.

[159] Besançon, "Anatomy of a Spectre," *Survey*, Vol. 25, n. 4 (Autumn 1980), 156-158, emphasis added.

[160] Draper, "Soviet Reformers," 289.

[161] See A. J. Polan, *Lenin and the End of Politics* (Berkeley: University of California Press, 1984), 128, where he states:

> The problem of the simple state of Lenin's model, simply put, is that the fewer institutions there are that make up the body politic, the greater the proportion of the total sum of power that will be lodged in each institution. If these institutions are reduced to one, or to a set of institutions that are not significantly separated, power is unitary, not distributed. This, then, is the negation of the field of democratic politics.

[162] Harrison, "Why Did NEP Fail?," *Soviet Industrialization and Soviet Maturity*, ed. Keith Smith (London: Routledge and Kegan Paul, 1986), 21.

[163] Alexander Gerschenkron in *Economic Backwardness in Historical Perspective* (Cambridge: Harvard University Press, 1962), 143 ff.), while he gives some economic reasons that I do not support, he argues that it was predominantly a political crisis that led to forced collectivization and industrialization. Also see 188 ff.

[164] Though Cohen's misinterpretation of the war communism period, in my opinion, seriously distorts the meaning of the Soviet experience, he presents a cogent and persuasive discussion of Stalin's militarization of Soviet life. Cohen states:

> Military rather than traditionally Marxist in inspiration, Stalin's intensification theory was perhaps his only original contribution to Bolshevik thought; it became a *sine qua non* of his twenty-five-year rule. In 1928, applied to kulaks, "Shakhtyites," and anonymous "counter-revolutionaries," it rationalized his vision of powerful enemies within and his "extraordinary" civil-war politics. By the thirties, he had translated it into a conspiratorial theory of "enemies of the people," and the ideology of mass terror.

See Cohen, *Bukharin and the Bolshevik Revolution*, 314-315. What Cohen misses in his analysis, however, is any discussion of how this militarization of social life could be the unintended undesirable outcome of the attempt to realize the Marxian ideal of social unity through scientific planning of the economy.

[165] Polanyi, "The Foolishness of History," 33; emphasis added.

[166] For an interesting discussion of the challenge Gorbachev faces see Marshall Goldman, *Gorbachev's Challenge* (New York: Norton, 1987); *Gorbachev's Economic Plans*, 2 vols. (Washington, DC: Joint Economic Committee, 1987); Ed Hewett, *Reforming the Soviet Economy* (Washington, DC: Brookings Institute,

1988); Gertrude Shroeder, "Anatomy of Gorbachev's Economic Reform," *Soviet Economy*, Vol. 3, n. 3 (July-September 1987), 219-241; and Padma Desai, *Perestroika in Perspective* (Princeton: Princeton University Press, 1989). Also see the contrasting assessments of the meaning of reform found in Abram Bergson, "Perestroika Before and After," *New York Times Book Review* (May 29, 1988), 3 ff., and Paul Craig Roberts, "The Soviet Economy: A Hopeless Cause ?" *Reason* (July 1988), 56-57. In addition, see Boettke, "The Political and Economic Challenges of Perestroika," *Market Process*, Vol. 8 (1990) and the references cited therein.

[167] As quoted in David Remnick, "Gorbachev Proposes President System," *The Washington Post* (June 28, 1988), A22.

[168] As quoted in Gary Lee, "Soviet Delegate Calls for Gromyko's Ouster," *The Washington Post* (July 1, 1988), A18.

3

THE POLITICAL ECONOMY OF UTOPIA: COMMUNISM IN SOVIET RUSSIA, 1918-1921

Introduction

The Soviet experience from 1918 to 1921 represents a utopian experiment with socialism. The Bolshevik revolutionaries attempted to implement a Marxian social order. Examination of the texts of Lenin, Bukharin, Trotsky, and various other party documents of the time demonstrates the intent to build socialism immediately. The Bolshevik cadre possessed a strong faith in the imminent world revolution and therefore believed in the Trotskyite concept of "permanent revolution."[1] As Trotsky pointed out, "The Bolsheviks categorically rejected as a caricature the idea imputed to them by the Mensheviks of creating a 'peasant socialism' in a backward country. The dictatorship of the proletariat in Russia was for the Bolsheviks a bridge to a revolution in the West. The problem of a socialist transformation of society was proclaimed to be in its very essence international."[2]

The civil war represents not so much a distraction in the building of socialism, but rather a method by which socialism will be brought to the West.[3] "Reasoning from the premises of permanent revolution," Robert Daniels points out, "the Bolshevik left wing—Lenin now included—envisioned vast but independent possibilities of revolution in Europe as well as in Russia. *Europe was ripe for revolution, and Russia would shake the tree*."[4]

This faith in sparking the international revolution was demonstrated at the Sixth Congress of the Russian Social-Democratic Workers' Party (Bolsheviks) held in August 1917. "History is working for us," Bukharin declared. "History is moving on the path which leads inevitably to the uprising of the proletariat and the triumph of socialism....[W]e will wage a holy war in the name of the interests of all the proletariat, and...by such a revolutionary war *we will light the fire of world socialist revolution*."[5] The draft resolution on the current movement and the war accepted at the Congress merely reiterated Bukharin's thesis.[6]

The civil war was not a surprise to the Bolsheviks, but rather an expected response from the bourgeoisie. But while it was expected as part of the transition period and, in fact, was the raison d'être of the dictatorship of the proletariat, the civil war did shape the implementation of policy. As Paul Craig Roberts argues: "It was not the policy [of war communism] but the manner in which it was applied that was determined by civil war."[7] The policies of war communism, I hope to demonstrate, were not born "in the crucible of military expediency," as Stephen Cohen argues, but were born instead in the political economy of Karl Marx and were transformed into praxis by Vladimir Ilyich Lenin from 1918 to 1921 in Soviet Russia.

The Economic History of War Communism

There is no real dispute over the economic facts. As Michael Polanyi wrote with regard to Maurice Dobb: "Mr. Dobb's account of the events does not materially differ from that given in my text ..."[8] What differs between the standard account and the one offered here is the *meaning* of these facts. The problem is one of intellectual history, not better fact-finding or statistical manipulation. Substantial agreement exists concerning the chronology of events following the October uprising and the implementation of certain economic policies.

The Bolsheviks rose to power with the promise of advancing Russia toward socialism. Between October 1917 and May 1918 the Bolsheviks carried out several policies intended as steps toward socialism. As Charles Bettelheim points out:

> Changes of this sort took concrete form in certain decisive measures concerning industry and trade. Of these, the most important were the decree on workers' control, published on November 19, 1917, the decree on the formation of the Supreme Economic Council of National Economy (VSNKh), the decree on the nationalization of the banks (December 28), the decree on consumers' organizations, placing consumers' cooperatives under the control of the soviets (April 16), and the decree on the monopoly of foreign trade (April 23).[9]

The nationalization drive, which the standard account argues did not begin until after the urgency of civil war became apparent, was already in preparation in March and April of 1918; plans were being made to nationalize both the petroleum and metal industries.[10] But the sugar industry, with the decree of May 2, 1918, became the first entire industry to be nationalized. Three hundred enterprises were nationalized on May 15, and by the beginning of June, that number exceeded 500, half of which represented concerns in heavy industry. This was followed by the general decree nationalizing large-scale industry issued on June 28, 1918.[11] By August 31 the number of nationalized enterprises reached 3,000. The pace of the nationalization of industry grew throughout the war communism period to such an extent that by November 1920, 37,000 enterprises were nationalized, 18,000 of which did not use mechanical power and 5,000 of which employed only one person.[12]

Efforts to nationalize the economy were deemed necessary for the replacement of market methods of allocation by centralized allocation and distribution. Although the standard account views this substitution as a product of war, I contend that it is the consistent application of Marxian ideology, and this is where the difference in interpretation lies.

A November 21, 1918, decree forbade internal private trading, and a monopoly of trade was granted to the Commissariat of Supply.[13] By March 1919 the consumer cooperatives lost their independent status and were merged with the Commissariat of Supply. Labor mobilization measures, that is, the militarization of the labor force, were introduced to insure the appropriate allocation of the work force. Stern labor discipline was introduced and "deserters" were accordingly penalized.[14]

Efforts were also undertaken during this period to eliminate monetary circulation. An August 1918 decree of the Supreme Economic Council declared that all transactions had to be carried out by accounting operations without using money. The figures concerning the emission of currency during this period are shocking: 22.4 billion rubles were in circulation on November 1, 1917; 40.3 billion by June 1, 1918; and 60.8 billion by January 1, 1919. In 1919 the quantity of money tripled; in 1920 it quadrupled, leaving the purchasing power of the ruble in October 1920 at only 1 percent of what it had been in October 1917.[15]

Perhaps the most ambitious effort of the Bolsheviks during the war communism period was the attempt to organize the planning apparatus of the national economy. The Supreme Economic Council (VSNKh) was established on December 2, 1917, and three weeks later the Councils of the National Economy (the Sovnarkozes) were created by the Supreme Economic Council to coordinate the activities of all economic units within their provinces and districts. As the nationalization continued to increase, the management of nationalized enterprises called for central administrations. Special departments within the Supreme Economic Council, called Glavkis, were formed for this task. Enterprises were integrated vertically through the Glavki system and horizontally through the Sovnarkozes.[16]

This system of planning attempted to provide ex ante coordination of economic activities in place of the chaotic and ex post coordination provided by the market system. This planning system, although not provided in blueprint form from Marx, was nevertheless influenced by him. As Silvana Malle writes: "Marxist ideology did not provide concrete guidance about economic organization, but it did provide a general hint about what had to be kept and what had to be dropped on the path of economic development. This hint was not irrelevant in the selection of alternatives facing the leadership."[17]

From Marx to Lenin

Although Marx did not wish to write "recipes for the cookshops of the future," no doubt exists about the broad outline of his project. It entailed the rationalization of politics and economics. Both spheres were interdependent within the Marxian system. The interpreter of Marx cannot merely concentrate on either Marx's economics or his politics if he wants to understand his project. Marx was a *political economist* in the broadest sense of the term.

Rationalization of the economy required the substitution of a "settled plan," which achieved ex ante coordination, for the "anarchy of the market" and the substitution of production for direct use for production for exchange. As Marx wrote:

> The life-process of society, which is based on the process of material production, does not strip off its mystical veil until it is treated as production by freely associated men, and is consciously regulated by them in accordance with a settled plan.[18]

The abolition of private property in the means of production and the substitution of a settled plan for the market has the consequence of rationalizing economic life and transcending man's alienated social existence. Marx's various criticisms of the "chaotic" and "irrational" process of market coordination suggest an alternative that is more orderly and rational. Within his negative view of the capitalist process of exchange and production there lies a positive view of how the socialist mode of production would work; otherwise, by what point of reference would he be criticizing the anarchy of capitalism?

Rationalization of politics, on the other hand, required the establishment of "classless" politics. Marx's political vision was one of radical democracy, one that included universal suffrage and insured full participation.[19] Since to Marx the state was an instrument of class conflict, the disappearance of class meant the disappearance of the state and political power. But this did not mean the disappearance of social or "classless" politics. As Marx argued in *The Poverty of Philosophy*:

> The condition for the emancipation of the working class is the abolition of all classes.... The working class, in the course of its development, will substitute for the old civil society *an association which will exclude classes and their antagonism, and there will be no more political power properly so-called*, since political power is precisely the official expression of antagonism in civil society....Do not say that social movement excludes political movement. There is never a political movement which is not at the same time social. *It is only in an order of things in which there are no more classes and class antagonisms that social evolutions will cease to be political revolutions.*[20]

Marx also argued clearly that the rationalization process of both politics and economics would be conducted in the transition period by the "dictatorship of the proletariat." Moreover, it is quite clear that Marx believed the transition from capitalism to socialism would not be peaceful, but violent. "The first step in the revolution by the working class," Marx and Engels wrote, "is to raise the proletariat to the position of ruling class, to win the battle of democracy.... The proletariat will use its political supremacy to wrest, by degrees, all capital from the bourgeoisie, to centralise all instruments of production in the hands of the State, that is, of the proletariat organized as the ruling class; and to increase the total of productive forces as rapidly as possible."[21]

And, though violent, Marx was of the opinion that the transition would be short-lived. As he argued in *Capital*:

> The transformation of scattered private property, arising from individual labour, into capitalist private property is, naturally, a process, incomparably more protracted, violent, and difficult, than the transformation of capitalistic private property, already practically resting on socialised production, into socialised property. In the former case, we had the expropriation of the mass of the people by a few usurpers; in the latter, we have the expropriation of a few usurpers by the mass of the people.[22]

There have been many recent attempts to understand Marx's project and assess its relationship to the Soviet experience with socialism.[23] Many of these attempts, however, focus exclusively on the relationship between Marx's political vision and Soviet authoritarianism. David Lovell, for example, concludes, after a thorough analysis and comparison of Marx's political project with that of Lenin's, that while "Lenin supplied the theoretical foundations for Soviet authoritarianism[,] Marx's contribution to them was not decisive. While there are many cogent reasons for rejecting Marx's project as a panacea for society's ills, the project's direct and necessary association with Soviet illiberalism is not one of them."[24]

Others, such as the critical theorists of the Frankfurt School (Horkheimer, Adorno, and Marcuse), consider it one of their fundamental tasks as social theorists to explain the relationship between the Marxian promise of emancipation and the Soviet reality of illiberalism. David Held, in his informative history on the development of critical theory, points out that one of the central problems of concern to the members of the Institute of Social Research, that is, the Frankfurt School, was to address the following questions:

> Given the fate of Marxism in Russia and Western Europe, was Marxism itself nothing other than a stale orthodoxy? Was there a social agent capable of progressive change? What possibilities were there for effective socialist practice?[25]

Positive answers to these questions have not always been forthcoming from the critical theorists or Western Marxism in general. As a result, negativism and a sense of despair burdens Western Marxist discussion of the project of emancipation. Martin Jay expresses this sense of frustration when he asks: "Is it too much to hope that amidst the debris there lurks, silent but still potent, the germ of a truly defensible concept of totality—and even more important, the potential for a liberating totalization that will not turn into its opposite?"[26] Jay and Western Marxism, in general, find hope in the research program of Jürgen Habermas and the positive alternative the Habermasian system suggests. Habermas wishes to focus on Marx's rationalization of politics. In this regard, Habermas has developed his idea of "uncoerced discourse" as a model for politics.[27] Habermas, however, does not provide a cogent discussion of Marx's responsibility (if any) for Soviet authoritarianism.

Perhaps the most insightful discussion on the subject of Marx's political project and the Soviet experience is to be found within the Praxis group philosophers of Yugoslavia. Svetozar Stojanovic, for example, argues that modern Marxists must accept that Marx's fundamental ambiguity toward the concept of the dictatorship of the proletariat is responsible for the perversion of politics under Soviet rule.[28]

All these interpretations, however interesting they are, have a fundamental problem: they forget the economic sphere of Marx's project, and they ignore unintended consequences in social life. In this regard, the attempt by Radoslav Selucky to understand Marx's project is much more satisfying.[29] Selucky suggests that central economic planning and full democratic participation are mutually exclusive.[30] He seems to understand the institutional requirements of economic rationalization and their unintended consequences.

Those who argue that there is continuity between Marx's project and Lenin's praxis need not argue that either Marx or Lenin was an authoritarian. The argument, rather, is that Marx's project of rationalization has the unintended, and undesirable, consequence of totalitarianism. The old Bolsheviks—Lenin, Bukharin, Trotsky, Zinoviev, and so forth—believed they were faithfully implementing Marx's project of social transformation.[31] Bolshevik proposals were filled with intentions of radical democracy, both economic and political, for the working man. To accomplish the process of social transformation, it would have to be directed by the dictatorship of the proletariat, that is, the Bolshevik party, which represented the true interests of the working class.

Among recent interpretations, Don Lavoie provides perhaps the most cogent understanding of Marx. Lavoie presents the project as an attempt to broaden the scope of democracy and public life. He states:

> Karl Marx conceived of central planning as an attempt to resolve this inherent contradiction between the private and public spheres of society. As in any genuinely radical perspective, his particular diagnosis of the problem is inextricably bound up with his utopia,

> his notion of the cure. Marx saw the problem as being located in the competitive private sphere, the market system, where separate, divided, or "alienated" interests contend with one another for resources. He argued that, so long as democratic institutions tried to merge themselves with this competitive sphere, they would invariably succumb to it. The solution, then, was to eradicate competitive market relations and to replace them with a broadening of the democratically based public sphere to encompass all of social life. No longer would politicians stoop to being tools of special and conflicting interests, since the private sector would cease to exist as a separate component of society. All social production would be carried out by the "associated producers" in conjunction with a common plan. Production would no longer be a private act of war by some market participants against others in a competitive struggle for wealth, but would instead be the main task of the self-coordinated democratic institution....The reason for our pervasive social ills, culminating in the modern threat of total destruction in war, is perceived to be the fact that we have narrowly confined the function of democratic institutions to a tiny part of social life and have left the bulk of economic activity to the unplanned outcome of non-democratic private struggles for wealth in the market. The proposed solution is to widen democracy to the whole sphere of economics and completely abolish private ownership of the means of production, thereby eliminating the competitiveness of market relations as a basis for economic decisionmaking.... [S]cientists would devise rational comprehensive planning procedures to implement these goals. Since this planning, to be meaningful and scientific, must obtain control over all the relevant variables, Marx consistently foresaw it as centralized and comprehensive. The commonly owned means of production would be deliberately and scientifically operated by the state in accordance with a single plan. Social problems would henceforth be resolved not by meekly interfering with a competitive market order but by taking over the whole process of social production from beginning to end.[32]

This task of abolishing market relations and "taking over the whole process of social production from beginning to end" constitutes the economic policies followed by the Bolsheviks from 1918 to 1921. The policies of war communism represent the conscious and deliberate attempt to realize Marx's utopia.

Ripeness and the Rise to Power

Much has been made of the issue of "ripeness" or whether Russia was sufficiently developed. Marx's model of dialectical materialism and the debate between the Mensheviks and the Bolsheviks are usually invoked to demonstrate Lenin's deviation from "real" Marxism. It is argued that Russia's backward political and economic traditions precluded a successful Marxist revolution, and that Lenin's political maneuvering was a gamble—the attempt to skip over the important historical stage of the bourgeois revolution—with the result being a net loss to the Russian people.[33] Russia became stuck, as a result of Lenin's hurried attempt to achieve utopia, in the Asiatic mode of production or "oriental despotism."[34] The tyranny under Stalin, from this perspective, is the outcome of the intentional gamble by Lenin to rush the revolution in a backward country. What is noteworthy in this analysis is that Marx's project of rationalization is understood; what is disappointing is that the economic problem this rationalization process would have to confront, no matter what stage of development the country of revolution found itself, is misunderstood. Discussion instead focuses on the proper historical conditions conducive to the world revolution.

Robert Daniels, for example, argues that the key to understanding the development of communism is the importance of historical conditions. The Soviet experience—a historical accident—could not possibly have succeeded in establishing socialism because it lacked the necessary conditions. What resulted in the Soviet Union was not the unintended outcome of attempting to implement Marx's rationalization project, but rather a different system determined by the historical stage of development. As Daniels argues in *The Conscience of the Revolution*:

> The important concern from the standpoint of understanding the development of Communism is to see how the ideal proved to be unrealizable under the *particular Russian conditions* where it was attempted. The Marxian theory underlying the ideal, whenever applied objectively, actually foretold the failure: proletarian socialism required a strong proletariat and an advanced economy; Russia lacked the strong proletariat and the advanced economy. Therefore, the ideal could not be attained, and any claims to the contrary could only mask the establishment of some other kind of social order.[35]

In contrast to Daniels, I contend that the preoccupation with the historical stages of development actually leads to misunderstanding the meaning of the Soviet experience with socialism. As Don Lavoie points out:

> The reasons for Lenin's failure to achieve either democratic political goals or a prosperous economy are seldom traced to

> intrinsic elements of his socialist aspirations. Russia, it is pointed out, began without democratic political traditions and with a backward economy. These special difficulties and not flaws within socialism itself, it is widely believed, brought Lenin's dream to its rude awakening. This interpretation of Soviet history in effect lets socialism off the hook for whatever political crimes or economic irrationalities the USSR is shown guilty of.

But this should not be the case. Rather, as Lavoie points out, we should see that: "In the failure of War Communism and the retreat to NEP the impossibility of planning as articulated theoretically in the Mises-Hayek critique was directly demonstrated in practice."[36]

What is disappointing about much of the analysis of the Bolshevik rise to power is the almost exclusive emphasis upon historical pre-conditions for successful socialist practice and the differences in *political strategy* that existed between the Mensheviks and Socialist-Revolutionaries, on the one hand, and the Bolsheviks, on the other. Besides the issue of whether Marx would or would not have agreed with Lenin's use of his doctrine to come to power, this focus in scholarly literature is symptomatic of two shortcomings. First, it represents an *uncritical* acceptance of Marx's interpretation of historical development. Second, because of the latent historicism of the first shortcoming, the approach represents a bias on the part of historians and social theorists to view historical events only as the intentional outcome or design of the major actors, and to disregard unintended consequences in human interaction.[37]

The Mensheviks and Socialist-Revolutionaries, after the February Revolution, originally wanted to work with the Kadet government, as a critic of policy, in the belief that Russia needed to go through the bourgeois revolution before the possibility of the workers' revolution could be discussed.[38] The April days and the July demonstrations, however, brought a closer coalition between the Mensheviks, the Socialist-Revolutionaries, and the provisional government.[39] The Bolsheviks, on the other hand, wanted no part of the compromise with the government and grew more anxious throughout 1917 to take state power and, from their perspective, bring relief (and political power) to the suffering masses. This proved to be a tactical coup d'etat, for as conditions became worse through the summer of 1917, the Bolsheviks were the only political group to remain untainted by association with the government. Lenin and the party took full advantage of this "higher moral ground."[40]

Lenin, for example, in April 1917 set out to answer questions about the political positions of the four major political factions.[41] There existed, according to Lenin, (1) a group to the right of the Constitutional Democrats, (2) the Constitutional Democrats, (3) the Social Democrats and the Socialist-Revolutionaries, and (4) the Bolsheviks. The Constitutional Democrats and the group to their right represented the interests of the bourgeoisie, while the Social Democrats and the Socialist-Revolutionaries represented the interest of the petty bourgeoisie. The Bolsheviks represented the interests of the proletariat and demanded all power to the Soviets: "undivided power to the Soviets from the bottom up all over the country" (24: 99). The major difference between the political platform of the Social Democrats and the Socialist-Revolutionaries and the Bolsheviks was *pace*; the Bolsheviks demanded power to the Soviets *now*, while the Social Democrats argued that it was not time—Russia must wait until the bourgeois revolution was completed.

"The masses must be made to see," Lenin argued on arrival in Russia in April 1917, "that the Soviets of Workers' Deputies are the only possible form of revolutionary government, and that therefore our task is, as long as this government yields to the influence of the bourgeoisie, to present a patient, systematic, and persistent explanation of the errors of their tactics, an explanation especially adapted to the practical needs of the masses" (24: 23). This is where he set out his famous "April Theses."[42]

As long as the Bolsheviks remained in the minority[43] their primary task was that of "criticising and exposing" the errors of the government, and to "preach the necessity of transferring the entire state power to the Soviets of Workers' Deputies" (24: 23). It was not the task of the proletariat at that time (April 1917) to introduce socialism immediately, according to Lenin, but rather to bring social production and distribution under the control of the Soviets.[44] The Bolsheviks were urged by Lenin to take the initiative in creating the revolutionary international. "It must be made clear that the 'people' *can* stop the war or change its character," Lenin wrote, "*only* by changing the class character of the government."[45]

Lenin believed that the workers could and should take state power immediately. His belief was justified, he argued, because of the existence of two governments; the existence of "dual power" within Russia.[46] The provisional government existed—this was the government of the bourgeoisie—but at the same time another government had arisen: the government of the proletariat—the Soviets of Workers' and Soldiers' Deputies. "This power is of the same type," Lenin argued, "as the Paris Commune of 1871" (24: 38). The workers' state must assume power.

It is not a problem of ripeness, argued Lenin.[47] The problem with the Paris Commune was not that it introduced socialism immediately (a bourgeois prejudice). "The Commune, unfortunately," Lenin argued, "was too slow in introducing socialism. The *real essence* of the Commune is not where the bourgeois usually looks for it, but in the creation of a state of a special type. *Such a state has already arisen in Russia, it is the Soviets of Workers' and Soldiers' Deputies!*"[48]

The existence of dual power and the circumstances of the time led Lenin to declare at the Seventh (April) All-Russia Conference that the crux of the matter can be summed up as follows: "We [Bolsheviks] put the issue of socialism not as a jump, but as a practical way out of the present debacle" (24: 308). World War I had ripened the conditions for the revolution. Economically, the necessities of war planning had created greater concentration of capital and brought production under the conscious control of society.[49] Politically, the war had intensified the exploitation of the working class in the name of the capitalist war.[50] "But with private ownership of the means of production abolished and state power passing completely to the proletariat," Lenin argued, "these very conditions are a pledge of success for society's transformation that will do away with the exploitation of man by man and ensure the well-being of everyone" (24: 310). Lenin argued that it was an utter mistake to suggest, because of some preconceived notion that conditions were not ripe, that the working class should support the bourgeois government, or that the proletariat should renounce its leading role in convincing the people of the urgency of taking practical steps toward the establishment of socialism. The time was ripe.

The steps Lenin advocated were: nationalization of land, state control over banks and the establishment of a single state bank, control over the big capitalist syndicates, and a progressive income tax. "Economically," Lenin argued, "these measures are timely; technically, they can be carried out immediately; politically they are likely to receive the support of the overwhelming majority of the peasants, who have everything to gain by these reforms" (24: 311).

Praxis and Catastrophe

Concentration on questions of historical ripeness results in a failure to discuss, within the usual analysis of these conflicts among the different political groups, the economic content of their respective platforms and what they hoped to accomplish by implementing their programs. As Lenin pointed out, though, in the "Impending Debacle" (24: 395-397), there were no substantial differences between the Narodniks and Mensheviks, on the one side, and the Bolsheviks, on the other, over the *economic* platform. What Lenin's complaint amounted to, therefore, was that the other groups were only socialists in word, but bourgeois by deed. The declaration of the "new" provisional government (issued on May 6, 1917, by the first coalition provisional government), for example, states that the "Provisional Government will redouble its determined efforts to combat economic disorganization by developing *planned state and public control of production, transport, commerce and distribution of products, and where necessary will resort also to the organization of production*."[51] Moreover, Lenin quotes at length from a resolution of the provisional government concerning economic policy:

> Many branches of industry are ripe for a state trade monopoly (grain, meat, salt, leather), others are ripe for the organization of state-controlled trusts (coal, oil, metallurgy, sugar, paper); and, finally, present conditions demand in the case of nearly all branches of industry state control of the distribution of raw materials and manufactures, as well as price fixing....Simultaneously, it is necessary to place all banking institutions under state and public control in order to combat speculation in goods subject to state control....At the same time, the

> most energetic measures should be taken against the workshy, even if labour conscription has to be introduced for that purpose....The country is already in a state of catastrophe, and the only thing that can save it is the creative effort of the whole nation headed by a government which has consciously shouldered the stupendous task of rescuing a country ruined by war and the tsarist regime (24: 396).

"We have here," Lenin commented, "state-controlled trusts, the combating of speculation, labour conscription—in what way does this differ from 'terrible' Bolshevism, what more could these 'terrible' Bolsheviks want?" Lenin answers his rhetorical question by simply stating that the provisional government has been "forced to accept the programme of 'terrible' Bolshevism because no other programme offers a way out of the really calamitous debacle that is impending" (24: 396). But Lenin charged the provisional government (the capitalists) with only accepting the program "in order not to carry it out." Even though "all this can be introduced by decree which can be drafted in a single day" the new provisional government possessed no intention of taking the correct action. Disaster was imminent, Lenin warned, and action should have been immediate.[52]

Lenin summarized his argument in "Lessons of the Revolution" (25: 229-243). He argues that Russia was ruled as a "free" country for about four months after the overthrow of the tsarist regime on February 27, 1917. While the bourgeoisie (Kadet Party) was able to "capture" the government, Soviets were elected in an absolutely free way—genuine organizations of the people, of the workers and peasants. Thus, there arose a situation of dual power. The Soviets should have taken state power in order to stop the war and stop the capitalists who were getting rich on the war. But only the Bolshevik social democrats demanded that state power be transferred to the Soviets. The Menshevik Social Democrats and the Socialist-Revolutionaries opposed the transfer of power. "Instead of removing the bourgeois government and replacing it by a government of the Soviets," Lenin argued, "these parties insisted on supporting the bourgeois government, compromising with it and forming a coalition government with it. This policy of compromise with the bourgeoisie pursued by the Socialist-Revolutionary and the Menshevik parties, who enjoyed the confidence of the majority of the people, is the main content of the entire course of development of the revolution during the first five months since it began" (25: 234).

This policy of compromise, according to Lenin, represented the complete betrayal of the revolution. By April a spontaneous workers' movement was ready to assume power, but the Socialist-Revolutionaries and Mensheviks instead compromised with the capitalists' government, betraying the trust of the people and allowing the capitalists to maintain state power.[53] The events of 1917, Lenin argued, merely confirmed old Marxist truths about the petty bourgeoisie, and prepared the way for a true workers' revolution. The lesson was all too clear.

> The lesson of the Russian revolution is that there can be no escape for the working people from the iron grip of war, famine, and enslavement by the landowners and capitalists unless they completely break with the Socialist-Revolutionary and Menshevik parties and clearly understand the latter's treacherous role, unless they renounce all compromises with the bourgeoisie and resolutely side with the revolutionary workers. Only the revolutionary workers, if supported by the peasant poor, are capable of smashing the resistance of the capitalists and leading the people in gaining land without compensation, complete liberty, victory over famine and the war, and a just and lasting peace (25: 242-243).

This theme is reiterated in "The Impending Catastrophe and How to Combat It" (25: 327-369). There Lenin argues that six months had passed since the revolution, and despite promises to the contrary, the catastrophe was closer than ever before. Unemployment had increased, shortages of food and other goods persisted, and yet the "revolutionary" government did nothing to avert the catastrophe. Russia could wait no longer. The imperialist war was driving the country nearer to ruin at an ever-increasing speed. Yet the government did not carry out the measures necessary to combat catastrophe and famine. The only reason, Lenin argued, that no movement was made to avert catastrophe was "exclusively because their [that is, the proper measures] realisation would affect the fabulous profits of a handful of landowners and capitalists" (25: 328).

What was needed, according to Lenin, was for the government (a real revolutionary government) to take steps toward introducing the socialization of production; only such steps would avert catastrophe.[54] The principal measure of combating, of averting, catastrophe and famine was to increase control of the production and distribution of goods, i.e., rationalize the economic process. "Control, supervision, accounting, regulation by the state, introduction of a proper distribution of labour-power in the production and distribution of goods, husbanding of the people's forces, the elimination of all wasteful effort, economy of effort"—these are the measures necessary, Lenin argued, "for combating catastrophe and famine." That this is so, Lenin stated, was "indisputable and universally recognized" (25: 328).

The Mensheviks and the Socialist-Revolutionaries did nothing in the face of catastrophe. Their coalition with the government, and the government's sabotage of all attempts at control, made the Mensheviks and the Socialist-Revolutionaries "politically responsible to the Russian workers and peasants for winking at the capitalists and allowing them to frustrate all control" (25: 330).[55] It is no wonder, given the increased suffering of the masses, that such energetic condemnations swung support from the provisional government toward the Bolsheviks.

The crux of the matter, to Lenin, was the need for a revolutionary dictatorship. "We cannot be revolutionary democrats in the twentieth century and in a capitalist country," he wrote, "if we fear to advance toward socialism" (25: 360). Those who argued that Russia was not ripe for socialism, and therefore, that the current revolution was a bourgeois revolution, had failed to "understand (as an examination of the theoretical basis of their opinion shows) what imperialism is, what capitalist monopoly is, what the state is, and what revolutionary democracy is. For anyone who understands this is bound to admit that there can be no advance except towards socialism" (25: 361).

Capitalism in Russia, Lenin argued, had become monopoly capitalism due to the imperialist war. This was evidenced by the development of the syndicates, such as in sugar. Monopoly capitalism develops into state monopoly capitalism. The state, on the other hand, is nothing but the organization of the ruling class. If you substitute a revolutionary democratic state for a capitalist state "you will find that, given a really revolutionary-democratic state, state-monopoly capitalism inevitably and unavoidably implies a step, and more than one step, toward socialism!" Lenin continued by arguing:

> For socialism is merely the next step forward from state-capitalist monopoly. Or, in other words, socialism is merely state-capitalist monopoly *which is made to serve the interests of the whole people* and has to that extent *ceased* to be capitalist monopoly....The objective process of development is such that it is *impossible* to advance from *monopolies* (and the war has magnified their number, role and importance tenfold) without advancing towards socialism (25: 361-362; emphasis in original).

From Imperialism to Socialism

Lenin's political position can be understood more clearly if one considers his two theoretical works that basically bracket the revolutionary activity of 1917, *Imperialism, The Highest Stage of Capitalism* and *The State and Revolution*.[56] *Imperialism* set out to explain how the world economic system had changed, and how the war was the inevitable outcome of this change. *The State and Revolution* concerned itself with the discussion of the nature of the state, its use in the revolution and later dictatorship of the proletariat, and its inevitable "withering away" in the postrevolutionary world.

"Competition," Lenin argued in *Imperialism*, "becomes transformed into monopoly....The result [of this increased monopolization of the economy] is immense progress in the socialisation of production. In particular, the process of technical invention and improvement becomes socialised" (22: 205). The natural operation of the capitalist mode of production leads to increased concentration of industry because of the profit advantage inherent in economies of scale.[57] The monopolization of the economy, to Lenin, is not just the result of a state-granted privilege, but inherent in the capitalist process of production.[58] The state can only affect the form the monopoly takes.

The increased concentration of industry that occurs in the highest stage of capitalism has the advantage of bringing economic life under conscious control. The chaotic process of free competition is overcome. "Capitalism in its imperialist stage," Lenin argued, "leads directly to the most comprehensive socialisation of production; it, so to speak, drags the capitalists, against their will and consciousness, into some sort of a new social order, a transitional one from complete free competition to complete socialisation" (22: 205).

The system no longer relied on the businessman's ability to compete and satisfy consumer demand. The concentration of banking had made business more and more dependent on pleasing finance capital to stay in operation.[59] "At the base of these manipulations and swindles," Lenin observed, "lies socialised production; but the immense progress of mankind, which achieved this socialisation, goes to benefit...the speculators" and not the people (22: 207). The system must be made to serve the interest of the people instead.

One of the key factors in the socialization of the economic process under imperialism was the increased role of banks in economic life. "We see the rapid expansion of a close network of channels which cover the whole country," Lenin commented, "centralising all capital and all revenues, transforming thousands and thousands of scattered economic enterprises into a single national capitalist, and then into a world capitalist economy" (22: 213). This "banking network," which under imperialism increases the power of the monopolistic giants, will provide the technical precondition for full socialization of the economy.[60]

All of industry has become interconnected (not scattered as under free competition) and dependent on the central nerve of economic life: the bank. "As regards the close connection between banks and industry," Lenin stated, "it is precisely in this sphere that the new role of banks is, perhaps, most strikingly felt." The result of this new role "is that the industrial capitalist becomes more completely dependent on the bank" (22: 220).

Lenin sees this, economically, as a good and natural development. It enables control over the economic life process.[61] "Finance capital," Lenin argued, "has created the epoch of monopolies, and monopolies introduce everywhere monopolist principles: the utilisation of 'connections' for profitable transactions takes the place of competition on the open market" (22: 244). The era of finance capital had laid the necessary economic groundwork for socialization.

On the other hand, the increased monopolization generated war as capitalists fought over economic territory and the division of the world market. "The capitalists divide the world, not out of any particular malice," Lenin stated, "but because the degree of concentration which has been reached forces them to adopt this method in order to obtain profits" (22: 253). The inevitable striving of finance capital to expand its influence leads directly to colonialism and colonial conquest. Lenin's argument here is that colonization supplies low-cost labor and natural resources, which allow the capitalist to receive increased profits.[62] This increases the misery individuals suffer under capitalist rule and brings to consciousness the antagonism of the classes. The imperialist war had laid the necessary ground work for political revolution.

Lenin argued that imperialism was capitalism in transition. As he stated:

> Imperialism emerged as the development and direct continuation of the fundamental characteristics of capitalism in general. But capitalism only became capitalist imperialism at a definite and very high stage of its development, when certain of its fundamental characteristics began to change into their opposites, when the features of the epoch of transition from capitalism to a higher social and economic system had taken shape and revealed themselves in all spheres. Economically, the main thing in this process is the displacement of capitalist free competition by capitalist monopoly. Free competition is the basic feature of capitalism, and of commodity production generally; monopoly is the exact opposite of free competition, but we have seen the latter being transformed into monopoly before our eyes, creating large-scale industry and forcing out small industry; replacing large-scale by still larger-scale industry, and carrying concentration of production and capital to the point where out of it has grown and is growing monopoly: cartels, syndicates and trusts, and merging with them, the capital of a dozen or so banks, which manipulate thousands of millions. At the same time the monopolies, which have grown out of free competition, do not eliminate the latter, but exist above it and alongside it, and thereby give rise to a number of very acute, intense antagonisms, frictions and conflicts. Monopoly is the transition from capitalism to a higher system (22: 265-266).

The epoch of imperialism had, according to Lenin, confirmed Marx's theory of the increased socialization of production under capitalism. Socialism was to be born in the womb of capitalism, and the transition phase would have all the pains associated with birth.[63] Imperialism signaled the advent of transition.

The interlocking of business and banking interests and the world economy signified to Lenin the changing of social relations of production. As he wrote:

> When a big enterprise assumes gigantic proportions, and, *on the basis of an exact computation of mass data, organizes according to plan* the supply of primary raw materials to the extent of two-thirds, or three-fourths, of all that is necessary for tens of millions of people; when the raw materials are transported in a systematic

> and organised manner to the *most suitable places of production*, sometimes situated hundreds or thousands of miles from each other; when *a single centre directs* all the consecutive stages of processing the material right up to the manufacture of numerous varieties of finished articles; when these products are distributed *according to a single plan* among tens and hundreds of millions of consumers ... then it becomes evident that *we have socialisation of production* and not mere 'interlocking' (22: 302-303; emphasis added).

The shell of private ownership and private enterprise no longer fit the content of the socialized mode of production; it must either decay (if its removal is artificially delayed) or be removed, but nevertheless it will inevitably fall away, opening the door for men to exist in social relation with one another.

The process of removing the shell and preparing for postrevolutionary social relations constitutes the subject of Lenin's *The State and Revolution*. This essay is perhaps one of the most fateful political tracts for humanity written in the twentieth century. "The Soviet state," A.J. Polan writes, "that emerged after 1917 bore the stamp of *The State and Revolution* in all its subsequent phases, before and after the Bolsheviks secured the monopoly of power, before and after the decline of the Soviets as significant institutions, before and after the rise of Stalin."[64]

Yet there is some controversy surrounding Lenin's essay and its place within his political thinking. Robert Daniels, for example, has argued that *The State and Revolution* represents a utopian aberration in Lenin's political career—a product of revolutionary fervor—and therefore views it as a mistake to treat the text as representative of Lenin's political philosophy. Daniels's argument amounts to pointing out that the essay's "argument for a utopian anarchism never actually became official policy after the revolution," and that the text only served as "the point of departure for the Left Opposition." It was the Leninism of 1902, the *What Is To Be Done* Lenin, "which prevailed as the basis for the political development of the USSR."[65]

Rodney Barfield, however, in challenging Daniels's interpretation, has pointed out that Lenin's essay cannot be viewed as a product of revolutionary fervor because at the time he was researching it Lenin had no idea that revolution was looming for Russia. "If *State and Revolution* is divorced from the revolutionary period and viewed as a theoretical work written for the future, a work intended to be Lenin's 'last will and testament,' consisting of ideas which were formulated not in the heat of revolution but in the cool detachment of the Zurich Library," Barfield argued, "then there is sufficient reason to interpret it as representing an integral part of the whole of Lenin's revolutionary thought and personal make-up. *The book may then be viewed as a serious revelation of the end to which Lenin had devoted his life.*"[66]

Alfred Evans has recently argued that "*State and Revolution* has been misinterpreted in most of the scholarly literature on Lenin's thought."[67] Lenin is simply not the utopian or quasi-anarchist, Evans argues, that people make him out to be in *State and Revolution*. Lenin did not possess a blind faith in the masses nor did he reject authority from above. Evans argues:

> In 1917 he did not in theory or practice throw all caution to the winds and stake everything on the unskilled wisdom of the masses. Lenin's essay was vulnerable to the charge of being unrealistic, not because he failed to allow for authority from above, but because he expected centralized planning and guidance to be easily compatible with enthusiastic initiative from below.[68]

Thus *State and Revolution* is neither the crazy utopian tract depicted by Daniels nor the humanistic utopian tract depicted by Barfield, but a polemic in defense of the Marxian utopia of a politically and economically rationalized society. Lenin saw his "prime task" as that of re-establishing "what Marx really taught" (25: 391). Once Lenin established, to his own satisfaction, what Marx really taught on the subject of the state, he turned his attention to clarifying the role of the state in the transition from capitalism to communism and the tasks that the proletariat vanguard must confront in socioeconomic transformation.

Lenin defends the thesis of the withering away of the state against both the opportunists (Kautsky, for instance), who argue that the proletariat needs the state, and the anarchists, who argue that the state must be abolished without first transforming the economic system. The state—that special apparatus of coercion—is necessary during the transition, but it is a state that is withering away. Lenin argued:

> The proletariat needs the state only temporarily. We do not at all differ with the anarchists on the question of the abolition of the state as the aim. We maintain that, to achieve this aim, we must temporarily make use of the instruments, resources and methods of state power against the exploiters, just as the temporary dictatorship of the oppressed class is necessary for the abolition of classes (25: 441).

The proletarian state would be modeled on the Paris Commune, Lenin argued, which could not be properly labeled a state because it no longer operated as a instrument for the suppression of the majority, but the minority (see 25: 444-447). The proletarian state must conduct the process of social transformation along the lines of democratic centralism.

From this point of reference Lenin argued, following Marx, that the proletarian must win the battle of democracy in order to overcome mere bourgeois democracy. "Fully consistent democracy," Lenin wrote, "is impossible under capitalism, and under socialism all democracy will wither away."[69] But "to develop democracy to the utmost, to find the forms for this development, to test them by practice, and so forth, all this is one of the component tasks of the struggle for the social revolution" (25: 457). Democracy, though, is merely "a state which recognizes the subordination of the minority to the majority, i.e., an organization for the systematic use of force by one class against another, by one section of the population against another" (25: 461). And, as Lenin pointed out, the goal of the social revolution was to transcend such a social existence.

However, during the special historical stage of development, where the revolutionary dictatorship of the proletariat assumes state power, capitalist democracy (democracy for the few) will be transformed into democracy for the majority. The vanguard of the oppressed ruling class must suppress the oppressors. "Simultaneously," Lenin wrote, "with an immense expansion of democracy, which for the first time becomes democracy for the poor, democracy for the people, and not democracy for the money-bags, the dictatorship of the proletariat imposes a series of restrictions on the freedom of the oppressors, the exploiters, the capitalists.... We must," Lenin emphasized, "suppress them in order to free humanity from wage slavery, their resistance must be crushed by force." Thus, Lenin concluded:

> Democracy for the vast majority of the people, and suppression by force, i.e., exclusion from democracy, of the exploiters and oppressors of the people—this is the change democracy undergoes during the transition from capitalism to communism. Only in the communist society, when the resistance of the capitalists has been completely crushed, when the capitalists have disappeared, when there are no classes (i.e., when there is no distinction between the members of society as regards their relation to the social means of production), only then 'the state...ceases to exist', and 'it becomes possible to speak of freedom.' Only then will a truly complete democracy become possible and be realised, a democracy without exceptions whatever. And only then will democracy begin to wither away...(25: 466-467).

The extension of democracy under the dictatorship of the proletariat will not be without economic consequences. The political development in the transition period "will exert its influence on economic life" and "stimulate its transformation; and in its turn it will be influenced by economic development....[T]his is the dialectics of living history" (25: 458).

The epoch of finance capital and the imperialist war had transformed capitalism into monopoly capitalism and provided the necessary prerequisites for transforming the social relations of production. "The proximity of such capitalism," Lenin wrote, "to socialism should serve genuine representatives of the proletariat as an argument proving the proximity, facility, feasibility and urgency of socialist revolution..."

(25: 448). The "mechanism of social management" necessary for social transforn tion was at hand and demonstrated in such state-capitalist monopoly busin organizations as the postal service. Lenin argued that once the workers overthr the bourgeoisie they would inherit a "splendidly-equipped mechanism" that cou easily be run by the united workers. This presented the proletariat with a "concre practical task which [could] immediately be fulfilled....To organize the *whc* economy," Lenin wrote, "on the lines of the postal service so that the techniciar foremen, and accountants, as well as *all* officials, shall receive salaries no high than 'a workman's wage', all under the control and leadership of the arme proletariat—that is our immediate aim. This is the state and this is the econom foundation we need" (25: 431-432; emphasis in original).[70]

Or, as Lenin put the matter of economic readiness later in the text:

> Given these *economic* preconditions, it is quite possible, after the overthrow of the capitalists and the bureaucrats to proceed immediately, overnight, to replace them in the *control* over production and distribution, in the work of *keeping account* of labour and products, by the armed workers, by the whole of the armed population....Accounting and control—that is *mainly* what is needed for the 'smooth working', for the proper functioning, of the *first phase* of communist society (25: 478; emphasis in original).

Once all have learned to administer and control social production, then "the door will be thrown wide open for the transition from the first phase of communist society to its higher phase, and with it the complete withering away of the state" (25: 479).

With the political and economic task of overthrowing the bourgeoisie and bringing social life under rational control in mind, Lenin broke off from completing *The State and Revolution.* The events of the fall of 1917 had transformed Lenin's activity from theorizing about revolution to revolutionary praxis. As Lenin put it on November 30, 1917: "It is more pleasant and useful to go through the 'experience of the revolution' than to write about it" (25: 497). Utopia had come to power.[71]

Utopia in Power

The revolutionary midwife—the party—had assisted in a successful delivery. The socialist child was born, and Lenin and associates were faced with the task of insuring its development and maturation. Overnight the new revolutionary government sought to implement its program by decree.[72] Referring to the Bolsheviks' economic program, K. Leites stated that "it [was] safe to say that from the beginning of history humanity [had] never witnessed so complicated an experiment in government."[73] Having wrested political control from the provisional government the Bolsheviki were now "in a position to carry out the great economic revolution to which the political revolution was only a prelude, introduce socialism forthwith and transform the whole order of Society."[74]

The economic transformation of Russian society consisted of carrying out five major principles of social organization. First, private property in land and the means of production was eliminated, and state ownership extended to the maximum. This included working-class control of the banks, railways, shipping, mining, large-scale industry, foreign trade, and so on. Second, labor was forcibly allocated and mobilized. The strictest militarization of labor was necessary to construct socialism. Third, management of economic production was centralized. Centralized planning of production and distribution of resources was deemed necessary for rationalizing the economic life process. Fourth, class and socialist principles of distribution were introduced. Rationing according to class was considered necessary for the achievement of an equitable distribution of resources. Fifth, commodity and money relations were abolished and a "natural economy" substituted for the market economy. These measures were deemed necessary for the "defetishization" of economic life and the transcendence of man's alienated social existence.[75]

Taken in combination, these policies constituted the economic program of the Bolsheviks from 1917 to 1921, though for purposes of exposition it is perhaps more accurate to place its beginning at December 1917 or January 1918 when the Supreme Economic Council was formed and the nationalization of industry increased in pace. This period is known to economists and historians today as war communism, but at the time it was known simply as communism.[76]

This system attempted to substitute a unified plan of economic life, that is, rational social relations of production, for the chaotic and exploitative relations of production that existed under monopoly capitalism. As Leo Pasvolsky stated in 1921: "The plan, underlying the whole Soviet economic mechanism, is made up, primarily, of two elements, viz., unity and hierarchy. The first of these elements calls for an effective coordination of the various phases of the whole country's economic life and a concentration of the control over these various factors. The second makes it imperative that these various factors be classified and then subordinated one to another in an ascending order."[77] The task the Bolsheviks took on themselves consisted not of "rebuilding the economic apparatus and organizing productive effort, but in placing both upon an entirely new basis. The Bolshevik[s] set out to purge the economic organization of Russia of its capitalist spirit and to breathe into it their version of the Socialist spirit."[78]

This program of socialist construction was presented in the party platforms and other writings of the leading Bolsheviks during this time. Various decrees were announced and resolutions passed with the intention of building socialism in Russia.[79] Theoretical works, socialist polemics, and party propaganda were issued to clarify and explain the Bolshevik program to the masses.

Lenin, for example, in his pamphlet *The Immediate Tasks of the Soviet Government* (27: 235-277), argued that "For the first time in history a socialist party has managed to complete in the main the conquest of power and the suppression of the exploiters, and has managed to *approach directly* the task of *administration*" (27: 242; emphasis in original). Having convinced the majority of the people that their program and tactics were correct and having captured political power, the Bolsheviks were faced with the immediate task of organizing social administration. The decisive aspect in accomplishing this task was organizing "the strictest and country-wide accounting and control of production and distribution of goods" (27: 245).

The successful carrying out of accounting and control, alongside the amalgamation of all banks into a single state bank, would transform the banking system into "nodal points of public accounting under socialism" and allow the Soviets to organize "the population into a single cooperative society under proletariat management" (27: 252, 256). But because the introduction of accounting and control had lagged behind the expropriation of the expropriators, Lenin argued, socialist construction would be slower than was originally expected. "The possibility of building socialism," Lenin wrote, "depends exactly upon our success in combining the Soviet power and the Soviet organisation of administration with the up-to-date achievements of capitalism."[80]

The possibility of socialism also required, according to Lenin, the subordination of the desires of the many to the unity of the plan. The rhetoric of workers' control and workers' democracy meant something entirely different from the model of decentralization that is promulgated today. To Lenin, as to most Marxists at that time, workers' control was a method by which central planning could be accomplished and not a decentralized alternative. As Silvana Malle points out: "In Lenin's model of power, workers' control would not evolve in any decentralized form, but, on the contrary, would facilitate the flow of information to the centre and the correct implementation of central guidelines."[81]

Centralized planning and control were considered the essential element of socialist construction. "It must be said," Lenin wrote, "that large-scale machine industry—which is precisely the material source, the productive source, the foundation of socialism—calls for absolute and strict *unity of will*, which directs the joint labours of hundreds, thousands and tens of thousands of people.…The technical, economic and historical necessity of this is obvious…and all those who have thought about socialism have always regarded it as one of the conditions of socialism.…But how can strict unity of will be ensured?" Lenin asked rhetorically. "By thousands subordinating their will to the will of one," he answered (27: 268-269).

This theme of the strict unity of the plan was echoed throughout various speeches and writings. Lenin, in fact, declared that anyone who challenged this view could not be properly considered a Marxist and was therefore not worth talking to. "Socialism," he wrote, "is inconceivable without large-scale capitalist engineering based on the latest discoveries of modern science. It is inconceivable without planned state organization which keeps tens of millions of people to the strictest observation of a unified standard in production and distribution. We Marxists have always spoken of this, and it is not worth while wasting two seconds talking to people who do not understand even this."[82]

Such policy prescriptions were not limited to Lenin, but were pronounced by all the leading Bolsheviks. Trotsky, for example, during a speech to the Central Executive Committee on February 14, 1918, repeated the necessity of rationalizing the economic life of Russia through strict conformity to the plan. "Only a systematic organization of production," he said, "that is, one based on a universal plan—only a rational and economical distribution of all products can save the country. And that means socialism."[83] The chaotic process of market exchange and production must not merely be tampered with but abolished. "Socialist organization of production," Trotsky declared in 1920, "begins with the liquidation of the market....Production shall be geared to society's needs by means of a unified economic plan."[84]

The ubiquity of monetary calculation under capitalist methods of production was to be replaced by the introduction of strict accounting and control within state enterprises. Proposals for the nationalization of the banks and the amalgamation of all banks into a single state bank was not, as Leon Smolinsky argues, a means to maintain money as the "lifeblood of the new planned economy" where "planners were to utilize the price system, making their choices on the basis of monetary values rather than physical terms." The economic transformation did not amount to using "regulated markets" as a "medium through which plans would work themselves out."[85] The transformation demanded instead the abolition of "the alienated ability of mankind," that is, money, and the substitution of moneyless accounting for monetary calculation.[86]

Yuri Larin, who was commissioned by Lenin to study the operation of the German economy and ways to implement that model in Russia, argued fervently for the most extreme centralization of the economy and the elimination of all market exchange and production.[87] Larin declared in the spring of 1918 that the moneyless system of accounting should be pursued posthaste. The nationalization of banks provided the framework to eliminate hand-to-hand currency and to transform the financial institutions of Soviet Russia into, as Lenin put it, "nodal points of public accounting." Larin declared, "Money as a circulating media can already be got rid of to a considerable degree."[88] And at the plenary session of the Supreme Economic Council in April 1918, Larin said: "We have made up our minds to establish commodity exchange on new bases, as far as possible without paper money, preparing conditions for the time when money will only be an accounting unit."[89]

By May of 1918 the party commanded all state enterprises to hand over all circulating media to the People's Bank. An August 1918 decree of the Supreme Economic Council instructed the management of industries that from then on, all settlements of deliveries and receipts of commodities should consist of book entries; on no account should money be used in transactions. The intent of the policy was to establish a cashless clearing system where circulating media would be replaced by bank money.[90] Osinskii, who was the manager of the State Bank and the first chairman of the Supreme Economic Council, described the monetary policy of the

Bolsheviks as follows:

> Our financial policy has been aimed recently at building up a financial system based on the emission of paper money, the *ultimate objective of which is the natural transition to distribution of goods without using money and to transform the money tokens into accounting units....* [W]hen introducing the system of cashless clearing, our financial policy *does not wish thereby to restore the disorder of monetary circulation. Its main aim is to create normal conditions of exchange without money between parts of the uniform and mostly socialized national economy.*[91]

This program of the Bolsheviks was perhaps best articulated in the Program of the Communist Party of Russia adopted at the Eighth Party Congress in March of 1919, and the popular exposition of that program by Nikolai Bukharin and Evgeny Preobrazhensky.[92] Bukharin gave a detailed presentation of the economic organization of communist society in his chapter "Communism and the Dictatorship of the Proletariat." He argued that "the basis of communist society must be the social ownership of the means of production and exchange." Under these circumstances "society will be transformed into a huge working organization for cooperative production." The anarchy of production will cease as rationality is imposed on economic life.

> No longer will one enterprise compete with another; the factories, workshops, mines, and other productive institutions will all be subdivisions, as it were, of one vast people's workshop, which will embrace the entire national economy of production. It is obvious that so comprehensive an organisation presupposes a general plan of production. If all the factories and workshops together with the whole of agricultural production are combined to form an immense cooperative enterprise, it is obvious that everything must be precisely calculated. We must *know in advance* how much labour to assign to the various branches of industry; what products are required and how much of each it is necessary to produce; how and where machines must be provided. These and similar details must be thought out beforehand, with approximate accuracy at least; and the work must be guided in conformity with our calculations. This is how the organisation of communist production will be effected.[93]

The planning process was to be entrusted to "various kinds of book-keeping offices and statistical bureaux." Accounts would be kept (day to day) of production and its needs. All decisions for the allocation and distribution of resources necessary for social production would be orchestrated by the planning bureaus. "Just as in an orchestra all the performers watch the conductor's baton and act accordingly," Bukharin wrote, "so here all will consult the statistical reports and will direct their work accordingly."[94]

By achieving ex ante coordination of economic activity through the substitution of production-for-direct-use for production-for-exchange, Bukharin understood that, organizationally, "money would no longer be required."[95] The rationalization of economic life under communism would eliminate the waste of capitalist production and lead to increased productivity. This burst of productivity would free individuals from the "chains imposed upon them by nature." The utopian promise of this project was that "concurrently with the disappearance of man's tyranny over man, the tyranny of nature over man will likewise vanish. Men and women will for the first time be able to lead a life worthy of thinking beings instead of a life worthy of brute beasts."[96]

Only the scientific organization of production under the direction of a unified plan constructed by the dictatorship of the proletariat could put an end to the capitalist anarchy of production and eliminate the tyranny of man over man. With the breakdown of commodity production and its replacement by the "socio-natural system of economic relations, the corresponding ideological categories also burst, and once this is so, the theory of the economic process is confronted with the need for a transition to natural economic thinking, i.e., to the consideration of both society and its parts as systems of fundamental elements in their natural form."[97] Social relations would no longer be veiled by the commodity fetishism of the monetary exchange system.

This project of rationalization and emancipation is spelled out in the party program adopted at the Eighth Congress. In the realm of economic affairs this amounted to expropriating the expropriators, increasing the productive forces of society by eliminating the contradictions of capitalism, mobilizing labor, organizing the trade unions, educating the workers, and securing "the maximum solidarisation of the whole economic apparatus."[98] To accomplish this goal, the Bolsheviks seized the banks and merged them into a single state bank. The bank thus "became an instrument of the workers' power and a lever to promote economic transformation." The bank would become an apparatus of unified book-keeping. "In proportion as the organization of a purposive social economy is achieved, this will lead to the disappearance of banks, and to their conversion into the central book-keeping establishment of communist society." The immediate elimination of money was not yet possible, but the party was moving in that direction. "Upon the basis of the nationalisation of banking, the Russian Communist Party endeavours to promote a series of measures favouring a moneyless system of account keeping, and paving the way for the abolition of money."[99]

The Bolsheviks did not just accept this program in the heat of civil war, as many historians assert. The civil war no doubt affected the way the program was carried out, but the program itself was clearly ideological in origin. It emerged out of the conscious attempt to achieve Marx's utopia. Even after the civil war had ended the Bolsheviks embarked on continued efforts to rationalize the economy. For example, the "Outstanding Resolutions on Economic Reconstruction" (adopted by the Ninth Congress of the Russian Communist Party in April 1920) argued that "the basic condition of economic recovery of the country is the undeviating carrying out of a *unified economic plan*."[100] And in November 1920, V. Milyutin, then assistant president of the Supreme Economic Council, announced the decree of the Council to nationalize even small industrial enterprises and bring them under conscious control.[101] Only the insurgency of the sailors at Kronstadt convinced the Bolsheviks to reconsider their policy.

Utopia in Disarray

The result of this policy of socialist transformation was an economic disaster.[102] "Considered purely as an economic experiment," William Henry Chamberlin commented, "war communism may fairly be considered one of the greatest and most overwhelming failures in history. Every branch of economic life, industry, agriculture, transportation, experienced conspicuous deterioration and fell far below the pre-War levels of output."[103] Economic life completely fell apart. "Never in all history," declared H.G. Wells, "has there been so great a debacle before."[104] As Moshe Lewin points out, "The whole modern sector of urbanized and industrialized Russia suffered a severe setback, as becomes obvious from the population figures....By 1920," he reports, "the number of city dwellers had fallen from 19 percent of the population in 1917 to 15 percent. Moscow lost half its population, Petrograd two-thirds."[105] After only three years of Bolshevik rule, "The country lay in ruins, its national income one-third of the 1913 level, industrial production a fifth (output in some branches being virtually zero), its transportation system shattered, and agricultural production so meager that a majority of the population barely subsisted and millions of others failed even that."[106] This debacle is recorded in various memoirs and novels of the time.[107] Statistically the economic disaster can be represented in table 3-1.

Table 3-1. Statistical Representation of the Economic Disaster

	1913	*1921*
Gross output of all industry (index)	100.00	31.00
Large-scale industry (index)	100.00	21.00
Coal (million tons)	29.00	9.00
Oil (million tons)	9.20	3.80
Electricity (million Kwhs)	2,039.00	520.00
Pig Iron (million tons)	4.20	0.10
Steel (million tons)	4.30	0.20
Bricks (millions)	2.10	0.01
Sugar (million tons)	1.30	0.05
Railway tonnage carried (millions)	132.40	39.40
Agricultural production (index)	100.00	60.00
Imports ("1913" rubles)	1,374.00	208.00
Exports ("1913" rubles)	1,520.00	20.00

Source: Alec Nove, *An Economic History of the U.S.S.R.* (New York: Penguin Books, 1984[1969]), 68.

The burst of productivity expected from the rationalization of economic life was not forthcoming. Instead, economic life and social relations under communist rule merely worsened the condition of the masses of people. If "Lenin was the midwife of socialism," then the "mother's belly had been opened and ransacked, and still there was no baby."[108] The socialist project proved unrealizable; utopia became dystopia within three years.

The Soviet socialist failure bore full witness to the Mises-Hayek criticism of socialist planning. The economic disorganization of Bolshevik Russia was, as Lancelot Lawton pointed out, a result of the "disregard of economic calculation."[109] The attempt to have a moneyless accounting system replace the monetary calculation of capitalism proved to be futile.[110] "With moneyless accounting, as with all Bolshevik innovations, the simplicity of theory vanished in the unavoidable complications of practice."[111] The Bolsheviks had attempted to eliminate, by decree, the only means to achieve the economic knowledge necessary for advanced industrial production: the monetary calculation embedded within the dynamic process of exchange and production. The "attempts of the Bolsheviks to establish moneyless accounting ended with no accounting at all." In striving "to make all men wealthy, the Soviet state had made it impossible for any man to be otherwise than poor."[112] What had happened under the rule of Lenin and Trotsky was, as Mises said, "merely destruction and annihilation."[113]

Throughout 1920 Soviet power was threatened as the social order of production was destroyed. The political protests and uprisings culminated in March 1921 with the Kronstadt uprising. The "waves of uprisings of workers and peasants," the Kronstadters declared, "have testified that their patience has come to an end. The uprising of the labourers has drawn near. The time has come to overthrow the commissarocracy.... Kronstadt has raised for the first time the banner of the uprising for the Third Revolution of the toilers.... The autocracy has fallen. The Constituent Assembly has departed to the region of the damned. The commissarocracy is crumbling."[114]

The Kronstadt rebellion represented an attempt by disillusioned revolutionaries to halt what they perceived to be a perversion of the revolution at the hands of the Bolsheviks. "In its economic content," Paul Avrich points out, "the Kronstadt program was a broadside aimed at the system of War Communism. It reflected the determination of the peasantry and working class to sweep away the coercive policies to which they had been subjected for nearly three years."[115] The Bolshevik government—and the government alone—was responsible for the hardship. Little to no blame was placed by the Kronstadters on the civil war or the Allied intervention and blockade. "All the suffering and hardship, rather, was laid at the door of the Bolshevik regime."[116]

The Bolshevik regime must be rejected, the Kronstadters argued. Only by overthrowing the Bolsheviks could the Russian worker and peasant expect to live a humane existence. "Communist rule has reduced all of Russia," they declared, "to unprecedented poverty, hunger, cold, and other privation. The factories and mills are closed, the railways on the verge of breakdown. The countryside has been fleeced to the bone. We have no bread, no cattle, no tools to work the land. We have no clothing, no shoes, no fuel. The workers are hungry and cold. The peasants and townsfolk have lost all hope for an improvement of their lives. Day by day they come closer to death. The Communist betrayers have reduced you to this."[117]

The "new serfdom" associated with Bolshevik political power was condemned throughout the land. "Faced with a simultaneous revolt of both the proletariat and the peasants," Leonard Shapiro has pointed out, the Bolsheviks were "prepared for drastic measures aimed at preserving party rule."[118] It was at this time that Lenin, and his associates decided to shift gears. The New Economic Policy was introduced, but at the same time, it is important to remember, the Bolsheviks declared a political monopoly.

"From the standpoint of the development of the experiment in the economics of Communism," Leo Pasvolsky wrote, "these measures [that is, NEP] are very significant. They represent the first official, generalized acknowledgement of the breaking down of the state monopoly of distribution."[119] Never again did the Soviets dare to implement such a project of economic centralization. Never again did they attempt to realize the Marxian utopia of a completely centrally planned organization superseding market modes of production and eliminating monetary calculation.

Even under the most extreme policies of Stalinism, monetary calculation, though highly interfered with, served as the basis of "planning." Marxism, instead, became *merely* a mobilizing ideology to maintain political power for the party.

Conclusion

The Soviet experience with communism from 1918 to 1921 bears directly on the calculation argument advanced by Mises. The Marxian project of economic rationalization proved unrealizable in practice. Today very few advocates of socialism would argue for comprehensive central planning, but they hold fast to the Marxist criticism of the anarchy of the market. "But," as Don Lavoie has argued, "the modification from comprehensive planning, which seeks to completely replace market competition as the coordinating process of the economy, to noncomprehensive planning, which seeks to reconcile planning with market institutions, is hardly an alteration of analysis. *It is the toppling of the basic pillar of Marxist analysis.... To preserve money, prices, and so on is to abandon Marx's whole system.*" And as a result, Lavoie concludes, "It is by no means evident that the Marxist critique of the market order which modern planners still implicitly employ, can stand up once it is admitted that markets are necessary and that planning is to consist merely of interference in this unplannable system."[120]

Besides the point that Marx's critique is relevant only if the point of reference from which he made the critique is valid, that is, the future socialist world, there is another fundamental criticism that must be considered. The very experience of attempting to "do the market one better" has important lessons for the interventionist policies that were followed under NEP (and those advocated today under *perestroika*). The same fundamental problem that confronts socialist proposals also confronts market-socialist proposals—that is, the knowledge problem, which manifests itself in calculational chaos. This will be examined in the next chapter, as I discuss the political-economic experience under the New Economic Policy in Soviet Russia from 1921 to 1928.

Notes

[1] For Leon Trotsky's views on the proletariat revolution and the importance of the European revolution for Russian success, see *Our Revolution (1906): Extracts*, in *Marxism in Russia: Key Documents 1879-1906*, ed. Neil Harding (New York: Cambridge University Press, 1983), 337-352. Also see Trotsky, *Permanent Revolution* (Calcutta: Atawàr Rahman, 1947) and *The History of the Russian Revolution*, 3 vols. (New York: Pathfinder Press, 1987[1932]), especially III: 351 ff.

I would also like to point out that in the preface to the second Russian edition of the *Communist Manifesto* Marx and Engels wrote: "If the Russia Revolution becomes the signal for a proletarian revolution in the West, so that both complement each other, the present Russian common ownership of land may serve as the starting-point for a communist development." See Marx and Engels, *Selected Works*, 3 vols. (Moscow: Progress Publishers, 1969), I: 100-101.

[2] Trotsky, *The History of the Russian Revolution*, III: 381.

[3] See Mikhail Heller and Aleksandr Nekrich, *Utopia in Power* (New York: Summit Books, 1986), 50-110. Heller and Nekrich argue:

> Lenin believed that the spark of the Russian revolution would ignite the fire of world revolution. In his view, conflict with Poland, a potential "Red bridge" to the West, was inevitable. None of the Bolsheviks doubted the necessity of "forcing the Polish bridge"; the only question was when and how to do it. Trotsky, who had said, "The road to London and Paris goes through Calcutta," declared at the end of 1919: "When we have finished off Denikin, we will throw all the strength of our reserves against the Polish front" (93).

By such a continued assault Lenin became convinced he could bring communist independence to the world.

This perspective can also help us understand the debate between Lenin and the left wing (Bukharin and others) within the Bolshevik party over the Brest-Litovsk peace agreement (signed March 3, 1918). At the time, Lenin agreed to peace with Germany in order to regroup the country's resources and hold out until the world revolution began (which he argued might be within a few days or weeks). The peace was a necessary strategic retreat for Lenin, a retreat that would, in a short time, be reversed. Bukharin, on the other hand, argued that the conditions of peace would reduce the international significance of the Russian Revolution to nothing and that, therefore, the peace treaty should be annulled and the proper preparations be made to create a combat-ready Red Army that would help bring the revolution to the West. Both Lenin and Bukharin believed that the international workers' revolution was essential to the success of the Russian Revolution. See the discussion between Lenin and Bukharin on the peace agreement in *A Documentary History of Communism*, 2 vols., ed. Robert V. Daniels (New York: Vintage Books, 1960), I: 135-143. Also see Robert V. Daniels, *The Conscience of the Revolution* (Cambridge, MA: Harvard University Press, 1960), 70-80.

[4] Daniels, *The Conscience of the Revolution*, 53; emphasis added.

[5] From Bukharin's report on the War and the International Situation excerpted in *A Documentary History*, I: 95-96; emphasis added.

[6] See *A Documentary History*, I: 97.

[7] See Roberts, *Alienation and the Soviet Economy* (Albuquerque: University of New Mexico Press, 1971), 26.

[8] Polanyi, *The Logic of Liberty* (Chicago: University of Chicago Press, 1980[1951]), 132, fn. 1.

[9] Bettelheim, *Class Struggles in the USSR, 1917-1923* (New York: Monthly Review Press, 1976), 144.

[10] See Eugene Zaleski, *Planning for Economic Growth in the Soviet Union, 1918-1932* (Chapel Hill: University of North Carolina Press, 1971[1962]), 17.

[11] This is where the standard account usually begins discussion of the nationalization of industry discounting the earlier nationalization efforts of the Bolsheviks; doing so has the effect of making the emergency interpretation more cogent.

[12] See Zaleski, *Planning for Economic Growth in the Soviet Union, 1918-1932*, 16-20. Also see Maurice Dobb, *Soviet Economic Development Since 1917* (New York: International Publishers, 1948), 106. The armistice with Poland was signed in October 1920, and the decree nationalizing small-scale industry was published in November 1920, *after* the civil war. As V. Sirotkin recently wrote:

> It has become a copybook maxim to assert that the policy of "War Communism" was imposed on the Bolsheviks by the Civil War and the foreign intervention. This is completely untrue, if only for the reason that the first decrees on introducing the "socialist ideal" exactly "according to Marx" in Soviet Russia were issued long before the beginning of the Civil War (the decrees of Jan. 28

and Feb. 14, 1918, on the nationalization of the merchant fleet and of all banks), while the last decree on the socialization of all small handicraftsmen and artisans was issued on Nov. 29, 1920, i.e., after the end of the Civil War in European Russia.

See Sirotkin, "Lessons of NEP," *Izvestia* (March 9, 1989), reprinted in *The Current Digest of the Soviet Press*, Vol. XLI, n. 10 (1989), 6.

[13] Dobb, *Soviet Economic Development*, 107.

[14] See Thomas Remington, *Building Socialism in Bolshevik Russia, 1917-1921* (Pittsburgh: University of Pittsburgh Press, 1984), 78 ff., for a discussion of the militarization of labor during this period.

[15] See Zaleski, *Planning for Economic Growth in the Soviet Union, 1918-1932*, 18, fn. 27. While Dobb and Carr, as I documented in the last chapter, see this emission of paper money as a result of war emergency, Preobrazhensky argued that the breakdown of the capitalist system could be accomplished through inflationary destruction of the currency. See Preobrazhensky, *Paper Money During the Proletarian Dictatorship* (Moscow, 1920). The importance of monetary policy for understanding the ideological interpretation of war communism will be brought out later in this chapter.

[16] See Zaleski, *Planning for Economic Growth in the Soviet Union, 1918-1932*, 24 ff. Also see Silvana Malle, *The Economic Organization of War Communism, 1918-1921* (New York: Cambridge University Press, 1985), 202 ff.

[17] Malle, *The Economic Organization of War Communism*, 202.

[18] Marx, *Capital: A Critique of Political Economy* (New York: The Modern Library, 1906[1867]), 92.

[19] See Karl Marx and Frederick Engels, "Manifesto of the Communist Party," *Selected Works*, I: 98-137; Marx, "The Class Struggles in France," *SW*, I: 186-299; "The Eighteenth Brumaire of Louis Bonaparte," *SW*, I: 394-487; "The Civil War in France," *SW*, II: 178-244.

[20] Marx, *The Poverty of Philosophy* (Moscow: Progress Publishers, 1978), 161; emphasis added.

[21] Marx and Engels, "Manifesto of the Communist Party," 126.

[22] Marx, *Capital*, I: 837. Marx at times does not seem to recognize the "free rider"

problem of collective action and the cost of revolution. Mancur Olson, in *The Logic of Collective Action* (Cambridge: Harvard University Press, 1965), 102-110, argues that this aspect of Marx's thought represents a fundamental flaw in his theory of the state and class analysis. "Marxian class action," Olson says, "takes on the character of any endeavor to achieve the collective goals of a large, latent group" and "as in any large, latent group, each individual in the class will find it to his advantage if all of the costs or sacrifices necessary to achieve the common goal are borne by others" (106). However, I do not think that Olson's or Gordon Tullock's *The Social Dilemma* (Blacksburg, VA: Center for the Study of Public Choice, 1974) analysis that "revolutions are carried out by people who hope for private gain and produce such public goods as they do produce as a byproduct" (46) captures fully the essence of revolutionary activity. The overcoming of the free-rider problem depends on the force of an ideological movement that serves as a point of unification; this might explain both Marx's and Lenin's emphasis on the educational role of the revolutionary party. This is also consistent with the work of Michael Taylor, *Anarchy and Cooperation* (New York: Wiley and Sons, 1976), who has suggested that free-rider problems can be overcome when a strong sense of community of purpose exists. Marx at times also seemed to recognize the importance of community of purpose in building revolutionary consciousness. "But the maintenance of wages, this common interest," Marx stated, "which they have against their boss, unites them in a common thought of resistance—combination....In this struggle—a veritable civil war—all the elements necessary for a coming battle unite and develop. Once it has reached this point, association takes on a political character." See Marx, *The Poverty of Philosophy*, 159.

[23] Some of the classic treatments of this question can be found in R.N. Carew Hunt, *The Theory and Practice of Communism* (Baltimore: Penguin Books, 1969[1950]); Edmund Wilson, *To the Finland Station* (New York: Doubleday and Co., 1940); and Nicolas Berdyaev, *The Origin of Russia Communism* (Ann Arbor: University of Michigan Press, 1972[1937]). Also see Leszek Kolakowski, *Main Currents of Marxism*, 3 vols. (New York: Oxford University Press, 1985[1978]), II: 304-527; Alexander Rüstow, *Freedom and Domination: A Historical Critique of Civilization* (Princeton, NJ: Princeton University Press, 1980[1950-57]), 537-558, 564-584; Paul Johnson, *Modern Times* (New York: Harper and Row, 1983), 49-103, 261-308; and Alain Besançon, *The Rise of the Gulag: Intellectual Origins of Leninism* (New York: Continuum, 1981).

[24] Lovell, *From Marx to Lenin: An Evaluation of Marx's Responsibility for Soviet Authoritarianism* (New York: Cambridge University Press, 1984), 197.

[25] Held, *An Introduction to Critical Theory* (Berkeley: University of California Press, 1980), 35.

[26] Jay, *Marxism and Totality: The Adventures of a Concept From Lukacs to Habermas* (Berkeley: University of California, 1984), 537.

[27] Habermas's latest attempt to articulate this program can be found in *The Theory of Communicative Action: Reason and the Rationalization of Society*, Vol. 1, translated by Thomas McCarthy (Boston: Beacon Press, 1984). An excellent discussion of Habermas's project can be found in Thomas McCarthy, *The Critical Theory of Jürgen Habermas* (Cambridge: The MIT Press, 1985).

[28] Stojanovic, "Marx and the Bolshevization of Marxism," *Praxis International*, Vol. 6, n. 4 (January 1987), 450-461. Stojanovic argues that:

> No matter how we look at it, Marx's idea of the dictatorship of the proletariat was practicable only by having one group rule in the name of the proletariat as a whole. In the best of cases, it would rule in its interest and under its control. In the worst case, it would rule without any kind of supervision and against its vital interests. In conceiving a new state it is no small oversight to set out from the most optimistic assumptions, where no real thought is given to measures and guarantees against the abuse of power (453).

Marxists need to deal with the terror inflicted upon the proletariat by the dictatorship in its name that occurred during the early years of the Soviet regime.

[29] See Selucky, *Marxism, Socialism, Freedom* (New York: St. Martin's Press, 1979).

[30] This line of reasoning is also consistent with basic Marxian materialist philosophy which argued that the material base (economic life) determines the super-structure (the realm of ideas). See Selucky, *Marxism, Socialism, Freedom*, 74-80.

[31] Alexander Rüstow provides an insightful discussion of the evolution of the Marxian heritage among the political elite within the first decade of Soviet rule, though I believe he does not address clearly enough the subtle point of how Stalinism can be seen as an unintended consequences of Marx's project. See *Freedom and Domination*, 571-572.

[32] Lavoie, *National Economic Planning: What Is Left?* (Cambridge, MA: Ballinger Press, 1985), 18-19.

[33] The gambling metaphor is important to keep in mind. It is not that the despotism was an unseen consequence of rationalization, just as it is not an unseen consequence of poker that one may lose a hand or money. Rather, the despotism in the

gambling story was the possible outcome that the Bolsheviks, and specifically Lenin, were trying to avoid, just as the poker player tries to avoid losing. This has the result, I contend, of obscuring the economic problem that the Marxian social relations of production would have to confront in any socioeconomic situation no matter how favorable.

[34] The classic presentation of this thesis is found in Karl Wittfogel, *Oriental Despotism: A Comparative Study of Total Power* (New Haven: Yale University Press, 1964[1957]), especially 369 ff. Wittfogel argues that Russia's development since 1917 deserves the most careful scrutiny. For reasons of historical development, Wittfogel supports the February Revolution, but opposes October.

[35] Daniels, *The Conscience of the Revolution*, 9, emphasis added.

[36] See Lavoie, "Political and Economic Illusions of Socialism," *Critical Review*, Vol. 1, n. 1 (Winter 1986-1987), 1-2, 10.

[37] For a criticism of this approach to social theory see F. A. Hayek, *The Counter-Revolution of Science* (Indianapolis: Liberty Press, 1979[1952]), especially 111-152. Also see Ludwig von Mises, *Theory and History*, 195, where he argues:

> History is made by men. The conscious intentional actions of individuals, great and small, determine the course of events insofar as it is the result of the interaction of all men. But the historical process is not designed by individuals. It is the composite outcome of the intentional actions of all individuals. No man can plan history. All he can plan and try to put into effect is his own actions which, jointly with the actions of other men, constitute the historical process. The Pilgrim Fathers did not plan to found the United States.

Neither Marx nor Lenin planned to found the Soviet society of Joseph Stalin. Nevertheless that should not absolve them from responsibility or deny the important role they (or their ideas) played in the establishment of the system.

[38] In fact, it is the belief that Russia had already begun its capitalist development that lead George Plekhanov to move from a populist (who believed the peasant commune could serve as the foundation of anarcho-socialism) to a Marxist by 1883. See *Marxism in Russia*, edited by Neil Harding, 41 ff., especially the extracts from Plekhanov's writings. Also see Samuel Baron, "Between Marx and Lenin: George Plekhanov," in *Revisionism: Essays on the History of Marxist Ideas*, ed. Leopold Labedz (New York: Praeger Publishers, 1962), 42-54, and his more elaborate treatment, *Plekhanov: The Father of Russian Marxism* (Stanford, CA: Stanford

University Press, 1963).

[39] See Trotsky, *The History*, I: 332 ff.

[40] See Alexander Rabinowitch, *The Bolsheviks Come to Power* (New York: Norton, 1978), for an excellent discussion of the events from the July uprisings to the October revolution. In particular, see Rabinowitch's reflections upon the reasons for the Bolshevik success in 1917, 310 ff.

[41] V.I. Lenin, "Political Parties in Russia and the Task of the Proletariat," in *Collected Works*, 45 vols.(Moscow: Progress Publishers, 1977), Vol. 24: 96-106. Hereafter cited as *CW* and within the text, for example, as (24: 96-106).

[42] Lenin, "The Tasks of the Proletariat in the Present Situation," *CW* (24: 21-26).

[43] It is interesting to note that the name *Bolshevik* was an accident of history; during the 1903 conference Plekhanov sided with Lenin on the organization of the party and, thus, created the Bolshevik (majority in Russian) wing of the Social Democratic party. In reality the Bolsheviks constituted a minority of Social Democrats until their assumption of power in 1917.

[44] Among other things, Lenin called for the immediate amalgamation of all banks into a single national bank, and that control over the bank be immediately turned over to the Soviets of Workers' Deputies. The importance of this proposal will be brought out throughout this chapter.

[45] Lenin, "Notes for an Article or Speech in Defense of the April Theses," *CW* (24: 33; emphasis added).

[46] Lenin, "Dual Power," *CW* (24: 38-41). Also see Trotsky, *The History*, I: 206-215.

[47] I am mainly documenting Lenin's convictions on the ripeness issue, but it should be emphasized that Marx during his lifetime was constantly watching for revolutionary chances—even in France and Germany of the 1840s. Commenting on the rigid interpretation of historical preconditions that many "revisionist" Marxists held, Trotsky argued: "Apparently Marx in 1848 was a Utopian youth compared with many of the present-day infallible automata of Marxism!" as quoted in Richard Day, *Leon Trotsky and the Politics of Economic Isolation* (New York: Cambridge University Press, 1973), 8. Moreover, from a Marxist perspective this ripeness question represents a meek argument (allowing any failure of Marxism to be in principle excusable) and should be rejected as undialectical and not sufficiently materialist in its analysis. It represents an evasion for a theory that claims to be a *critical* social theory. Marxian theory is built (supposedly) on the connection

between theory and praxis and any analysis that is neither grounded in historical praxis nor sufficiently self-critical is to be rejected. The historical-precondition response does not answer the questions raised by critical Marxists concerning the problems of the Soviet experience. See the discussion above of both the Frankfurt School and especially the Praxis group philosophers for a more fruitful approach to the problem at hand.

[48] Lenin, "Letters on Tactics," *CW* (24: 53), written in April 1917.

[49] Lenin did not intend to abolish war planning but to transform it into a model of socialist organization. As he wrote in December 1916:

> The war has reaffirmed clearly enough and in a very practical way...that modern capitalist society, particularly in the advanced countries, has fully matured for the transition to socialism. If, for instance, Germany can direct the economic life of 66 million people from a single, central institution...then the same can be done, in the interests of nine-tenths of the population, by the non-propertied masses if their struggle is directed by the class-conscious workers....All propaganda for socialism must be refashioned from abstract and general to concrete and directly practical; expropriate the banks and, relying on the masses, carry out in their interests the very same thing the W.U.M.B.A. [i.e., the Weapons and Ammunition Supply Department] is carrying out in Germany.

"*Chernovoi proekt tezisov obrashchenia k internatsional'noi sotsialisticheskoi komissii i ko vsem sotsialisticheskim partiiam,*" *Polnoe sobranie sochinenii*, Vol. 30, 278-279, as quoted in Alfred Evans, "Rereading Lenin's *State and Revolution,*" *Slavic Review*, Vol. 46, n. 1 (Spring 1987), 18, fn. 79.

[50] Lenin, "Resolution on the Current Situation," *CW* (24: 309-312).

[51] This reference is supplied in the explanatory reference notes of Lenin's *CW* (24: 603, fn. 106; emphasis added).

[52] Also see, Lenin, "Inevitable Catastrophe and Extravagant Promises," *CW* (24: 424-430).

[53] "The 'April days'" Trotsky argued, "were the first candid warning addressed by the October to the February revolution. The bourgeois Provisional Government was replaced after this by a Coalition whose fruitlessness was revealed on every day of its existence. In the June demonstrations summoned by the Executive Committee

on its own initiative, although perhaps not quite voluntarily, the February revolution tried to measure strength with the October and suffered a cruel defeat." See Trotsky, *The History*, I: 458.

[54] Lenin's program of control, which he argued could be established by a workers' state by decree "in the first weeks of its existence," consisted of: (1) nationalization of all banks and the creation of a central bank, (2) nationalization of syndicates, (3) abolition of commercial secrecy, (4) compulsory syndication, and (5) compulsory organization of population. The creation of a central bank, in particular, was essential to Lenin because the principal nerve center of modern economic life was the bank and one cannot regulate economic life without taking over banks—control over the bank allowed the unification of accountancy. See Lenin *CW* (25: 333 ff.).

[55] Also see Lenin, "Who Is Responsible?" *CW* (25: 151-152), where he argues : "In times of revolution, procrastination is often equivalent to a complete betrayal of the revolution. Responsibility for the delay in the transfer of power to the workers, soldiers and peasants, for the delay in carrying through revolutionary measures to enlighten the ignorant peasants, rests wholly on the Socialists-Revolutionaries and Mensheviks. They have betrayed the revolution...."

[56] *Imperialism*, *CW* (22: 185-304), was written from January to June 1916 and was published in Petrograd in late April 1917. *The State and Revolution*, *CW* (25: 384-497), was written in August and September 1917.

[57] This standard Marxist analysis of the operation of capitalism is based on faulty reasoning for the same theoretical reasons presented in chapter 2. Also see Murray N. Rothbard, *Man, Economy and State: A Treatise on Economic Principles*, 2 vols. (Los Angeles: Nash Publishing, 1970[1962]), II: 547 ff. and 585-586. The problem of economic calculation puts a limit on the potential size of any firm within an economic system—the evolution of the economy into one big firm is not technically possible from an economic point of view.

[58] In contrast, see the discussion of the economic and political reasons why the most meaningful definition of monopoly is a state grant or privilege given to a business enterprise to be the sole producer of a commodity or service: Rothbard, *Man, Economy and State*, II: 560-660; Dominick T. Armentano, "A Critique of Neoclassical and Austrian Monopoly Theory," in *New Directions in Austrian Economic*, edited by Louis M. Spadaro (Kansas City: Sheed, Andrews and McMeel, 1978), 94-110; Harold Demsetz, "Barriers to Entry," *American Economic Review*, Vol. 72, n. 1 (March 1982), 47-57. For an historical discussion of "political capitalism" and the strategic use of the state by businessmen to either guarantee or protect their profits see Gabriel Kolko, *The Triumph of Conservatism* (New York: The Free Press, 1964) and James Weinstein, *The Corporate Ideal in the Liberal State, 1900-1918* (Boston:

Beacon Press, 1968).

[59] Although Lenin is a harsh critic, he gets most of his theoretical insights on the operation of finance capital from the Austro-Marxist Rudolf Hilferding, *Finance Capital: A Study of the Latest Phase of Capitalist Development* (London: Routledge & Kegan Paul, 1985[1910]).

[60] Lenin concludes that "again and again the final word in the development of banking is monopoly" and he points to America where "two very big banks, those of the multimillionaires Rockefeller and Morgan, control" most of the capital (22: 219-220). It is true that the Morgan banks dominated the financial system in the United States, but this situation resulted from the system of political capitalism. The New York (Morgan) banks were losing their market share to the St. Louis and Chicago banks prior to 1913. They tried to keep their market share through a cartel arrangement, which would have allowed them to overissue notes, but the cartel could not be maintained. So they sought to establish a government enforced cartel and the Federal Reserve System (established in 1913) supplied just that for the "House of Morgan." See Murray N. Rothbard, "The Federal Reserve as a Cartelization Device: The Early Years, 1913-1930," in *Money in Crisis*, edited by Barry N. Siegel (Cambridge, MA: Ballinger Publishing, 1984), 89-136.

[61] For the same theoretical reason that the realization of socialism is impossible and the assessment of increasing concentration of capital under capitalism is flawed, Lenin's assessment of the desirability of central banking is also questionable. Central banking is not capable of bringing the economic life process under control—in fact, central banks operate in the dark. They are not well equipped to *know* whether an adjustment in the supply of money is needed or not because they lack the necessary economic knowledge. See George Selgin, *The Theory of Free Banking* (Totawa, NJ: Rowman and Littlefield, 1988), 89-107. The problem facing the central bank is a microcosm of the problem facing the comprehensive central planning board—neither can obtain the requisite knowledge to effectively accomplish the task it sets out to do, and, therefore it ends up relying on political rationales and not economic ones.

[62] This argument of the economic logic of imperialism should be kept in mind, especially later when we discuss the internal imperialism advocated by Preobrazhensky, and later Stalin, during the Industrialization Debate.

[63] As Marx argued in the "Critique of the Gotha Programme," *SW*:

> What we have to deal with here is a communist society, not as it has developed on its own foundations, but, on the contrary, just as it emerges from capitalist society; which is thus in every

> respect, economically, morally and intellectually, still stamped with the birth marks of the old society from whose womb it emerges. The "first phase of communist society," Marx later added, will have certain inevitable defects as it has "just emerged after prolonged birth pangs from capitalistic society" (III:19).

[64] Polan, *Lenin and the End of Politics* (Berkeley: University of California Press, 1984), 57.

[65] Daniels, *The Conscience of the Revolution*, 51-52.

[66] Barfield, "Lenin's Utopianism: *State and Revolution*, *Slavic Review*, Vol. 30, n. 1 (March 1971), 45-56; emphasis added. Barfield argued that Lenin researched the book from January to February 1917, the notebooks that constitute 'Marxism on the State.' Barfield's argument suggests that the utopianism evidenced in the *State and Revolution* permeates all of Lenin's political writings—a sort of anarcho-libertarian belief in the masses. Though I would agree, I think Barfield places his finger upon the wrong utopianism. Lenin's utopianism is better represented by the ease with which he thought Marx's project of rationalization could be accomplished.

[67] Evans, "Rereading Lenin," 3.

[68] Evans, "Rereading Lenin," 3.

[69] Lenin here is discussing the idea that full democratic participation is impossible under capitalism because the state will be used to exploit the many for the benefit of the few, that is, the capitalists. Under socialism, however, classes will disappear, and with their disappearance formal institutions of democracy will also disappear. Polan has suggested that this theory of the state eliminates all possible checks against abuse and results in the lodging of power in the hands of a few—exactly what happened under Bolshevik rule. The crime of Lenin's text, Polan argues, is not that it did not work; the crime is that it did work. Lenin's theory eliminated any of the possible checks that would have made the Gulag less likely. See Polan, *Lenin and the End of Politics*, 129-130.

[70] Lenin seems completely naive in his understanding of the complexity of economic organization. As Polan, *Lenin and the End of Politics*, states:

> Lenin seems to suggest that the economic problem that can be resolved by the adoption of the model of the "postal service" is simply one of efficiency: where the multi-faceted confusions of the competitive mechanism have been removed, there is no "economic" problem of organization. However, the problem

> remains that the capitalist mechanism, in the form of the market, accomplished the task of allocation and distribution of rewards and resources, while this task remains to be performed in the absence of the market. Confident assertions of the possibility of extending the "postal" model to embrace the whole economy ignore the fact that the absence of a market forces the state to *inherit a task of immense complexity* (61-62; emphasis added).

This is essentially the point of departure for Michael Polanyi's criticism of central administration of economic life: see "The Span of Central Direction," in *The Logic of Liberty* (Chicago: University of Chicago Press, 1980[1951]), 111 ff. On the nature of complexity in social relations also see Hayek, "The Theory of Complex Phenomena," *Studies in Philosophy, Politics and Economics* (Chicago: University of Chicago Press, 1980[1967]), 22-42; *Law, Legislation and Liberty*, I: 35-54 and II: 107-132.

[71] The Bolsheviks and their allies among the Left Socialist-Revolutionaries overthrew the Kerensky government on October 25 [November 7], 1917. The Council of People's Commissars (Sovnarkom) was established with Lenin as Chairman and Trotsky as the Commissar of Foreign Affairs. The Revolutionary Military Committee of Petrograd Soviet of Workers' and Soldiers' Deputies declared that the provisional government had been overthrown and that "the cause for which the people have fought—the immediate proposal of a democratic peace, the abolition of landed proprietorship, workers' control over production and the creation of a Soviet government—is assured." See *A Documentary History*, 117. Also see Lenin, "The Bolsheviks Must Assume Power," "Marxism and Insurrection," "The Tasks of the Revolution," and "Can the Bolsheviks Retain State Power?" all in *CW* (26: 19 ff.) and Trotsky, *The History*, III: 124 ff.

[72] Trotsky provides an eloquent discussion of Lenin's first appearance before the Congress after taking power:

> Lenin, whom the Congress has not yet seen, is given the floor for a report on peace. His appearance in the tribune evokes a tumultuous greeting. The trench delegates gaze with all their eyes at this mysterious being whom they had been taught to hate and whom they have learned without seeing him to love. "Now Lenin, gripping the edges of the reading-stand, let little winking eyes travel over the crowd as he stood there waiting, apparently oblivious to the long-rolling ovation, which lasted several minutes. When it finished, he said simply, 'We shall now proceed to construct the socialist order.'"

See Trotsky, *The History*, III: 325. Also see John Reed, *Ten Days That Shook the World* (New York: Penguin Books, 1985[1919]), 117 ff.

[73]Leites, *Recent Economic Developments in Russia* (New York: Oxford University Press, 1922), 65.

[74] Arthur Shadwell, *The Breakdown of Socialism* (Boston: Little, Brown, and Co., 1927), 23.

[75] See Laszlo Szamuely, *First Models of the Socialist Economic Systems: Principles and Theories* (Budapest: Akademiai 1974), 10 ff. Also see William Henry Chamberlin, *The Russian Revolution*, 2 vols. (Princeton: Princeton University Press, 1987[1935]), II: 96 ff. Notice that prominence is not given to grain requestioning in this outline of the socialist program of the Bolsheviks from 1918 to 1921. Although grain requestioning was undoubtedly a major policy, it *was not* the major element in the program of socialist transformation. Concentration on the food-procurement policy of requisitioning while ignoring the various other components of the Bolsheviks economic and social policy leads to an overemphasis on the emergency aspect of gathering food for the Red Army. Cf., Lars Lih, "Bolshevik *Razverstka* and War Communism," *Slavic Review*, Vol. 45, n. 4 (Winter 1986), 673-688. Also see Malle, *Economic Organization of War Communism*, 322-465, for a discussion of the ideology of food procurement and the military expediency of *prodrazverstka*.

[76]See Glenn Paul Holman, "'War Communism,' or the Besieger Besieged" (unpublished PhD thesis, Georgetown University, 1973), 7-10, for a discussion of the evolution of the terminology from communism (Bukharin and Kritsman) to militant communism (Alfred Meyer) to military communism (Trotsky) to war communism (Dobb, Carr, and others). Also consider the following statement by Victor Serge, *Memoirs of a Revolutionary, 1901-1941* (New York: Oxford University Press, 1963), 115: "The social system in these years was later called 'War Communism.' At the time it was called simply 'Communism', and any one who, like myself, went so far as to consider it purely temporary was looked upon with disdain." Also see Vasil Selyunin, "Sources," *Novy Mir* (May 1988), reprinted in *The Current Digest of the Soviet Press*, Vol. XL, n. 40 (1988), 14-17, and V. Sirotkin, "Lessons of NEP," *Izvestia* (March 9, 1989), reprinted in *The Current Digest of the Soviet Press*, Vol. 41, n. 10 and n. 11 (1989), 6-7, 11-12.

[77] Pasvolsky, *The Economic of Communism: With Special Reference to Russia's Experiment* (New York: Macmillan Co., 1921), 21.

[78] Pasvolsky, *The Economics of Communism*, 26.

[79]The following is a list and dates (Western calendar) of some of the major economic decrees and resolutions following the Bolshevik rise to power:
November 8, 1917: The Council of People's Commissars is formed.
November 8, 1917: Decree on Land; abolished the landlords' right of property and confiscated landed estates.
November 27, 1917: Decree on Workers' Control over production.
December 15, 1917: Supreme Economic Council is established.
December 27, 1917: Declaration of the Nationalization of Banks.
January 15, 1918: Dividend and interest payments and all dealings in stocks and bonds are declared illegal.
January 16, 1918: Declaration of the Rights of the Working and Exploited People; abolished the exploitation of man by man.
February 10, 1918: Repudiation of all foreign debt.
April 22, 1918: Nationalization of foreign trade.
May 1, 1918: Abolition of inheritance.
May 9, 1918: Decree giving the Food Commissariat extraordinary powers to combat village bourgeoisie who were concealing and speculating on grain reserves.
June 9, 1918: Labor mobilization for the Red Army.
June 28, 1918: Nationalization of large-scale industry and railway transportation.
November 2, 1918: Decree on the Extraordinary Revolutionary Tax to support the Red Army and the International Socialist Revolution.
March 22, 1919: The Party Programme of the Eighth Party Congress; called for increased centralization of economic administration.
March 29 to April 4, 1920: The Outstanding Resolution on Economic Reconstruction is passed; called for increased centralization of economic administration to insure the unity of the plan necessary for the economic reconstruction after civil war and foreign intervention.
November 29, 1920: Decree of the Supreme Economic Council on the nationalization of small industrial enterprises; all enterprises with mechanical power who employed five or more workers and all enterprises without mechanical power who employed ten or more workers were nationalized.
March 1921: The Kronstadt Rebellion.
March 8-16, 1921: Resolution on Party Unity abolishing factionalism within the party is accepted.
March 23, 1921: The Tax in Kind is established and the New Economic Policy is introduced.

[80] *CW* (27: 259). Lenin invokes the Taylor system as an example of the technological innovations of capitalism that the Soviet system must experiment with and adopt. The Taylor system was expected to increase the productivity of labor, which was deemed a necessary condition for socialist construction. The Taylor system fit neatly into the social engineering bias of the Bolsheviks and other socialist thinkers at that time. Trotsky, for example, argued that the Minister of Trade and Industry

should be a technician, an engineer, who would work under the overall control of the Council of People's Commissars. See Trotsky's memo to Commarade Sljapnikov in *The Trotsky Papers,* Vol. 1, 1917-1919 (London: Mouton & Co., 1964), 3. Also see the discussion in Remington, *Building Socialism in Bolshevik Russia*, 113-145. This is also connected to Lenin's reliance on the model of German War Planning as a means to achieve socialist planning. See Judith A. Merkle, *Management and Ideology* (Berkeley: University of California, 1980), 172 ff. The principle of one-man management (OMM) represents, both in military organization and technological management within the industry, the latest stage of scientific development.

[81] Malle, *The Economic Organization of War Communism*, 32-33.

[82] "'Left-Wing' Childishness and the Petty-Bourgeois Mentality," *CW* (27: 339). Lenin argues here that the Soviet dictatorship of the proletariat provides the political basis for social transformation, while the German war-planning machine provides the economic basis. The task of the Soviets, therefore, was to study the German system and "spare no effort in copying it and not shrink from adopting dictatorial methods to hasten the copying of it" (27: 340). Compare this with Adam Kaufman, "The Origin of 'The Political Economy of Socialism,'" *Soviet Studies*, Vol. 4, n. 3 (January 1953), 243-272, and Leon Smolinsky, "Planning Without Theory, 1917-1967," *Survey*, n. 64 (July 1967), 108-128, who argue that neither Lenin nor the other Bolsheviks had any theoretical framework from which to develop an approach to economic planning.

[83] As quoted in Shadwell, *The Breakdown of Socialism*, 24.

[84] Trotsky, *Sochinenia* (Moscow, 1927), XV: 215, as quoted in Smolinsky, "Planning without Theory," 113.

[85] Smolinsky, "Planning without Theory," 112. Neither was the nationalization of the banks nor the inflationary monetary policy intended to be "simply used to finance government expenditures, just as in so many other countries," as Malle seems to suggest, in *The Economic Organization of War Communism*, 175.

[86] See Marx *Economic and Philosophic Manuscripts of 1844* (Moscow: Progress Publishers, 1977), 127 ff., and *Grundrisse* (New York: Vintage Books, 1973), 115 ff. Also see W. Francis Vorhies, "Marx and Mises on Money: The Monetary Theories of Two Opposing Political Economies" (unpublished PhD thesis, University of Colorado, 1982).

[87] His reports were published in several articles and pamphlets during this time. See Nikolai I. Bukharin, "The Economics of the Transition Period," in *The Politics and*

Economics of the Transition Period, ed. Kenneth J. Tarbuck (Boston: Routledge & Kegan Paul, 1979[1920]), 212, fn. 5. These articles were collected and later (1928) published in the Soviet Union as *Gosudarstvennyi kapitalizm voennogo vremeni v Germanii (1914-1918)*. Larin, who was a Bukharin's father-in-law, died in 1932 before "the Terror" destroyed the rest of his colleagues of the war communism period. He was buried in the Kremlin Wall with honors. See Remington, *Building Socialism in Bolshevik Russia*, 30. Also see the interview with Anna Mikhailovna, the widow of Bukharin, "He Wanted to Remake Life Because He Loved It," *Ogonyok*, n. 48 (November 1987), reprinted in *The Current Digest of the Soviet Press*, Vol. 40, n. 5 (1988), 6-8.

[88] As quoted in Lancelot Lawton, *An Economic History of Soviet Russia*, 2 vols. (London: Macmillan, 1932), I: 108.

[89] As quoted in Malle, *The Economic Organization of War Communism*, 165.

[90] Malle explains the policy of all-out nationalization of industry pursued in November 1920, after the armistice with Poland in October 1920, as an attempt to extend this cashless payment system. As she states: "One of the reasons for the overall nationalization of industry in November 1920 was the attempt to extend the system of non-monetary accounts to the sphere of small-scale and kustar' industry, which had been working under war communism on the system of cash payments. A decree of Sovnarkom in July 1920 did, in fact, extend the rules of non-monetary payments to contracts negotiated with private institutions." See Malle, *The Economic Organization of War Communism*, 172.

[91] "*Bezdenzhnye raschety i ikh rol v finansovom khozyaistve*," *Narodnoe Khozyaistvo*, n. 1 and n. 2 (1920), as quoted in Szamuely, *First Models of the Socialist Economic System*, 34; emphasis added. Also see Malle, *The Economic Organization of War Communism*, 174, where she quotes Krestinskii, who was one of the Commissars of Finance, as arguing that the Bolshevik's financial policies during war communism were a result of their conviction that "the period had begun in which monetary tokens would become unnecessary and it would be possible to get rid of them without any damage to the economy. From such a perspective originated our easy attitude towards monetary issue and our lack of concern to increase the value of the ruble."

[92] See Bukharin and Preobrazhensky, *The ABC of Communism* (Ann Arbor: University of Michigan Press, 1966[1919]). The appendix of this book contains the adopted party program, 373 ff. Bukharin wrote all of Part One, the theoretical exposition on the decay of capitalism. He also wrote the introduction to Part Two, which concerns itself with the dictatorship of the proletariat and the building of

communism. Bukharin also wrote the chapters on the organization of industry, the protection of labor, and public hygiene. Preobrazhensky wrote the remaining chapters.

[93] *The ABC of Communism*, 70; emphasis added. It is this program of rationalization that Milyutin announced with pride in June 1920 had been accomplished. "All enterprises and all industrial branches," he stated, "are considered like a single enterprise. Instead of competition, instead of struggle, Soviet Power with determination implements the principle of unity of the national economy in the economic field." As quoted in Malle, *The Economic Organization of War Communism, 1918-1921*, 320, fn. 27. It is also this very project of achieving ex ante coordination that Mises directly challenged; while Bukharin stated that the planner would know in advance how, what and for whom to allocate resources, Mises merely asked the planners how, in the absence of monetary calculation, they would know which projects are economically feasible and which ones were not. As we will see, it is the Bolsheviks' disregard of economic calculation that finally led to the collapse and the retreat to NEP.

[94] *The ABC of Communism*, 74. Bukharin does, however, admit that two or three generations would have to grow up under the new conditions before the project is fully realizable, and "the bureaucracy, the permanent officialdom, will disappear" and the state would wither away. Bukharin, at least here, did not seem to understand the threat of the growing bureaucracy associated with the communist scheme. For a discussion of the bureaucratization of social life under Soviet rule, see Bruno Rizzi, *The Bureaucratization of the World* (New York: The Free Press, 1985[1939]); Milovan Djilas, *The New Class* (New York: Praeger, 1957); and George Konrad and Ivan Szelenyi, *The Intellectuals on the Road to Class Power* (New York: Harcourt Brace Jovanovich, 1979).

[95] *The ABC of Communism*, 72. Also see Bukharin, "The Economics of the Transition Period," 155, where Bukharin argues that: "Money represents the material social ligament, the knot which ties up the whole highly developed commodity system of production. It is clear that during the transition period, in the process of abolishing the commodity system as such, a process of 'self-negation' of money takes place. It is manifested in the first place in the so-called devaluation of money and in the second place, in the fact that the distribution of paper money is divorced from the distribution of products, and vice versa. Money ceases to be the universal equivalent and becomes a conventional—and moreover extremely imperfect—symbol of the circulation of products."

[96] *The ABC of Communism*, 77.

[97] Bukharin, "The Economics of the Transition Period," 155.

[98] "Program of the Communist Party of Russia (adopted at the Eighth Party Congress Held March 18 to 23, 1919)," in *The ABC of Communism*, 390.

[99] "Program of the Communist Party of Russia," 397. Also see Lenin, "Draft Programme of the R.C.P.(B.)," *CW* (29: 98-140). Lenin proposed that "the R.C.P. will strive as speedily as possible to introduce the most radical measures to pave the way for the abolition of money, first and foremost to replace it by savings-bank books, cheques, short-term notes entitling the holders to receive goods from the public stores and so forth...." (115-116). Lenin argued for the eventual elimination of hand-to-hand currency and its replacement by a system of cashless accounting, that is, sophisticated barter.

[100] See the Appendix: Documents of the Revolution in Chamberlin, *The Russian Revolution*, II: 490.

[101] "Decree of the Supreme Economic Council on the Nationalization of Small Industrial Enterprises, of November 29, 1920," Chamberlin, *The Russian Revolution*, II: 494.

[102] Bukharin would try to "apologize" for the economic destruction—not by reference to civil war or foreign intervention, but by reference to the dialectics of the transition period. This goes for his theory of expanded negative reproduction as well as his justification of noneconomic coercion. The contradiction inherent in the transition period —"where the proletariat has already left the confines of capitalist compulsion, but has not yet become a worker communist society"—demand it. See Bukharin, "The Economics of the Transition Period."

[103] Chamberlin, *The Russian Revolution*, II: 105.

[104] Wells, *Russia in the Shadows* (New York: George H. Doran, 1921), 137. Wells, however, blames the debacle upon the civil war and foreign blockade. This reminds me of the scene in the movie *Reds* where Emma Goldman and John Reed are having a conversation over the debacle of war communism. Reed argued that the 4 million deaths from famine between 1919 and 1920 were a result of the capitalist (imperialist) blockade. Goldman, however, responds that the people did not starve to death because of the blockade, but because of a system that cannot work. My sympathies lie with Goldman's interpretation of the Soviet experience with Marxian socialism.

[105] Lewin, *The Making of the Soviet System* (New York: Pantheon Books, 1985), 211.

[106] Stephen Cohen, *Bukharin and the Bolshevik Revolution* (New York: Oxford

University Press, 1980[1971]), 123.

[107] For example, Boris Pasternak's *Doctor Zhivago* and Ayn Rand's *We the Living* give explicit details of the destruction of economic and social life under Soviet rule during this period. Also see the memoirs of Emma Goldman, *My Disillusionment in Russia* (New York: Doubleday, Page and Co., 1923) and *My Further Disillusionment in Russia* (New York: Doubleday, Page and Co., 1924) and Arthur Ransome, *Russia in 1919* (New York: B.W. Huebsch, 1919).

[108] Besançon, *The Rise of the Gulag*, 278.

[109] Lawton, *An Economic History of Soviet Russia*, I: 107.

[110] As early as 1912 Mises had argued the essential organizational connection between private property in the means of production and monetary calculation. See Mises, *The Theory of Money and Credit* (Indianapolis: Liberty Press, 1980[1912]), 41, where he states: "The phenomenon of money presupposes an economic order in which production is based on division of labor and in which private property consists not only in goods of the first order (consumption goods), but also in goods of the higher order (production goods)."

[111] Lawton, *An Economic History of Soviet Russia*, I: 108.

[112] Lawton, *An Economic History of Soviet Russia*, I: 111.

[113] Mises, "Economic Calculation in the Socialist Commonwealth," [1920] reprinted in *Collectivist Economic Planning*, ed. and introduced by F.A. Hayek (New York: Augustus M. Kelley, 1975[1935]), 125.

[114] "*Etapy revoliutssi*," *Izvestiya* (March 12, 1921), as quoted in Daniels, *The Conscience*, 144.

[115] Avrich, *Kronstadt 1921* (New York: Norton, 1970), 163.

[116] Avrich, *Kronstadt 1921*, 163. Avrich seems to think this naive, but given the evidence presented above concerning the economic program of the Bolsheviks, and the economic coordination problems that program ran into, the Kronstadter's assessment might not be so naive after all. Avrich also seems to suggest that the Kronstadt rebellion was a result of the "failure" of the Bolsheviks to implement a Marxian socialist program, but this is because he interprets the socialist project to be one of a radical democratic decentralization of economic and political life. The Marxian ideal of both the rationalization of economic and political life is thus misunderstood. Nevertheless, Avrich provides perhaps the best history of the

rebellion. Also see Daniels, *The Conscience*, 137-153.

[117] *Pravda o Kronshtadte* (The Truth about Kronstadt), 1921, pp. 164-165, as quoted in Avrich, *Kronstadt 1921*, 163-164.

[118] Shapiro, *The Communist Party of the Soviet Union* (New York: Vintage, 1971[1960]), 211.

[119] Pasvolsky, *The Economics of Communism*, ix.

[120] Lavoie, *National Economic Planning*, 214; emphasis added.

4

THE POLITICAL ECONOMY OF NEP: MARKET RELATIONS AND INTERVENTIONISM IN SOVIET RUSSIA, 1921-1928

Introduction

The political unrest of 1920 and 1921, which produced turmoil in the countryside, in the city, and within the party itself, forced the Bolsheviks to change course. The move toward a new course was not easy in that it required a fundamental rethinking of the basic tenets of Bolshevism and socialist construction. Trotsky, for example, had introduced a proposal for the substitution of a tax-in-kind for requisitioning as early as February 1920, but only received four out of 15 votes within the Central Committee in support.[1] Even as late as December 1920 the All-Russian Congress of Soviets rejected a proposal for the introduction of a tax-in-kind on the grounds that it would betray the principles of Bolshevism and allow free trade, in other words, it would represent a retreat to capitalism.

But by February 1921 Lenin had become convinced that the concession was the only way to maintain political power. As Alec Nove states:

> [A]ll the way up to February 1921, Lenin kept stubbornly on the course of all-round nationalization, centralization, the elimination of money, and above all, the maintenance of prodrazverstka [grain requisitioning]. *There was no pressure on him from his colleagues to change this policy. Events, rather than the central committee, provided a potent means of persuasion.*[2]

Lenin became convinced that the relationship between the peasant and the industrial worker (the proletariat) was essential for continued political control. This relationship was expected to have taken care of itself because of the burst of productivity in economic life that was to come from the rationalization of production. But calculational chaos left economic life in misery instead.

As I tried to demonstrate in the last chapter, Lenin did not deviate from Marx by coming to power in a country that was both politically and economically backward or by attempting to rationalize the economy through centralization. In his goals of the revolution and his policies of war communism, Lenin was a faithful interpreter of Marx. Lenin advanced various arguments concerning the ripeness of Russia for socialist revolution. The imperialist war had created the necessary economic and political conditions for effective socialist praxis. The social ills that resulted in Soviet Russia from 1918 to 1921 were not a consequence of economic or political backwardness, but a consequence of a backward political economy. The economic-rationalization project of Marxism could not (and cannot) solve the fundamental economic problem of how to use the knowledge in society "which is not given to anyone in its totality."[3]

Lenin's deviation was the New Economic Policy. The interventionist policies of NEP were an outright denial of Marx's organizational scheme. Lenin did not just allow prices and profits to arise; he also abandoned the cardinal aim of socialism—the substitution of a settled plan for the anarchy of the market.

The Economic History of NEP

As with the war communism period, there is no dispute over the facts surrounding the economic situation under NEP. The dispute is in understanding what NEP represented and why it failed. But first, I will briefly go over the chronology of the economic policies and their consequences.

The substitution of a tax-in-kind for the forced requisitioning of peasant surplus was first discussed by Lenin in February 1921 to appease political unrest. At the Tenth Congress of the Russian Communist Party (Bolsheviks) in March 1921 the issue received full consideration and was adopted.[4] The economic reasons given for the change were the "acute crisis of peasant farming" and consequences that the crisis had on "the restoration of [the Soviet] transport system and [Soviet] industry."[5] Politically, any hesitation toward the change was quickly overcome when peasant uprisings culminated in the Kronstadt revolt in early March 1921. "As emergency military measures were improvised to crush the revolt, so Lenin proposed the substitution of food tax (*prodnalog*) for confiscation of surpluses (*prodrazverstka*)."[6]

As the 1939 edition of the *History of the Communist Party of the Soviet Union* states:

> The resolution of the congress dealt with the substitution of a tax in kind for the surplus-appropriation system. The tax in kind was to be lighter than the assessments under the surplus-appropriation system. The total amount of the tax was to be announced each

> year before the spring sowing. The dates of delivery under the tax were to be strictly specified. All produce over and above the amount of the tax was to be entirely at the disposal of the peasant, who would be at liberty to sell these surpluses at will.[7]

Thus while the delivery quota for 1920-1921 was 423 million poods of grain, the grain tax-in-kind was fixed at 240 million poods.[8] Similarly, the tax-in-kind for potatoes was well below the delivery quota (which was 110 million poods in 1920-1921) being fixed at 60 million poods for 1921-1922. For meat, the respective figures are 25.4 under requisitioning and 6.5 under the tax-in-kind.[9]

At first, NEP was primarily an agricultural reform intended to restore the alliance (*smychka*) between the proletarian and the peasant to secure an increased production of food.[10] But within a few months after the introduction of the tax-in-kind, the span of NEP increased to include industrial reform. Lenin argued, "Want and destruction have gone so far that we cannot at once restore large scale, factory, state, socialist production," and therefore "it is indispensable in a certain measure to help the restoration of small industry."[11] On May 17, 1921, the decree of November 1920, which nationalized small industry, was revoked.[12] In another decree of May 17 it was stated that the Bolsheviks would "take necessary measures to develop rural and small industries, whether in the form of private enterprises or of cooperatives," and "avoid the excessive regulation and excessive formalism which crush the economic initiative of individuals or groups of the population."[13] A July 5, 1921, decree called for the leasing of nationalized enterprises, and on July 7, 1921, the Soviet government authorized citizens to undertake handicraft production and organize small-scale industrial enterprises (20 or less workers).[14]

Instructions for running the national economy were released on August 9, 1921. The Soviet state, to prevent any further industrial decline, reorganized industry along the following lines:

1. The Supreme Economic Council, and its local branches, were to concentrate on direct administration of only those large-scale industries whose output was considered important for the state as a whole, along with the industries that supplement and supply these important industrial enterprises.
2. These enterprises were to be managed on the principle of rational economic budgeting.
3. Production in these enterprises could only begin with the permission of the Supreme Economic Council and only when the necessary supply of raw materials, technical equipment, and working capital was assured.
4. Enterprises not under the direct administration of the Supreme Economic Council were to be operated by cooperatives or private persons. Soviet institutions were to support this policy of leasing enterprises that the state could not at present organize rationally.
5. Enterprises that would neither be leased nor taken over for administration by

the Supreme Economic Council were to be closed. The workers of these enterprises were to be allocated to working enterprises and public works, or registered as unemployed (with unemployment compensation).

6. All enterprises that should have been nationalized by the November 1920 decree, but were not, were to be considered as not nationalized and their ownership restored to the former owner.

7. Large enterprises were to be organized in industrial combines, but the organization of industrial combines was permitted only for state-owned and state-administered enterprises.[15]

The result of this industrial reorganization was that by 1923, of the 165,781 enterprises accounted for in an industrial census 147,471 or 88.5 percent were owned by private persons, 13,697 or 8.5 percent were state owned, and 4,613 or 3.1 percent were cooperative enterprises. Although these private enterprises amounted to 88.5 percent of the total enterprises, they employed only 12.4 percent of the total number of workers employed in industry, while the state-owned enterprises, which comprised only 8.5 percent of the total enterprises, employed 84.1 percent of employed workers. Thus the state was freed from administrating small enterprises, while at the same time holding fast to the industrial base of Russian society. The "commanding heights" of industry remained state property.[16]

Thus, the Supreme Economic Council "became primarily an administrative coordinator for the socialized sector and a centre of macroeconomic policy" for the national economy.[17] The private enterprises, on the other hand, having received their organizational independence from the Supreme Economic Council, operated on the basis of the principles of supply and demand.[18]

Along with agricultural and industrial reform, the introduction of NEP led to monetary reform in an attempt to stabilize the currency. The reintroduction of the market as an allocating device demanded a stable currency.[19] The monetary system, however, had suffered throughout the war communism period, and stabilizing the currency was not an easy task. The attempt was made first to use pre-war rubles to draw up the 1922 budget, but with the 1922 ruble valued at some 60,000 to 1 pre-war ruble, this proved impractical. By July 1922 the decision was made to create a new unit, the *chervonets*, which were to be backed by gold.[20] The Soviet government hoped to create a stable currency, maintain a balanced budget, and practice sound public finance based on a form of the gold standard. At the same time, however, the older monetary unit retained its legal-tender status. The *chervonets* and the paper ruble, as a result, coexisted uneasily throughout 1922 and 1923 on a sort "bi-paperism" standard.[21] But the issue of paper rubles continued to increase to such an extent that it was rendered almost worthless. Figures for ruble currency in circulation are shown in table 4-1.

Table 4-1. Ruble Currency in Circulation, 1921-1922

	Milliards
January 1921	1,169
1 October 1921	4,529
1 September 1922	696,141
1 January 1923	1,994,464

Source: Alec Nove, *An Economic History of the U.S.S.R.* (New York: Penguin, 1984[1969]), 91.

This continued emission of rubles led finally to a situation where 100,000 rubles equalled only 1 pre-war kopeck. As a result, this monetary devaluation led to the substitution of grain poods as the unit of account in many villages.[22]

The government undertook several steps to try and rectify the situation and in 1924 the chervonets became the sole currency.[23] Alexander Baykov states that the monetary reform consisted of five main decrees:

1. Decree of February 5, 1924, ordered the issue of new paper currency—State Treasury notes in the denomination of 1, 3, and 5 gold rubles, which were accorded the right of legal tender. The amount of these, moreover, was not to exceed 50 percent of the amount of *chervontzy* in circulation.
2. Decree of February 14, 1924, ordered the cessation of the printing and issue of paper rubles (*sovznaks*), although those already in circulation were to remain.
3. Decree of March 7, 1924, ordered the redemption of the *sovznak*. The rate of redemption was fixed at 50,000 rubles (1923) or 50,000,000 rubles (pre-1921) and the redemption period was fixed at three months (April to June 1924).
4. Decree of February 22, 1924, ordered the minting and issue of silver and copper coins in the denomination of 10, 15, and 20 kopecks and half-rubles in silver, and 1, 2, 3, and 5 kopecks in copper coins.
5. Decree of July 1, 1924, ordered cessation of the emission of paper money to cover deficits in the state budget.[24]

Along with the monetary reform of 1924, changes also occurred in the public-finance system. A monetary tax, for example, was substituted for the tax-in-kind in 1924. The agricultural tax between 1924 and 1927 was gradually transformed into a progressive income tax based on "class." Thus while the tax rose over these years the burden of tax fell increasingly heavier on the rich peasants (*kulaks*). Also the income-property tax was reformed in 1924 and 1926, reflecting highly progressive tax rates differing according to "class."[25]

The Results of NEP

Despite the re-establishment of aspects of the civil code, there was heavy and arbitrary interference by the government with this market-based economic system throughout NEP.[26] For example, a decree of August 5, 1921, established the Price Committee of the Commissariat of Finance which had the power to fix wholesale and retail prices for goods produced or sold by state enterprises and, more important, goods the government brought from other enterprises, for example, private peasants. Planning during NEP, as Nove points out, consisted "not in plans in the sense of orders to act, but 'control figures', which were partly forecasts and partly a guide for strategic investment decisions, a basis for discussing and determining priorities."[27] The quest to abolish the anarchy of the market and substitute for it a settled plan was forgotten. Economic planning was transformed into interventionist fine tuning or steering the economic system in the desirable direction, leaving the market system as the major method of resource allocation.

This "mixed system" produced varying results over its lifetime (1921-1927), with the high-water mark of economic recovery coming in 1925. The relative freedom of exchange and production produced a drastic recovery from the catastrophe of war communism.[28] This recovery did not go into effect immediately in 1921 because of a severe drought that affected Soviet agriculture, and, while large-scale industrial production did increase by 32 percent in 1921-1922, that represented a negligible recovery considering the abysmal level of production in 1920 (some 20 percent below pre-war levels).[29] But by 1922-1923 the recovery was well underway.

As Alec Nove records: "The 1922 harvest was fairly good; by 1923 the sown area reached almost 90 percent of the pre-war level, and while the harvest was still far below 1913 levels, the shortage of food was no longer desperate."[30] Grain harvests during NEP, for example, ranged from 50.3 million tons in 1922, 56.6 million tons in 1923, 51.4 million tons in 1924, 72.5 million tons in 1925, and 76.8 million tons in 1926.[31] By contrast, however, the industrial recovery was much slower at obtaining pre-war levels of output.[32]

The recovery of industry during NEP is represented in table 4.2. By 1924 industry had still not recovered to even 50 percent of the prewar level of output. But in 1925 industrial production increased by 66.1 percent and reached 75 percent of its pre-war level of output.

Table 4-2. Output of Large-Scale Industry in 1926-1927 Prices

Year	*Million Rubles*	*Percent of 1913*	*Annual increases*
1913	10,251	100.0	—
1920	1,410	13.8	—
1921	2,004	19.5	42.1
1922	2,619	25.5	30.7
1923	4,005	39.1	52.9
1924	4,660	45.4	16.4
1925	7,739	75.5	66.1
1926	11,083	108.1	43.2
1927	12,679	123.7	14.2

Source: Naum Jasny, *Soviet Economists of the Twenties* (Cambridge: At the University Press, 1972), 23.

Railway freight traffic also reflects the recovery of industry under NEP. Whereas it is estimated that 132.4 million tons were transported by rail in 1913, at the end of the war communism period, in 1920, that figure had fallen to an estimated 31.9 million tons. In 1919 the figure had fallen to 30.5 million tons. But under NEP the tonnage increased as industrial production bounced back after 1921-1922. In 1923, for example, the amount of traffic is estimated at 60.7 million tons, and that increases to 70.7 million in 1924, 92.4 million in 1925, 122.2 million in 1926, and 139.6 million in 1927.[33]

"During the years of NEP," as Mikhail Heller and Aleksandr Nekrich state, "the worst of the war-inflicted wounds were healed, the economy was restored despite the many difficulties, and life assumed a semblance of normality." They continue, however, by adding: "But these accomplishments were paid for dearly. The population lived in uncertainty, fearful of breaking the law, afraid of what was to come. Paradoxically, those who were considered the victors (the workers) lived in poverty, although without fear, while those who knew they were the vanquished (the middle peasants, Nepmen, intellectuals) enjoyed material comfort, but lived in fear."[34]

The relative economic recovery, though, was reflected in the lives and literature of the people. In Andrei Platonov's *Chevengur*, for example, the hero returns home during NEP and is surprised to find:

> There was a buffet at the train station where gray rolls were sold without a line and without ration cards. Near the station...there

> was a gray sign whose letters dripped because of the poor quality of the paint. The sign announced primitively and briefly:
>
> > EVERYTHING ON SALE, TO ALL CITIZENS!
> > PREWAR BREAD! PREWAR FISH! FRESH MEAT!
> > OUR OWN PRESERVES!
>
> ...In the store the owner explained in a very concise and sensible way, to an old woman who had just come in, the meaning of these changes: "We've lived to see the day. Lenin tooketh away, and now Lenin giveth."[35]

The reintroduction of the market, even in a limited form, was a happy moment to the Soviet citizens even though many Bolsheviks viewed this reintroduction of the market under NEP as a "bourgeois perversion." Lenin even commented on the "enormous danger harboured by NEP" (*CW*, 33: 271). But the economic recovery visa via war communism led observers, such as E. Karelsky (a Bolshevik sympathizer), to comment:

> We can indeed say that the time of the NEP...was perceived by every inhabitant of the Soviet Union as the happiest period of his life. It lasted only until 1926 and it ended abruptly with the ruthless persecution of those who had become newly enriched. It was the time of free trade and free production in which independent entrepreneurs sprang up like mushrooms from the earth, during which prices dropped to ridiculously low levels as a result of intensely growing competition and of an oversupply of commodities, whereas wages in relation to those prices were higher than they had ever been in czarist times—a time in which people who had earlier lived through the period of "war communism" seemed to have gotten a glimpse of heaven on earth.[36]

Retreat or Advance?

Many standard historians of the Soviet experience interpret the New Economic Policy as a return to the proper road of socialist construction. They argue that the policies of NEP were originally introduced in 1917 and 1918 until the emergency of civil war forced the regime to abandon state capitalism for more centralized control over economic life. Maurice Dobb, for example, emphasized that Lenin's position on state capitalism in early 1918 was similar to, if not identical with, the position he advanced from 1921 to 1923. "NEP," Dobb writes, "was no sudden novelty, invented overnight or forced upon intentions quite alien to it by the failure of a 'direct assault' upon the old regime. It fitted completely, where War Communism had not, into the conception Lenin had always held of 'a definite transition period.'"[37] NEP was the proper economic system for the victorious proletariat.

Dobb's interpretation was reinforced by E.H. Carr, although Carr is a little more sensitive to the existence of a dual interpretation among the Bolsheviks themselves. But Carr does not see the fundamental economic change that NEP signified. To Carr, NEP merely represented the establishment of a better alliance with the peasants. "The introduction of NEP required not so much the creation of new institutions as the transformation of existing institutions from instruments of compulsion into instruments of the new policy of encouraging the individual initiative of the peasant."[38] Carr's assessment, however, was due in large part to his failure to understand the institutional requirements of Marxian socialism, let alone the fundamental economic problem that all socioeconomic organizations have to solve. For Carr, all the problems the Bolsheviks confronted in the political or economic realm were a result of the backward tradition they inherited when they came to power. Even the dual interpretation of the significance of NEP, according to Carr, stemmed from the historical accident of the socialist revolution happening first in a backward country. "These uncertainties and inconsistencies in the attitude of the party and of Lenin himself towards NEP," Carr argued, "reflected the persistent duality of aims that lay behind it—the need at all costs to create a workable economy by way of agreement with the peasantry, and the desire to effect the long-delayed transition to a socialist order, which could be realized only through a radical transformation of the peasant economy. It involved the *fundamental problem* which had dogged the Bolshevik revolution from the outset—*the problem of building a socialist order in a country which had missed the stage of bourgeois democracy and bourgeois capitalism.*"[39]

Among current political historians, Stephen Cohen represents the strongest advocate of NEP as the true path in building socialism. "NEP," Cohen argues, "the years between the end of the Russian civil war in 1921 and the coming of Stalin's revolution from above in 1929 represent the first and still most far-reaching liberalization in Soviet political history—a kind of Moscow Spring."[40] NEP represented the "first dual economy," a model of "socialist humanism." Stalin destroyed, according to Cohen, "a model of Communist politics and economics that many citizens would long remember as the 'golden era' in Soviet history."[41]

It is ironic that Cohen would refer to this time as a period of "conciliatory politics" and as a model for "socialist humanism." The Bolsheviks had declared opposition factions illegal and established a political monopoly. Lenin declared all political activity outside of the party to be subversive. The Mensheviks and Socialist-Revolutionaries, dressed up in their modern, Kronstadt, nonparty attire, were helping, Lenin declared, "the vacillating petit-bourgeois element to recoil from the Bolsheviks, to cause a shift of power in favour of the capitalists and landowners." These individuals, Lenin argued, shall either be kept safely in prison or sent abroad, alongside Martov in Berlin, where they can enjoy all "the charms of democracy" (*CW*, 32: 361-362). Even within the party the Workers' Opposition was effectively silenced by Lenin (see *CW*, 32: 241 ff.). As Paul Johnson commented: "We have to assume that what drove Lenin on to do what he did was a burning humanitarianism, akin to the love of the saints for God, for he had none of the customary blemishes of the politically ambitious.... But his humanitarianism was a very abstract passion. It embraced humanity in general but he seems to have had little love for, or even interest in, humanity in particular."[42] It is this passion for abstract humanity, and the conviction that he was the designated interpreter of the Marxian "word," that led Lenin to sanction social institutions such as the Cheka, which by 1920 had already put to death an estimated 50,000 particular members of humanity.[43]

In his biography of Nikolai Bukharin, Cohen describes Bukharin's shift from war communism to NEP as requiring a process of rethinking. "Bukharin's enthusiasm for NEP," Cohen argues, "began to emerge as his criticism of war communism broadened."[44] But Cohen does not seem to appreciate his own evidence on Bukharin's position concerning the critique of war communism and the significance of NEP. Bukharin tied the economic irrationality of war communism to the bureaucratization of the economy. The system, he argued, was not more, but less rational than the anarchy of commodity production. As Bukharin argued:

> Taking too much on itself, it has to create a colossal administrative apparatus. To fulfill the economic functions of the small producers, small peasants, etc., it requires too many employees and administrators. The attempt to replace all these small figures with state chinovniki [bureaucrats]—call them what you want, in fact they are state chinovniki—gives birth to such a colossal apparatus that the expenditure for its maintenance proves to be incomparably more significant than the unproductive costs which derive from the anarchistic condition of small production; as a result, this entire form of management, the entire economic apparatus of the proletariat state, *does not facilitate, but only impedes* the development of the forces of production. In reality it flows into *the opposite of what was intended*, and therefore iron necessity compels that it be broken.... If the proletariat itself does not do this, then other forces will overthrow it.[45]

This quote, along with Bukharin's own admission that "the transition to the new economic policies represented the collapse of our illusions," should have alerted Cohen to the problems with his own historical interpretation.[46] Bukharin, for example, went on to state: "We thought then that our peacetime policy would be a continuation of the centralised planning system of that period....In other words war communism was seen by us not as military, i.e., as needed at a given stage of civil war, but as a universal, general, so to speak 'normal' form of economic policy of a victorious proletariat."[47]

If war communism was only necessitated by the civil war, what were the illusions that were shattered? Why did the Bolsheviks consider that the transition to NEP required "a radical modification in our *whole outlook on socialism*"?[48]

Moshe Lewin has pointed out the fundamental ambiguity that the Bolsheviks felt over the introduction and meaning of NEP. Lenin's embarrassment, Lewin has argued, was due to traditional Marxist attitudes toward "market categories." Though Lewin has interpreted war communism as an expedient brought on by the strain of civil war, he has understood the problematic nature of Lenin's and the other Bolsheviks' explanations of the new course. "If the NEP was only a temporary retreat from 'war communism' policies," Lewin has suggested, "it was necessary to reassert these latter policies as party objectives for the long run and to explain the failure to implement them by circumstances or by the premature character of the steps taken. But if, on the other hand, the precivil-war line made sense, what then was 'war communism'? Lenin said it was an error. *But he did not explain in what sense the NEP was a 'retreat' if 'war communism' was not an advance*."[49]

Lewin has argued, however, that the Bolsheviks, and Lenin especially, found an answer to the conundrum by viewing NEP as the policy of a prolonged transition period lasting a generation or so. NEP provided valid policies for the transition to socialism not only for Russia but for all countries. But if one recalls Bukharin's discussion in *The ABC of Communism*, the Bolsheviks expected the policies of war communism (then simply known as communism) to last a generation or so until they reached the higher phase of communism. Planning, and not the anarchy of the market, was to rule even in the transition between the first and higher phase of the communist society.[50] NEP abandoned the rationalization project altogether, and instead sought to control a basically market-governed economic system through the "commanding heights."[51]

With the establishment of NEP the Bolsheviks conceded in practice the theoretical argument advanced by Mises and later Hayek. They recognized in reality the need to use the knowledge embedded in money prices.[52] As Alec Nove has pointed out: "No more was heard of the abolition of money as a means of leaping into socialism." Instead, the Bolsheviks talked of the "urgent need for a stable currency, in which calculations and payments could be made."[53]

Lenin went as far as to admit in a secret letter of February 19, 1921, written to G.M. Krzhizhanovsky, that "the greatest danger is that the work of planning the state economy may be bureaucratised. This is a great one. Milyutin does not see it.... *A complete, integrated, real plan for us at present = 'a bureaucratic utopia.'*...Don't chase it" (35: 475; emphasis added).[54]

Lenin in March 1921, at the Tenth Congress of the R.C.P.(B.), argued that the Bolsheviks had made a mistake during war communism. They had "gone too far," he declared. "We overdid the nationalisation of industry and trade, clamping down on local exchange of commodities....Was this a mistake?" he asked rhetorically. "It certainly was" (32: 219). A constant theme throughout Lenin's speeches justifying NEP was that the Bolsheviks made a mistake by attempting to introduce communist relations of production immediately.

On the fourth anniversary of the October Revolution, for example, Lenin emphasized that the Bolsheviks "had expected—or perhaps it would be truer to say that we presumed without having given it adequate consideration—to be able to organize the state production and the state distribution of products on communist lines in a small peasant country directly ordered by the proletarian state. *Experience has proven that we were wrong*" (33: 58). Notice that the civil war is not invoked as a reason that the Bolsheviks pursued these "mistaken" policies. The reason for the mistake is insufficient attention paid to the transition period. As he continues: "It appears that a number of transitional stages were necessary—state capitalism and socialism—in order to prepare—prepare by many years of effort—for the transition to communism" (33: 58).

Moreover, in an article entitled "The New Economic Policy and the Tasks of the Political Education Departments," he explained that the mistake consisted of "deciding to go over directly to communist production and distribution" (33: 62). Always the master of political double-speak, however, Lenin is able to turn this admission into an excuse for why the decision was forced upon them.[55] It is the double-speak that caught commentators like Dobb and Carr.

It is clear that not only did Lenin consider war communism a mistaken policy (not a pragmatic policy forced on the Bolsheviks by war) but also that NEP was a strategic retreat.[56] In the same speech to the political education department, Lenin equated the NEP with military strategy:

> In attempting to go over straight to communism we, in the spring of 1921, sustained a more serious defeat on the economic front than any defeat inflicted upon us by Kolchak, Denikin or Pilsudski. This defeat was much more serious, significant and dangerous. It was expressed in the isolation of the higher administrators of our economic policy from the lower and their failure to produce that development of the productive forces which the Programme of our Party regards as vital and urgent (33: 63-64).

Moreover, at the Eleventh Party Congress in March 1922, Lenin referred repeatedly to NEP as a retreat.[57] "Retreat," Lenin explained, "is a difficult matter, especially for revolutionaries who are accustomed to advance..." (33: 280). But Lenin understood that retreat the Bolsheviks must. And while some communists, mostly abroad, Lenin argued, "burst into tears" over the fact that "the good Russian Communists were retreating" (33: 280-281), the Bolshevik cadre soon understood the necessity of the retreat.[58]

Bukharin, perhaps the most eloquent spokesmen for NEP, argued that the retreat was necessary because "a misunderstanding arose which threatened the whole system of the proletarian dictatorship." The political crisis found its expression in the Kronstadt rebellion in March of 1921. The rebellion, Bukharin argued, represented "a petty bourgeois rebellion against the socialist system of economic compulsion."[59] But as long as the state apparatus remained under Bolshevik control, catastrophe could be averted:

> When the State apparatus is in our hands we can guide it in any desired direction. But unless we are at the helm we can give no direction at all. Consequently we must seize power and keep it and make no political concessions. *But we may make many economic concessions in order to avoid making political concessions.*[60]

The economic retreat was not to be feared, Bukharin added. True, "it was proved economically" that the policies of war communism, and the grain requisitioning in particular, took "away almost all the incentive to further production" and that capitalist incentives must be reintroduced. But by maintaining the commanding heights of industry, Bukharin argued, the Bolsheviks could make the economic concessions to the peasants and small-scale industry and still direct the economy. "Our view," Bukharin stated, "is that capitalism will rise slowly from below, but we will keep under our control the chief branches of industry. *Once this is achieved all the industrial processes will assume their normal course.*"[61]

This understanding of NEP as a strategic economic retreat forced on the Bolsheviks by the political crisis of the spring of 1921 was not limited to Lenin and his eloquent theorist, Bukharin, but was also understood by the entire Bolshevik cadre. They would retreat for now, in the expectation that they would someday return to the "normal course" of socialist construction.

Trotsky, in *The Revolution Betrayed*, pointed out that: "The Soviet government hoped and strove to develop [the policies of war communism] directly into a system of planned economy in distribution as well as production. In other words, from 'military communism' it hoped gradually, but without destroying the system, to arrive at genuine communism." But, as Trotsky states, reality "came into increasing conflict" with this program and the country and the government found themselves "at the very edge of the abyss."[62]

Trotsky goes further. The war communism policies were not solely dictated by military emergency, but were understandable only as policies connected to the expected success of revolution in the West. As Trotsky argues:

> The theoretical mistake of the ruling party remains inexplicable, however, only if you leave out of account the fact that all calculations at the time were based on the hope of an early victory of the revolution in the West....And there is no doubt that if the proletarian revolution had triumphed in Germany—a thing that was prevented solely and exclusively by the Social Democrats—the economic development of the Soviet Union as well as of Germany would have advanced with such gigantic strides that the

> fate of Europe and the world would today have been incomparably more auspicious.[63]

But Trotsky's admission lies deeper than merely false expectations. He admits that even if the German revolution would have been successful, the Bolsheviks would have had to concede their defeat to the principles of commerce. "It can be said with certainty," Trotsky states, "that even in that happy event it would still have been *necessary to renounce* the direct state distribution of products in favor of the methods of commerce."[64]

Lenin's Theory of the State and State Capitalism

The writers who support the "emergency" interpretation of war communism rely on Lenin's description of NEP as a return to his 1918 position on "state capitalism." But is his post-war communism version of state capitalism really the same as his pre-war communism version? In his defense of the introduction of NEP, *The Tax in Kind: The Significance of the New Policy and its Conditions* (32: 329-365), Lenin argued that NEP was a return to his 1918 position that state capitalism was the transitional form of social organization between capitalism and socialism. But we must keep in mind Lenin's theory of the state and his theory of social relations of production under imperialism.[65]

In *The Tax in Kind*, Lenin reprints much of the argument contained in his 1918 pamphlet, *Left-Wing Childishness and the Petty-Bourgeois Mentality*, which was a broadside against Bukharin and other left-wing Bolsheviks on the Brest-Litovsk and the issue of "state capitalism." In his 1918 polemic Lenin argued that history had witnessed an unusual event. The Russian people had successfully introduced the proper political basis for communism with the dictatorship of the proletariat and the organization of the Soviets. But Russia was not fully developed economically. Germany, on the other hand, Lenin argued, was backward politically but advanced economically. The immediate task of the Russian people was to model their economy after the German war-planning machine. They were to "spare no effort in copying it and not shrink from adopting dictatorial methods to hasten the copying of it" (27: 340).

The German model, Lenin argued, was "the last word" in modern large-scale capitalism, incorporating advanced engineering and planned organization. But the system was subordinated to a "Junker-bourgeois imperialism." If the system could be made to serve the interest of the proletariat, then socialism was not only possible but immediate. "Cross out the words in italics [Junker-bourgeois imperialism], and in place of the militarist, Junker, bourgeois, imperialist state put also a state, but of a different social type, of a different class content—a Soviet state, that is, a proletariat state, and you will have the sum total of the conditions necessary for socialism" (27: 339). Thus, despite accounts that claim that Lenin, and his associates had no model of socialist organization because Marxism was confined to a criticism of capitalism, Lenin apparently had little doubt what socialist construction entailed. It had nothing to do with the reintroduction of market methods of production as under NEP.

The transition period up to the introduction of NEP did not refer to a period of market-based "socialism," but instead to the first phase of communism—which would last a generation or so—until the people had become so culturally ingrained with communism that the door would swing open for the advancement to full communism. This was explained by both Lenin and Bukharin in their theoretical works before 1921. The market was to be abolished and replaced by a unified plan that would achieve ex-ante coordination of production and distribution. The model of war communism was the deliberate attempt to achieve this desired outcome.[66] But, as Lenin wrote in 1921, this method of economic organization proved to be a mistake.

Lenin's Assessment and the Failure of NEP

Lenin argued that during war communism the Bolsheviks had failed to develop the productive forces that the party program deemed necessary and that the reason for the failure was the inability of the planning system to coordinate the activity of the higher administrations of economic planning with the lower. The Bolsheviks, he argued, must learn to plan the economy effectively. NEP was to provide the necessary "breathing spell" to regroup forces and acquire the necessary ability for the task of economic administration.[67]

The economic administrators had failed to produce a practical plan. Endless debates over first principles rather than praxis dominated economic planning discussions, and Lenin argued that the Bolsheviks should cease such discussions and develop a plan based on practical experience. There was also the matter of "administrative technique," which the Bolsheviks lacked. "Of planning commissions," Lenin wrote in February 1921, "we have more than enough....The whole point is that we have yet to learn the art of approach, and stop substituting intellectualist and bureaucratic projecteering for vibrant effort."[68]

This tendency toward "scholasticism" and bureaucratic "red tape" within the planning system lies behind Lenin's criticism in 1922 of the overconsideration of the administrative side of work. "The task," he argued, "is to learn to organize work properly, not to lag behind, to remove friction in time, not to separate administration from politics....For our administration and our politics," Lenin stressed, "rest on the ability of the entire vanguard to maintain contact with the entire mass of the proletariat and with the entire mass of the peasantry." This led him to conclude that "if anybody forgets these cogs and becomes wholly absorbed in administration, the result will be a disastrous one" (33: 299).[69]

To build a communist society, Lenin argued, the Bolsheviks should employ noncommunists in the state-planning apparatus and learn from these bourgeois specialists. "We Communists shall be able to direct our economy if we succeed in utilizing the hands of the bourgeoisie in building up this economy of ours and in the meantime learn from these bourgeoisie and guide them along the road we want them to travel" (33: 291). Only by doing so will the Bolsheviks "acquire the practical ability to do what is economically necessary" (33: 291). As Lenin wrote in 1922:

> Either we pass this test in competition with private capital, or we fail completely. To help us pass it we have political power and a host of economic and other resources; *we have everything you want except ability. We lack ability.* And if we learn this simple lesson from the experience of last year and take it as our guiding line for the whole of 1922, we shall conquer this difficulty, too, in spite of the fact that it is much greater than the previous difficulty, for it rests upon ourselves. It is not like some external enemy. The difficulty is that we ourselves refuse to admit the unpleasant truth forced upon us; we refuse to undertake the unpleasant duty that the situation demands of us, namely, to start learning from the beginning (33: 277).

To acquire the time to learn, the Bolsheviks must re-establish the link with the peasants. This led Lenin to command his comrades to "stop philosophising and arguing about NEP" and get on with the "serious business" of communist competition under NEP (33: 285, 289).

The Bolsheviks had to operate the economic system effectively from a business point of view. They had to learn how to operate as a capitalist would. As Lenin stated in his report on the tax-in-kind in April 1921, "Everyone knows, of course, that it is not the Soviet government's preference for some particular policy" that led to the adoption of NEP. Rather, it was "the grinding need and the desperate situation" (32: 289). The Bolsheviks needed to concede to the principles of commerce. He continued:

> Any salesman trained in a large capitalist enterprise knows how to settle a matter like that; but ninety-nine responsible Communists out of hundred do not. And they refuse to understand that they do not know how and that they must learn the ABC of this business. *Unless we realise this, unless we sit down in the preparatory class again, we shall never be able to solve the economic problem that now lies at the basis of our entire policy* (33: 298; emphasis added).

Lenin, however, did not understand that the economic policies of the Bolsheviks under war communism took away the only means available for accomplishing large-scale industrial production, that is, monetary calculation, and that the interventionist economic policies of NEP served only to impede the development of the productivity of industry by interfering with the everyday process of business through monetary mismanagement and arbitrary price controls and taxation. The system produced results which were the opposite of those intended.[70]

Lenin did not fully appreciate the problems in the economic system itself. He recognized the symptom, but misdiagnosed the sickness. Thus he prescribed the wrong cure for the ailing Russian economy.

Lenin had argued that there was no reason to fear the re-emergence of capitalists and capitalist relations because "the workers' state has enough resources to keep within the proper bounds and control these relationships."[71] In his arguments against the communist concerns over NEP, raised by the likes of Preobrazhensky, Osinskii, and Larin, Lenin simply replied that: "The capitalism that we have permitted is essential....If we were afraid to admit this our doom would be sealed." It is true, Lenin admitted, that capitalist relations had re-emerged and that they harbored inherent dangers, but it was "capitalism that we ourselves have permitted" and it "[was] essential."[72] Moreover, the workers' state had at its command the economic and political resources to keep capitalism under control and make it work in the interest of the proletariat.

The change in course was not a political mistake, Lenin argued. It was essential for the survival of the dictatorship of the proletariat. But Lenin started to recognize a problem with NEP by 1922. The problem was that the communists were not learning how to control the capitalist relations of production. Even though the main economic power rested in the hands of the proletariat, they were not controlling the economy. Instead, responsible communists succumbed to the giant bureaucracy, leading Lenin to comment that: "To tell the truth, they are not directing, they are being directed....They scatter orders and decrees right and left, *but the result is quite different from what they want*."[73] Lenin provided an eloquent example of what was going wrong:

> The machine refused to obey the hand that guided it. It was like a car that was going not in the direction the driver desired, but in the direction someone else desired; as if it were being driven by some mysterious, lawless hand, God knows whose, perhaps of a profiteer, or of a private capitalist, or of both. Be that as it may, the car is not going quite in the direction that the man at the wheel imagines, and often it goes in an altogether different direction (33: 279).

The Bolsheviks had not "yet learned to confine [capitalism] within [certain] bounds." They had political power and economic resources, but what they lacked was ability. "We have sufficient, quite sufficient political power; we also have sufficient economic resources at our command, but the vanguard of the working class which has been brought to the forefront to directly supervise, to determine the boundaries, to demarcate, to subordinate and not be subordinated itself, lacks sufficient ability for it" (33: 279).

This is Lenin's fundamental error in political economy. First of all, interventionist policies face the same economic problem as centralized economic planning: how to use the dispersed bits and pieces of economic knowledge in society to promote economic coordination. The market system serves this function in at least three ways by providing knowledge concerning economic decisions *ex ante* and *ex post* and generating the *discovery* of new knowledge. Market prices, for example, transmit knowledge about the relative scarcities of goods ex ante. If the price of a good goes up, for example, this informs economic actors that the good has become relatively more scarce and that they should economize on its use. By price rationing the market process serves to generate and reveal knowledge about the relative evaluations that various market participants possess. Thomas Sowell describes this function of market prices in *Knowledge and Decisions*:

> Prices convey the experience and subjective feelings of some as effective knowledge to others; it is implicit knowledge in the form of an explicit inducement. Price fluctuations convey knowledge of changing trade-offs among changing options as people weigh costs and benefits differently over time, with changes in tastes or technology. The totality of knowledge conveyed by the innumerable prices and their widely varying rates of change vastly exceeds what any individual can know or needs to know for his own purposes.

And: "How accurately these prices convey knowledge depends on how freely they fluctuate."[74] Interference with price fluctuation necessarily distorts the knowledge that is conveyed. While the free fluctuation of prices provides an ex ante service to economic actors by alerting them to current market conditions, the interference with the determination of prices distorts this ex ante role of prices.

Prices also serve an ex post function of ultimately revealing the profitability or unprofitability of economic decisions. Market prices not only convey knowledge about changing conditions and inform future market decisions, but they also reveal knowledge about past market decisions. Buying dear and selling cheap is penalized, while buying cheap and selling dear is rewarded.

In addition, the discrepancy between the current array of market prices and the possible future array generates the competitive market process. Prices serve as the basis of economic calculation only within the context of the entrepreneurial search for pure profit. Under those conditions, the active bidding up of prices when demand exceeds supply or down when supply exceeds demand generates the knowledge necessary to coordinate economic decisions. The very discrepancy between the current array and the anticipated future array of prices provides the incentive for entrepreneurs to discover previously unknown opportunities for economic profit. Of course, in this process of perceiving the future, entrepreneurs make errors, but these errors generate further activity aimed at allocating or reallocating resources in a more effective manner to obtain the desired ends.

So although market prices do not contain perfect information they nevertheless provide market participants with both *ex ante* and *ex post* information, concerning economic decisions, and perhaps most important, generate the incentive for the further *discovery* of, as of yet, unknown opportunities. Prices, within the context of the competitive struggle among market participants, serve to convey ever-new and fresh knowledge about the constantly changing conditions in the market and the imagined possibilities of the future. The essence of the coordinative property of the price system lies in "its ability to communicate information concerning its own faulty information-communication properties."[75]

It is this communicative and coordinating function of the market system that Lenin fundamentally misunderstood. Even if the best administrators in the world were in command of the economic centers, they could not plan the economy or interfere optimally with the market system because they lack the requisite economic knowledge.[76] It is beyond the ability of any one mind or group of minds to control the economic process of advanced industrial production.

Because Lenin misunderstood the nature of economic calculation, when faced with the economic disaster of war communism and the unintended and undesirable consequences of NEP, he was forced to lay blame on lack of ability or culture. This reveals Lenin's second fundamental error of political economy.

Lenin saw the problem of NEP running out of control as one of the lack of ability: "the ability to put the right man in the right place, the ability to avoid petty conflicts, so that state economic work may be carried on without interruption" (33: 300). The inability to effectively compete with capitalism and accomplish the ends sought by intervention was diagnosed not as a problem with the system but rather as a problem of the people running the system.

Lenin subscribed to a variant of the benevolent-despot theory of socioeconomic organization. "In connection with NEP some people are beginning to fuss around, proposing to reorganize our government departments and to form new ones. All this is pernicious twaddle. In the present situation *the key feature is people, the proper choice of people*" (33: 303; emphasis added). Lenin was like a manager of a bottle-processing plant who after discovering that the bottles are coming out only half filled with soda pop decides he should change the bottles rather than fix the machine. It was the machine, that is, the rules, that needed to be fixed, not the people.[77]

Lenin understood quite well the problem of bureaucratization of the Soviet system, stating at one point that the Soviet "state apparatus [was] deplorable, not to say wretched."[78] But his theme was always improving the culture of the people, not providing checks in the system.[79] This is why further disillusionment with the ability of the commanding heights to control the economic system under NEP led Lenin to view NEP increasingly as a long-term transition phase—lasting generations until the appropriate ability was developed to rationalize the economic life process. Lenin failed to understand the value of constitutional theory for economic restructuring and political reform. He was ignorant of the bourgeois tradition of classical political economy and, as such, failed to provide a workable political and economic system when his own proletarian system came into increasing conflict with economic and political reality. "It was for this reason," as Mises wrote, "that it was quite impossible for Lenin to realize the causes of the failure of his policy."[80]

The failure of NEP in the 1920s was not due to an inherent inability of market methods of production to promote economic growth. Neither was it solely a result of political manipulation. NEP failed because of a combination of political and economic reasons.[81]

Economically, the interventionist policies of monetary inflation and government manipulation of the price structure produced a distortion in the structure of prices which hampered economic development.[82] Also, the constant fear of reprisal by the government against private trading produced contradictory expectations. Throughout the period this had the undesirable effect, from an economic point of view, of reducing private trading and limiting such private trading as did go on to arbitrage activity and short-term speculation, rather than long-term entrepreneurial ventures.

Politically, NEP failed because far from being a period of liberalization, this was a period of suppression of the values and institutions that would have prevented the emergence of Stalin's "cult of personality." Lenin silenced all opposition within the party, as well as outside the party. In addition, he personally placed supreme power in Stalin's hands and eliminated all possible checks—believing instead in an ability of cultured communists to overcome the incentives to abuse power. Faced with the reality of bureaucratization, which he himself criticized, this flaw in his political outlook of the 1920s was more than a mere oversight.

Lenin's political and economic views enabled Stalin, now in control of the political power after Lenin's death, though he let Zinoviev appear in control, to easily defeat all opposition from the remaining Old Bolsheviks. Stalin was first able to charge Trotsky with a left deviation for views that harked back to the failed policy of war communism, and then, second, to charge Bukharin with a right deviation for supporting the capitalist re-emergence in Russia. Both, of course, were correct accusations in some strict sense.[83] But both positions were a product of the previous political and economic contradictions of Lenin's rule.[84]

Conclusion

These concerns with the failure of NEP as system of economic and political restructuring are not just of antiquarian interest. They are concerns of today. A failure to understand the problems with NEP in the 1920s will not only affect our understanding of the current reform movement in the Soviet Union, but also hinder that reform movement itself.

In a recent book, *The Economic Challenge of Perestroika*, Gorbachev's chief economic adviser, Abel Aganbegyan, describes NEP as the period of the peaceful development of the forces of production.[85] In *Perestroika*, Gorbachev describes his policy of economic restructuring as a return to the teachings of Lenin, a return to NEP. *Perestroika*, we are told, is the new NEP.[86]

Both books, however, argue that the collectivization under Stalin was necessary. Aganbegyan writes that the period of industrialization overcame the backwardness of the Soviet Union, and that by 1941 the "Soviet Union was already producing 10% of the world's industrial output and had caught up with the developed European countries."[87] And Gorbachev states that the "industrialization and the collectivization of agriculture was indispensable."[88] Neither Gorbachev nor Aganbegyan sees NEP as failing, but rather as giving way to the inevitable and necessary industrialization and collectivization drive.

To them, NEP today means increased economic incentives within the planning system. They do not explicitly question the system. Nor have they learned the lessons of history. Both authors have sections entitled "the lessons of history," but neither addresses the fundamental historical questions. War communism was merely a military emergency; NEP was the development of state capitalist relations of production that led to recovery after the civil war; and the five-year planning system achieved tremendous industrial growth.

Neither author recognizes the fundamental political and economic mistakes that Lenin made. For example, discussion of Stalin's abuses are always prefaced with the phrase "cult of personality," which takes full blame away from the political system and places it squarely on the person. Second, although there is talk of reform in terms of profit incentives and price reforms, how freely will prices be allowed to fluctuate? Aganbegyan argues that under *perestroika* a "radical and total reform of price formation is envisaged," but this does not apparently include a wholesale adoption of free pricing. As Aganbegyan states:

> With the implementation of the reforms intended for the 1989-90 period the whole method of price formation is to be radically changed. The number of prices set centrally is to be reduced, that is, to comprehend only the more essential staple products. And, moreover, they will not be set in a voluntaristic fashion. Rather they will be based on social costs and will take into consideration the cost effectiveness of production and the level of world prices shaped by the relations between supply and demand. The prices will be reviewed at least once every five years and will be closely tied to the indicators of five-year plans. Should the conditions change sharply prices will be reviewed before the end of a five-year period.
>
> At the same time the sphere of contractually set and free prices will rapidly expand....Thus to a large extent prices will be a

> matter of agreement. It is possible then that the state will set up a certain method for calculating prices, and the Price Committee is being invested with the task of assessing the rationale for contractual and free prices. In particular, speculative price increases aimed at excessive profits will not be permitted.[89]

It seems that neither the knowledge problem nor the totalitarian problem is being addressed within the current reform movement in a manner that will produce any real results. But unless Lenin's errors are explored and the possible alternative political and economic ideas of the Soviet theorists of the 1920s are understood, there is little hope for either understanding the Soviet system in its historical operation or in changing the system today in the direction of a more efficient and humane system of social cooperation. As Alec Nove states in his introduction to Aganbegyan's book, "In a world where economic problems worry us all, in east, west and south—a world increasingly interdependent—the efforts of the Soviet leadership to achieve *perestroika* can affect us all."[90]

Notes

[1] See E.H. Carr, *The Bolshevik Revolution, 1917-1923*; 3 vols. (New York: W. W. Norton, 1980[1952]), II: 280.

[2] Alec Nove, *An Economic History of the U.S.S.R.* (New York: Penguin Books, 1984[1969]), 83; emphasis added.

[3] F.A. Hayek, "The Use of Knowledge in Society," in *Individualism and Economic Order* (Chicago: University of Chicago Press, 1980[1948]), 78.

[4] Lenin, in his "Report on the Substitution of a Tax in Kind for the Surplus Grain Appropriation System," delivered on March 15, 1921, opens the discussion by stating: "Comrades, the question of substituting a tax for surplus grain appropriation is *primarily and mainly a political question*, for it is essentially a question of the attitude of the working class to the peasantry" (*CW*, 32: 214). This is important to keep in mind when assessing the economic concessions Lenin is willing to make to maintain political control.

[5] Lenin, "Report on the Tax in Kind Delivered at a Meeting of the Secretaries and Responsible Representatives of R.C.P.(B.) Cells of Moscow and Moscow Gubernia," April 9, 1921, *CW*, 32: 286.

[6] Nove, *An Economic History of the U.S.S.R.*, 83.

[7] *History of the Communist Party of the Soviet Union* (San Francisco: Proletarian Publishers, 1976[1939]), 256.

[8] A pood is a Russian unit of weight equal to about 36.11 pounds.

[9] See Nove, *An Economic History of the U.S.S.R.*, 84. Along with the substitution of the tax-in-kind for the requisitioning system, NEP also restored the freedom to trade. A decree of April 7, 1921, for example, recognized the cooperatives as independent trading organizations no longer subordinate to the Commissariat of Supply. By September 1, 1921, all the existing financial relations between the cooperatives and the state were severed and they became independent. And on October 20, 1921, all their former property and enterprises, which had been nationalized, were returned to the cooperatives.

[10] Maurice Dobb, *Soviet Economic Development Since 1917* (New York: International Publishers, 1948), 127, argues to the contrary:

> The crux of centralised supply, as we have seen, was the policy of compulsory requisitioning of the peasant surplus; and the crux of the restoration of commercial transactions in the economy at large, when this came, was to be the market-relationship between agriculture and industry. Curiously enough, the discussion from which NEP emerged *started, not with the relationship with the peasantry, but with the relationship between State industry and the industrial workers* (emphasis added).

Dobb's argument is referring to the trade-union controversy within the party in the fall of 1920. But compare his assessment with that of Robert Daniels, *The Conscience of the Revolution* (Cambridge: Harvard University Press, 1960), 119 ff., where Daniels argues that the decentralized and democratic alternative was presented by the Workers' Opposition and silenced by Lenin as a "anarcho-syndicalist" deviation. Also see Lenin's discussion at the Eleventh Party Conference in March 1922 where he argues that the crux of NEP was the alliance with the peasant: "Our aim is to restore the link, to prove to the peasant by deeds that we are beginning with what is intelligible, familiar and immediately accessible to him, in spite of his poverty, and not with something remote and fantastic from the peasant's point of view. We must prove that we can help him and that in this period, when the small peasant is in a state of appalling ruin, impoverishment and starvation, the Communists are really helping him. Either we prove that, or he will send us to the devil. That is absolutely inevitable" (*CW*, 33: 270).

[11] As quoted in Carr, *The Bolshevik Revolution*, II: 297.

[12] See Nove, *An Economic History of the U.S.S.R.*, 85.

[13] See Carr, *The Bolshevik Revolution*, II: 299.

[14] See Nove, *An Economic History of the U.S.S.R.*, 85.

[15] See Alexander Baykov, *The Development of the Soviet Economic System* (New York: Macmillan, 1948), 105-106.

[16] Baykov, *The Development of the Soviet Economic System*, 107. As Lenin wrote in 1922: "The main economic power is in our hands. All the vital large enterprises, the railways, etc., are in our hands. The number of leased enterprises, although considerable in places, is on the whole insignificant; altogether it is infinitesimal compared with the rest. The economic power in the hands of the proletarian state of Russia is quite adequate to ensure the transition to communism" (*CW*, 33: 288).

[17] V.N. Bandera, "Market Orientation of State Enterprises During NEP," *Soviet*

Studies, Vol. 22, n. 1 (July 1970), 111.

[18] A decree of August 16, 1921, had granted the right to individuals to manage financial and material resources, and a decree of October 4, 1921, permitted the free disposal of output. A decree of July 16, 1923, even stated that state industries (the trust system) should be operated and evaluated from the point of view of profit.

[19] At this time it became acceptable again to use the word *money*. During the period of war communism the term *sovznak* or "Soviet token" was used instead. This shift in terms is much more important than most observers grant. It represents the foregoing of the attempt to abolish the monetary economy and as such, represents the abandonment of the quest to eliminate the "alienated ability of mankind."

[20] On October 11, 1922, the State Bank was entrusted with the issuance of the chervonets, which were equal to ten of the pre-revolutionary gold rubles. The chervonets were fully secured (25 percent of the issue was to be covered by gold and stable foreign currency; 75 percent by short-term bills) and were issued in very limited amounts. See Baykov, *The Development of the Soviet Economic System*, 89.

[21] As Baykov points out: "On 1 January 1923, of the total volume of money in circulation, calculated in chervontzy, 97% consisted of sovznaks[roubles] and only 3% of chervontzy, but on 1 October 1923 the sovznak accounted only for 25% of the total and the chervonetz already for 75%." See *The Development of the Soviet Economic System*, 90.

[22] See Nove, *An Economic History of the U.S.S.R.*, 92.

[23] Chervonets equalled 10 new stabilized rubles. One of these new rubles equalled 50,000 1923 rubles, and one 1923 ruble equaled 1 million 1921 rubles. Remember that the purchasing power of the rouble in October 1920 was only 1 percent of what it had been in October 1917.

[24] Baykov, *The Development of the Soviet Economic System*, 91.

[25] The tax was lower, for example, for workers, employees, and cooperative home craftsmen, and higher for noncooperative individual home craftsmen and much higher for persons with unearned income. In 1926 an excess-profit tax on entrepreneurs was introduced.

[26] See N. Gubsky, "Economic Law in Soviet Russia," *Economic Journal*, Vol. XXXVII (June 1927), 226-236. Also see Nove, *An Economic History of the U.S.S.R.*, 102, for a discussion of the practice of price control during NEP. Also see 96 ff. for a discussion of the planning role of the Supreme Economic Council during

NEP.

[27] Nove, *An Economic History of the U.S.S.R.*, 101.

[28] Nepmen or private entrepreneurs acted on discrepancies in prices between the trusts and cooperatives to exploit opportunities for profit. In Moscow, for example, in 1922, Nepmen controlled 14 percent of the wholesale market, 50 percent of wholesale-retail market, and 83 percent of retail. Fifty percent of wholesale trade in textiles throughout the country until the spring of 1923 is estimated to have been under the control of private enterprise. In 1922-1923 it is estimated that 78 percent of retail trade was private, with that percentage falling to 57.7 percent in 1923-1924, 42.5 percent in 1924-1925, 42.3 percent in 1925-1926 and 36.9 percent in 1926-1927 as NEP comes to a close. See Nove, *An Economic History of the U.S.S.R.*, 103.

[29] See Nove, *An Economic History*, 86, where he points out that while the grain harvest in 1920 was only 54 percent of pre-war (1909-1913) average, the 1921 harvest was only 43 percent (or 37.6 million tons) of the pre-war average. As a result, uncounted millions died. Also see Jasny, *Soviet Economists*, 17.

[30] Nove, *An Economic History*, 93.

[31] Nove, *An Economic History of the U.S.S.R.*, 94. As Nove documents, the comparison year of 1913 was an unusually favorable harvest at 80.1 million tons.

[32] This relative recovery of agricultural production over industrial production produced what is termed "the scissors crisis" in 1923. This will be discussed in the context of the industrialization debate in the next chapter.

[33] See Jasny, *Soviet Economists*, 29.

[34] See Heller and Nekrich, *Utopia in Power: The History of the Soviet Union from 1917 to the Present* (New York: Summit Books, 1986), 217. This aspect of conflicting expectations between current market conditions and a possible future assault by the Bolsheviks on the market is rarely addressed within the usual analysis of NEP. This persistent fear led Boris Pasternak to describe NEP as "the most ambiguous and hypocritical of all Soviet periods." See Pasternak, *Doctor Zhivago* (New York: Signet Books, 1958), 387.

[35] Platonov, *Chevengur* (Ann Arbor: University of Michigan Press, 1978), 135, 137.

[36] As quoted in Alexander Rüstow, *Freedom and Domination: A Historical Critique of Civilization* (Princeton: Princeton University Press, 1980[1950-1957]), 575.

[37] Dobb, *Soviet Economic Development Since 1917* (New York: International Publishers, 1948), 146-147.

[38] Carr, *The Bolshevik Revolution, 1917-1923*, 3 vols. (New York: Norton, 1980[1952]), II: 282-283.

[39] Carr, II: 277; emphasis added. As I argued in the last chapter, I believe this concentration on historical preconditions produces a fundamental misinterpretation of the Soviet experience with socialism. In fact, I would go so far as to suggest that as a result of this concern within the scholarly literature, we have misunderstood completely the meaning of this historical episode for human cooperation and social existence.

[40] Cohen, *Rethinking the Soviet Experience: Politics & History Since 1917* (New York: Oxford University Press, 1985), 75.

[41] Cohen, *Rethinking the Soviet Experience*, 76. There is no doubt that the political relations under NEP where much more liberal than the perversion of politics under Stalin—though I think totalitarianism is an unintended undesirable consequence of socialism. It is also important to keep in mind that Lenin did establish the political institutions that Stalin inherited—even if Stalin was "too rude," Lenin clearly is responsible for purposefully eliminating checks against the possible abuse of power. Consider, for example, the following statement of Zinoviev from the Eleventh Party Congress concerning the political situation:

> We have a monopoly on legality. We have denied political freedom to our opponents. We do not permit legal existence to those who aspire to become our rivals....The dictatorship of the proletariat, as Comrade Lenin has said, is a very harsh thing. In order to assure the victory of the proletarian dictatorship there is no other way than to break the back of all opposition to this dictatorship....No one can foresee a time when we will be able to revise our opinion on this question (as quoted in Heller and Nekrich, *Utopia in Power*, 132).

Also it is untenable to argue that NEP represented a model of communist economics—at best it was only a transition stage between capitalism and communism, and at worst, from a Marxist perspective, it was a retreat to market relations of production even if heavily interfered with.

[42] See Johnson, *Modern Times* (New York: Harper and Row, 1983), 51. Stalin did not corrupt Soviet politics, he inherited and perfected it. Also see Heller and Nekrich, *Utopia in Power*, 162, where they point out that: "Stalin did not make

himself general secretary. Lenin did....Many reasons are given to explain Stalin's rise to power. The main reason was that he was Lenin's legitimate heir. The majority of the party perceived the situation that way. This was a necessary condition for his success...."

[43] See William Henry Chamberlin, *The Russian Revolution, 1917-1921*, 2 vols. (Princeton: Princeton University Press, 1987[1935]), II: 75.

[44] Cohen, *Bukharin and the Bolshevik Revolution* (New York: Oxford University Press, 1980[1973]), 140.

[45] Bukharin (December 20, 1921) as quoted in Cohen, *Bukharin*, 140; emphasis added.

[46] Bukharin (1924) as quoted in Cohen, *Bukharin*, 139.

[47] See Alec Nove, "Some Observations on Bukharin and His Ideas," in *Political Economy and Soviet Socialism* (Boston: George Allen & Unwin, 1979), 86, where he continues the quote of Bukharin cited in Cohen.

[48] Lenin, "On Co-operation" (written January 6, 1923), *CW* (33: 474).

[49] Lewin, *Political Undercurrents in Soviet Economic Debates* (Princeton: Princeton University Press, 1974), 87, emphasis added. Notice that Lewin does not mention that one of the possible explanations the Bolsheviks would have had to offer was the economic impossibility of Marxian socialism. Yet in many ways, as I am arguing, it is the recognition of this assessment that alone renders the Bolshevik ambiguity intelligible.

[50] Bukharin and Preobrazhensky, *The ABC of Communism* (Ann Arbor: University of Michigan Press, 1966[1919]), 75.

[51] This is the whole point of the discussion found in Lenin, Trotsky, and Preobrazhensky concerning the competition between the socialist sector and the private sector or between plan and market. They believed that eventually plan would win out and large-scale socialism would emerge. But Lenin was in many ways much more conscious of the fundamental organizational question than many current comparative political economists when he recognized that this "mixed" economy resulted in situation where one wonders "who beats whom." The essential contradiction of mixing market and plan resulted in the eventual economic failure of NEP. NEP did not just fail because of politics, though that was perhaps the major contributing factor, but because of monetary and other intervention (cf., Simon Johnson, "Inflation, Hyperinflation and Disinflation in Soviet Russia, 1921-1924,"

paper presented at the Fourth Annual Workshop on Soviet and East European Economics, University of California, Berkeley, May 1988).

[52] Mises's argument was *never* that one needed theoretical prices for rational economic calculation, but real-world money prices. The idea of "shadow prices," as employed in the theoretical response to Mises by market-socialist writers, does not address Mises's challenge. As he wrote in his original article: "As soon as one gives up the conception of a freely established *monetary price* for goods of a higher order, rational production becomes completely impossible. Every step that takes us away from the use of money also takes us away from rational economics." See Mises, "Economic Calculation in the Socialist Commonwealth," ed. F.A. Hayek, *Collectivist Economic Planning* (New York: August M. Kelley, 1975[1920]), 104; emphasis added.

[53] Nove, *An Economic History of the U.S.S.R.*, 87.

[54] Krzhizhanovsky was the president of the State Planning Commission (GOSPLAN). Bukharin, after his defeat in the Industrialization Debate, would argue along similar lines to Lenin. In a seemingly harmless review of Hermann Bente's book, *Organized Mismanagement: Economic Forms of Bureaucratized Economy and Their Changes in the Era of Collectivized Capitalism* (1929), Bukharin argued that: "The reasons for bureaucratic centralization are the complexity and the enormous size of economic enterprises, which makes direct personal supervision impossible. At the same time, the longer the chain of command, the more difficult it is to set the entire machine in motion....Bureaucratism is economic arteriosclerosis." Bukharin concludes his review with the admission: "The Soviet reader may be startled to find a certain formal resemblance between some of the organizational problems posed and solved by Bente and the problems raised and settled in Soviet practice." The problem of bureaucracy in the Soviet case, Bukharin wrote, is not "purely organizational, but is also one of class." And "our own experience of socialist construction raises similar problems for us with even greater urgency....It," he concludes, "has become essential for us to analyze them." See Bukharin, "Organized Mismanagement in Modern Society," *Pravda* (June 30, 1929), translated and reprinted in ed. Irving Howe , *Essential Works of Socialism* (New York: Bantam Book, 1970), 394-403.

[55] Lenin understood the power of literature and as a result mobilized the Soviet propaganda machine from the beginning. This also motivates his concern with the intellectuals and the reorganization of the educational system. It is, in addition, the reason behind his call during the debate over factions for individuals, such as Preobrazhensky and Larin, to write textbooks on Marxism rather than concern themselves with party battles. They would serve the party more faithfully, Lenin argued, if they educated the youth. Criticizing the use of literature to promote the

interest of the state is one of the points of Eugene Zamyatin's disturbing dystopian novel, *WE*, where in the future world literature becomes simply a branch of civil service. And, of course, this theme is again eloquently dealt with in George Orwell's *1984*.

[56] Mistaken about the timing of the policies, not the substance of the policies. As Charles Bettelheim states: "[T]he mistake that was made did not relate to the significance of the measures taken (which Lenin regarded as 'communist measures') but to the moment which they were adopted: they were apparently premature." See Bettelheim, *Class Struggles in the U.S.S.R., 1917-1923* (New York: Monthly Review Press, 1976), 452. Thus, the retreat of NEP was to regroup the forces and prepare for the time when the introduction of communist measures was right. The expected time horizon of NEP was originally fairly short—two or three years—and eventually expanded to a generation or longer in the minds of Lenin and Bukharin. This issue will be brought out in more depth in the discussion of the Industrialization Debate.

[57] At one point Lenin states that the time had come to put a halt to the retreat, but on the very next page he states that the Bolsheviks "can retreat still further." See "Political Report of the Central Committee of the R.C.P.(B.), March 27, 1922," in Lenin, *CW* (33: 280-281).

[58] But see the counter- evidence in Daniels, *The Conscience of the Revolution*, 155, where he points out both Larin's and Preobrazhensky's dissatisfaction with the "unavoidable evil" of NEP. At worst these writers, and Trotsky should be included, believed that the retreat would last two or three years before a vigorous offensive could be launched.

[59] Bukharin, "The New Economic Policy of Soviet Russia," in Lenin, Bukharin, and Rutgers, *The New Policies of Soviet Russia* (Chicago: Charles H. Kerr, 1921), 56.

[60] Bukharin, "The New Economic Policy of Soviet Russia," 57-58; emphasis added.

[61] Bukharin, "The New Economic Policy of Soviet Russia," 51, 60; emphasis added. Notice Bukharin's use of the term "normal course" to refer to the policies the Bolsheviks will return to *after* NEP. NEP was referred to as the "new course." Such a use of terms suggests that the model of war communism was conceived of as the "normal course" for socialist construction. Bukharin also adds that "if the tendencies of capitalist growth gain the upper hand over the tendencies to improve large industry, then we are doomed" (60). Lenin also referred to this period as "not competition but, if not the last, then nearly the last, desperate, furious, life-and-death struggle between capitalism and communism." The Bolshevik strength in this battle, Lenin continued, rests with the fact that they control the economic power of

the country—large-scale industry. See Lenin, "Political Report of the Central Committee of the R.C.P.(B.)," March 27, 1922, *CW* (33: 287).

[62] Trotsky, *The Revolution Betrayed: What Is the Soviet Union and Where Is It Going?* (New York: Pathfinder Press, 1972[1937]), 22.

[63] Trotsky, *The Revolution Betrayed*, 23.

[64] Trotsky, *The Revolution Betrayed*, 23. Trotsky was writing in hindsight in 1937. It should be remembered, however, that in 1923 Trotsky argued against the continuation of NEP and forcefully for increased economic planning to rationalize the Russian economy.

[65] The problem with the imperialist war-planning model, according to Lenin, was that it was serving the interests of the capitalist-imperialist. But with the transfer of political power to the proletariat, this model of economic organization would be made to serve the interests of the proletariat. This is what underlies Lenin's enthusiasm for the German War Planning model. Also consider Lenin's assessment of Karl Ballod's *The State of the Future: Production and Consumption in the Socialist State* (originally published in 1898, revised 1919 and appeared in Russian in 1920): "A look at Germany will bring out the dimensions and value of GOELRO's efforts [i.e., state planning for the electrification of Russia]. Over there, the scientist Ballod produced a similar work: he compiled a scientific plan for the socialist reconstruction of the whole national economy of Germany. But his being a capitalist country, the plan never got off the ground. It remains a lone-wolf effort, and an exercise in literary composition" ("Integrated Economic Plan," written February 21, 1921, *CW* [32: 140]).

[66] It should be emphasized again that this opinion was not limited to Lenin and Bukharin, but shared by the party as a whole. As Richard Day points out: "War Communism constituted a logical endeavour to unify thought with action, to rush headlong into an experiment in social engineering of unprecedented dimensions." See Day, *Leon Trotsky and the Politics of Economic Isolation* (Cambridge: At the University Press, 1973), 46.

[67] Lenin, in his discussion of the tax-in-kind at the Tenth Congress of the R.C.P.(B.) in March 1921, argued that the development of the peasantry along socialist lines would take a generation or so, not a century but decades (32: 217). His public assessment of the economic problem that forced NEP on the Bolsheviks was not yet the lack of administrative ability in managing the industrial economy, but the lack of incentives to the peasant to produce agricultural goods.

[68] Lenin, "Integrated Economic Plan," *CW* (32: 142-143).

[69] This is, of course, Lenin's criticism of Trotsky in his "Letter to the Congress," written in December 1922 and January 1923, *CW* (36: 595).

[70] For a general criticism of interventionist policies along these lines, see Ludwig von Mises, *A Critique of Interventionism* (New York: Arlington House, 1977[1929]), *Human Action*, 3rd rev. ed. (Chicago: Henry Regnery, 1966[1949]), 716 ff.; Murray Rothbard, *Man, Economy and State*, 2 vols. (Los Angeles: Nash Publishing, 1970[1962]), II: 765 ff.; *Power and Market* (Kansas City: Sheed, Andrews and McMeel, 1977[1970]); Israel Kirzner, *Discovery and the Capitalist Process* (Chicago: University of Chicago Press, 1985), 93-149.

[71] Lenin, "Instructions of the Council of Labour and Defence to Local Soviet Bodies, Draft," May 1921, *CW* (32: 385).

[72] Lenin, "Closing Speech on the Political Report of the Central Committee of the R.C.P.(B.)," March 28, 1922, *CW* (33: 310 ff.).

[73] Lenin, "Political Report of the Central Committee of the R.C.P.(B.)," March 27, 1922, *CW* (33: 289).

[74] Sowell, *Knowledge and Decisions* (New York: Basic Books, 1980), 167.

[75] Israel Kirzner, "Prices, the Communication of Knowledge, and the Discovery Process," in *The Political Economy of Freedom: Essays in Honor of F.A. Hayek*, ed. Kurt Leube and Albert Zlabinger (Munchen: Philosophia Verlag, 1985), 196.

[76] To quote Sowell again:

> The limitations and distortions of articulation revolve around the simple fact that third-party central planners cannot know what users want, whether those users be consumers or other producers acquiring raw materials, component parts or production-line machinery....It is not merely the enormous amount of data that exceeds the capacity of the human mind. Conceivably, this data might be stored in a computer with sufficient capacity. The real problem is that the knowledge needed is a knowledge of subjective patterns of trade-offs that are nowhere articulated, not even to the individual himself....Market transactions do not require any such knowledge in advance.

See *Knowledge and Decisions*, 217-218.

[77] The analogy of the political process and constitutional choice with the bottling

machine is found in Richard Wagner, "James M. Buchanan: Constitutional Political Economist," *Regulation*, n. 1 (1987), 13-17.

[78] Lenin, "Better Fewer, But Better," *CW* (33: 487).

[79] This is also his fundamental political error. Lenin entrusted enormous power to Stalin by making him General Secretary, and defending him against "charges" by Preobrazhensky that Stalin had too many responsibilities. It seems that Lenin only came to realize the amount of power that he had put at the disposal of Stalin too late. See A.J. Polan, *Lenin and the End of Politics* (Berkeley: University of California Press, 1984).

[80] Mises, *Socialism* (Indianapolis: Liberty Classics, 1981[1922]), 189.

[81] These two problems could be summarily stated as: (1) the knowledge problem and (2) the totalitarian problem.

[82] The manipulation of the price structure became increasingly apparent after the "sales crisis" of 1922, the "scissors crisis" of 1923, the "goods famine" of 1924 and 1925, and the "grain crisis" of the winter of 1927-1928. These crises and Bolshevik responses will be discussed in more depth in the next chapter.

[83] Needless to say, this in no way justified the show trials. Merely from standpoint of intellectual history it is true that in 1923 and after, Trotsky wished to reinstate many of the measures of war communism (he was not alone in this; many believed that the retreat was over), and Bukharin, who had become convinced that the superseding of the market by *ex-ante* planning was not possible at the moment, increasingly defended the economic activity of the Nepmen.

[84] Lenin, who in 1921 and 1922 argued that NEP was clearly a retreat from communist methods of production and that the Bolsheviks would again take the offensive, came to the position at the end of his life that NEP was an advance. See Lenin, "On Co-operation," written January 4, 1923, *CW* (33: 470) where he argues that his comrades should adopt the following rule: "as little philosophizing and acrobatics as possible....NEP is an advance." And he instructed his comrades to learn to trade, to combine a wide range of revolutionary enthusiasm with the ability to be an effective and capable trader, that is, cultured trader in the European manner.

[85] Aganbegyan, *The Economic Challenge of Perestroika* (Bloomington: Indiana University Press, 1988), 46.

[86] Gorbachev, *Perestroika* (New York: Harper and Row, 1987).

[87] Aganbegyan, *The Economic Challenge*, 47.

[88] Gorbachev, *Perestroika*, 41.

[89] See Aganbegyan, *The Economic Challenge*, 125 ff., for a discussion of the market reforms proposed for the planned economy.

[90] Nove, "Introduction," in Abel Aganbegyan, *The Economic Challenge*, xv.

5

THE POLITICAL ECONOMY OF DEVELOPMENT STRATEGY: THE SOVIET INDUSTRIALIZATION DEBATE, 1924-28

Introduction

With Lenin incapacitated from a series of strokes in 1922 and 1923, and then with his death in January 1924, a bitter power struggle occurred within the leadership of the Communist Party. On the level of ideas, the struggle took the form of the Soviet Industrialization Debate, where leading party economists and nonparty economists debated strategies for economic growth and development. Although much of the analysis of the debate focused on the political struggle for power, the consequence was more profound than just the political maneuvering of Stalin. The debates and controversies of the 1920s contain much that is of importance to economic and intellectual historians. As Alec Nove points out, "Development economics could be said to have been born here."[1]

Nove makes an interesting point of intellectual history. The emphasis in development economics on "growth" and "long-range" economic planning of a country follows directly from the Soviet discussion in the 1920s. The development of the Harrod-Domar model of economic growth, for which Robert Solow won the 1987 Nobel Prize, was directly influenced by the Soviet discussion and later experience.[2] Evsey Domar remarked that the study of the Soviet economy, and in particular the articles in the late 1920s in the journal *The Planned Economy*, were "a valuable source of ideas." Soviet society, Domar continued, represented a sort of economic laboratory where the social scientist could re-examine "his whole intellectual apparatus in light of a social and economic system sufficiently different from ours to make the experiment rewarding, and yet not so different as to make it impossible."[3]

But the unique character of Marxian economics is often obscured within standard accounts of the debate. As the Keynesian approach to economic analysis became dominant in the middle of this century, the concept of economic development became synonymous with economic growth.[4] Participants in the Industrialization Debate, as a result, are usually attributed neo-Keynesian positions instead of Marxian.[5] Although the neo-Keynesian interpretation has some appeal, because of the similarities in the social engineering mentality among the Russian debaters and the neo-Keynesians, the standard interpretation distorts both the theoretical positions of the debaters and the implications of the debate for understanding strategies for economic growth and development.[6]

Despite the abstract level of the debate, there were practical political considerations. The strategy that would convince the party would solidify political power in the hands of the victor.[7] The usual interpretation of the political events, an interpretation with which I have no quarrel, is that Stalin originally sided with Bukharin to eliminate the Trotsky left-wing threat, and then jumped sides to purge Bukharin of right-wing deviationism. By the end of the 1920s, as a result of his political maneuvering, Stalin reigned supreme. As Paul Gregory and Robert Stuart put it in their standard textbook on the Soviet economy:

> In a series of adroit political maneuvers, Stalin consolidated his power within a rather brief period of time after Lenin's death in 1924. First, he allied himself with the right wing of the party (Bukharin, Rykov, and Tomsky) to purge the leftist opposition led by Trotsky from positions of power—a phase completed in late 1927. Then Stalin turned his attention to the "right deviationist" Bukharinites, who were denounced by the Central Committee of the Communist Party in November of 1928. This occurred just one month after Stalin's adoption of the more ambitious alternative draft of the First Five Year Plan, which was supportive of the original left-wing industrialization program.[8]

The consequences of Stalin's "adroit political maneuvers" were horrifying. His mobilization of propaganda to purge both Trotsky and Bukharin not only from positions of power but also from Soviet history has been documented in photographic and documentary detail by Isaac Deutscher and David King.[9] In the end, only Stalin remained—the sole survivor of the Old Bolsheviks.

While this sums up the political events fairly accurately, it should not be taken to minimize the power of the economic ideas that were discussed during the debate by such thinkers as E. Preobrazhensky and Nikolai Bukharin, or their impact on the theory and policy of economic development. The Industrialization Debate signifies, as Maurice Dobb has pointed out, "the classic case study of a policy discussion about industrialisation in a socialist sector."[10] It encompassed such a wide range of developmental strategies that "it merits careful study by anyone interested in development problems and/or the considerations which have—for better or worse—decided the fate of one-third of mankind."[11] Political considerations cannot be overlooked, but the political ambition of the various participants did not dictate their position entirely. Concentration on Stalin's political ability distracts from the actual intellectual and economic history of the Soviet experience.

By reinterpreting the fateful industrialization debate in light of both the theoretical problems of socialist organization and the political consequences that follow from the attempt to realize such a policy, I hope to elucidate the issues involved in the various developmental strategies. If, as I have argued, war communism was the attempt to implement the Marxian program and NEP was the strategic retreat, then what were the issues of the industrialization debate?

The Ideological Background

Ideologically, the Old Bolsheviks were faced in 1921 and after with the collapse of their illusions. Illusions concerning immediate socialist construction had to be abandoned. The Bolsheviks had to begin anew. As Lenin wrote in March of 1922:

> Those Communists are doomed who imagine that it is possible to finish such an epoch-making undertaking as completing the foundations of socialist economy (particularly in a small-peasant country) without making mistakes, without retreats, without numerous alterations to what is unfinished or wrongly done. Communists who have no illusions, who do not give way to despondency, and who preserve their strength and flexibility "to begin from the beginning" over and over again in approaching an extremely difficult task, are not doomed (and in all probability will not perish).[12]

The Marxian project of rationalization of political and economic life had been turned against the Bolsheviks to produce nothing but political and economic irrationality. Politically, the irrationality was manifested in the growing bureaucracy (new class) that alienated not only the peasants but the workers. This was demonstrated in the political uprisings of 1920 and early 1921, and in the Kronstadt rebels' use of the term "the new serfdom" to describe life under the Bolshevik regime. It is also represented in the Workers' Opposition's "Declaration of the Twenty-Two" of February 1922, where they state: "Tutelage and pressure by the bureaucracy lead to the members of the party being constrained by the threat of expulsion and other repressive measures to elect not whom these Communists themselves want, but those whom the higher-ups, ignoring them, want. Such methods of work lead to careerism, intrigue, and toadying, and the workers answer this by quitting the party."[13] Lenin understood this problem of the Soviet proletarian dictatorship. To curb the political threat from peasant revolt and ensure the maintenance of power, Lenin introduced the New Economic Policy; but he also, in order to silence any socialist protest against his concession to capitalism, outlawed all political factions outside as well as inside the party. The party must maintain the strictest unity. In a letter dated March 26, 1922, to the Central Committee concerning the conditions necessary for admission into the party, Lenin wrote: "If we do not close our eyes to reality we must admit that at the present time the proletarian policy of the Party is not determined by the character of its membership, but by the enormous undivided prestige enjoyed by the small group which might be called the Old Guard of the Party. A slight conflict within this group will be enough, if not to destroy this prestige, at all events to weaken the group to such a degree as to rob it of its power to determine policy" (33: 257).

Economically, the irrationality was manifested in the destruction of industrial and agricultural output that resulted from the policies of war communism. But the New Economic Policy, though more rational than war communism, continued to impede the productive forces of the market through arbitrary intervention. This led Sergei Prokopovitch, a Russian economist, to comment in 1924, "It is hoped that the instinct of self-preservation will help the great Russian people to discover the ways and means of curing itself of the terrible disease from which it has been suffering for six long years."[14] Unfortunately, the disease became terminal with the ascendancy of Stalin.

Fundamentally, the problem was (and is) one of an essential tension between Marx's political and economic project.[15] Marx and Lenin relieved the tension between the two projects with their theory of proletarian class consciousness and the elimination of the division of *knowledge* in society. The importance of proletarian consciousness to Marxist-Leninism explains the vital role of the party and the international socialist movement. Although both Marx and Lenin were political revolutionaries, they were also educationalists in strategy. "By educating the workers' party," Lenin argued in *State and Revolution*, "Marxism educates the vanguard of the proletariat, capable of assuming power and leading the whole people to socialism, of directing and organising the new system, of being the teacher, the guide, the leader of all the working and exploited people in organising their social life without the bourgeoisie and against the bourgeoisie" (25: 409). It is perhaps this ability to generate both political activism and scholarship that explains the overwhelming success of Marxist-Leninism as a mobilizing ideological movement.

Reference to the assumption of generalizable knowledge and the ability of the proletarian system to eliminate the hierarchy of knowledge in society renders intelligible some of the more overtly utopian statements within Marxism. This, as I interpret it, for example, is the reason for the claim in *The German Ideology* that

> as long as man remains in natural society, that is, as long as a cleavage exists between the particular and the common interest, as long, therefore, as activity is not voluntarily, but naturally, divided, man's own deed becomes an alien power opposed to

> him, which enslaves him instead of being controlled by him. For as soon as the distribution of labour comes into being, each man has a particular, exclusive sphere of activity, which is forced upon him and from which he cannot escape. He is a hunter, a fisherman, a shepherd, or a critical critic, and must remain so if he does not want to lose his means of livelihood; while in communist society, where nobody has one exclusive sphere of activity but each become accomplished in any branch he wishes, society regulates the general production and thus makes it possible for me to do one thing today and another tomorrow, to hunt in the morning, fish in the afternoon, rear cattle in the evening, criticise after dinner, just as I have a mind, without ever becoming hunter, fisherman, shepherd or critic.[16]

The problem of bureaucratic abuse was one of bourgeois society, but with the advent of a successful proletarian revolution (the establishment of a proletarian dictatorship), such problems would be minimized and eventually wither away. The rise of proletarian class consciousness and the elimination of the hierarchy of knowledge in society would usher in an age of civil society in which man would finally be free of the tyranny of both nature and man.[17]

Economic administration was such a simple task that any worker could run the economy, according to Lenin. In *State and Revolution*, for example, Lenin states:

> Accounting and control—that is mainly what is needed for the 'smooth working', for the proper functioning, of the first phase of communist society....The accounting and control necessary for this have been simplified by capitalism to the utmost and reduced to the extraordinary simple observations—which any literate person can perform—of supervising and recording, knowledge of the four rules of arithmetic, and issuing appropriate receipts (25: 478).

With the breakdown of the capitalist system and the division of knowledge in society, the bureaucracy and eventually the state would wither away.

> In order to abolish the state it is necessary to convert the functions of civil service into simple operations of control and accounting that are within the scope and ability of the vast majority of the population, and subsequently, of every individual. And if careerism is to be abolished completely, it must be made impossible for 'honorable' though profitless posts in the civil service to be used as a springboard to highly lucrative posts in banks or joint-stock companies, as constantly happens in all the freest capitalist

> countries (25: 457).

There was no need for formal institutions of democracy within Lenin's simple model of social organization; bureaucracy would be checked by an ever-revolving proletarian administration. With the disappearance of class (only the proletariat remained, and thus there were no class distinctions), every individual would run (self-manage) the economy, and therefore no one group would possess economic power. Society would consciously control economic life. This project of political and economic emancipation and rationalization was articulated in Bukharin's and Preobrazhensky's popular exposition of the party platform adopted at the Eighth Party Conference in March 1919. Bukharin wrote:

> And inasmuch as, from childhood onward, all will have been accustomed to social labour, and since all will understand that this work is done according to a prearranged plan and when the social order is like a well-oiled machine, all will work in accordance with the indications of these statistical bureaux. There will be no need for special ministers of State, for police and prisons, for laws and decrees—nothing of the sort. Just as in an orchestra all the performers watch the conductor's baton and act accordingly, so here all will consult the statistical reports and will direct their work accordingly.[18]

The bureaucracy, Bukharin continued, will be checked because "in these statistical bureaux one person will work today, another tomorrow. The bureaucracy, the permanent officialdom will disappear." In another section of the book, Bukharin argues that the "first, the most important, function of the industrial (productive) unions is to an ever-increasing degree to ensure that the masses shall participate in the control of economic life....This introduction of the masses to participation in constructive work is also the best way of counteracting the tendency to bureaucracy in the economic apparatus of the Soviet Power."[19]

But these predictions proved too utopian. The reason for their failure, according to Lenin, and his associates was lack of culture. The solution was NEP. Under the controlled capitalism of NEP, Lenin believed, the people would learn to become cultured traders; comrades would learn to behave in a business-like manner. With the political dictatorship and the commanding heights of industry firmly in their control, the Bolsheviks could make controlled concessions to capitalism. But the attempt to mix market and plan did not go as was originally planned. It produced results opposite of those intended, leading Lenin to comment, at the Eleventh Congress of the R.C.P.(B.) in March 1922, that: "If we take Moscow with its 4,700 Communists in responsible positions, and if we take the huge bureaucratic machine, that gigantic heap, we must ask: who is directing whom?...I doubt very much," he concluded forcefully, "whether it can truthfully be said that the Communists are directing that heap. To tell the truth, they are not directing, they are being directed" (33: 288). The political and economic machine refused, Lenin argued, "to obey the hand that guided it" (33: 279). As Leonard Schapiro stated: "The conditions of NEP, which tolerated both a free market and free enterprise even if subjected to interference and restrictions, necessarily imposed limits on the extent to which the party could control and direct."[20]

Not only did NEP fail to produce the economic results that Lenin and his associates had envisaged, but the system actually increased the alienation of the worker from the Soviet regime. Ideologically, the concessions to capitalism were not greeted with applause. The "Workers' Truth" group, centered around Alexander Bogdanov, argued that the state capitalist system in Russia exploited the workers for the benefit of the party leaders:

> The working class is leading a miserable existence at a time when the new bourgeoisie (i.e., the responsible functionaries, plant directors, heads of trusts, chairmen of executive committees, etc.) and the Nepmen live in luxury and recall in our memory the picture of the life of bourgeoisie of all times....The Communist Party, which during the years of the revolution was a party of the working class, has become the ruling party, the party of the organizers and directors of the governmental apparatus and economic life on capitalist line....The party has more and more lost its tie and community with the proletariat....The Russian Communist Party has become the party of the organizer intelligentsia. The abyss between the Russian Communist Party and the working class is getting deeper and deeper, and this fact cannot be glossed over by any resolutions or decisions of the Communist congresses and conferences, etc....NEP, i.e., the rebirth of normal capitalistic relations and intensive economic differentiation among the peasantry, intensified by the famine of 1920-21, has contributed to the pronounced growth of the big kulak stratum in the Russian village....At the same time the state is growing in influence as the representative of the nation-wide interest of capital and as the mere directing apparatus of political administration and economic regulation by the organizer intelligentsia.[21]

Therefore, not only did the NEP system fail to produce the results the Bolsheviks had intended, but the system evolved into a bureaucratic embarrassment. No structural changes were introduced to the economic institutions that were the legacy of war communism; their economic tasks were re-arranged but they were not dismantled.[22] The problem of bureaucracy in the Soviet system led Lenin to devote his last two articles to suggestions for reform of the political and economic system.

In "On Cooperation" (January 6, 1923) Lenin argued that

> we have to admit that there has been a radical modification in our whole outlook on socialism. The radical modification is this; formerly we placed, and had to place, the main emphasis on the political struggle, on revolution, on winning political power, etc. Now the emphasis is changing and shifting to peaceful, organizational, "cultural" work.... the emphasis in our work is certainly shifting to education (33: 474).

And in "Better Fewer, But Better," Lenin offered both additional criticism of the bureaucracy and some organizational suggestions. With regard to the growth of the Soviet state, Lenin argued that the Bolsheviks "should now draw the conclusion from [their] past experience that it would be better to proceed more slowly" (33: 487). And since the "state apparatus [had become] so deplorable, not to say wretched, [the Bolsheviks] must first think very carefully how to combat its defects" (33: 487). They were "too prone to compensate (or imagine that [they could] compensate) [their] lack of knowledge by zeal, haste, etc." (33: 488).

To combat the problems of bureaucracy, Lenin proposed a streamlining of the state apparatus. "We must," he argued, "reduce our state apparatus to the utmost degree of economy. We must banish from it all traces of extravagance, of which so much has been left over from tsarist Russia, from its bureaucratic capitalist state machine" (33: 501). But while Lenin pleaded for a "sound scepticism" toward rapid growth of the state apparatus, he also empowered political institutions with the task of sorting out the "old lumber."

> Our Soviet Republic is of such recent construction, and there are such heaps of the old lumber still lying around that it would hardly occur to anyone to be shocked at the idea that we should delve into them by means of ruses, by means of investigations sometimes directed to rather remote sources or in a roundabout way. And even if it did occur to anyone to be shocked by this we may be sure that such a person would make himself a laughing-stock (33: 494).

Thus, although Lenin suggested bureaucratic reform, he also justified *in advance* the mentality of the Stalinist show trials of the 1930s.

With Lenin's health in question throughout 1922 and then his final stroke on March 10, 1923, which ended his political activity, the Soviet government was left without a leader.[23] On January 21, 1924, Vladimir Ilyich Lenin died, and with him (in many ways) so did the public ideology of Bolshevism. As Stephen Cohen states:

> The public ideology that had served so well from 1917 to 1920

> was in shambles by 1924. The rude dismantlement of war communism, the emergence of NEP with its 'extraordinary confusion of...socioeconomic relations,' the 'psychological depression' caused by the failure of European revolution, Lenin's death, and the spectacle of his successors claiming allegiance to different Leninisms—all shattered or seriously undermined earlier beliefs and certainties. The 'collapse of our illusions' had been the collapse of dearly held assumptions, of old theories. Disenchantment and pessimism came in the aftermath. There were many signs, some petty, some portentous: workers resented the finery of the nepman's wife; rural Communists were disoriented by the permissive agrarian policies; and, most serious, among the party faithful, especially the youth, NEP brought 'a sort of demoralization, a crisis of ideas.' In a sense, the sequence of disillusionments put an end to the Bolsheviks' innocent faith in the omnipotence of theory. Even Bukharin now liked to quote: 'Theory, my friend, is gray, but green is the eternal tree of life.' Nonetheless, party leaders felt strongly the need to rebuild and reassert Bolshevism as a coherent ideology.[24]

This ambiguity and despair toward socialist construction was the legacy Lenin left behind. He had criticized political bureaucracy, yet he established a political monopoly for the party. He argued for concessions to capitalism, but his mobilizing ideology demanded an assault on capitalism. Lenin ended his life-work staring at a stark contradiction; socialist construction, along whatever path, proved to be both politically and economically irrational. It was the struggle to overcome this despondent conclusion that served as the ideological background to the "great" debate in Soviet history.

The Economic Situation

Several important economic "crises" arose with which the different theorists and party leaders within the economic planning apparatus had to cope. The first was the "sales crisis" of 1922. The second was the "scissors crisis" of 1923. The third was the "goods famine" of 1924 and 1925. The final crisis was the "grain crisis" of the winter of 1927-1928. These crises produced various responses from the party, and in many ways each response created the next crisis.

The industrial sector of the Soviet economy in 1922 was faced with a sales crisis. Because of the famine in 1921, there was a shortage of agricultural goods to supply the industrial sector. Because of this shortage "a unit of industrial goods could produce no more than 65 percent of the pre-war equivalent in agricultural produce." And hence "the paradox of industries unable to find buyers even though industrial production was less than a quarter of the pre-war, while currency inflation was still proceeding at a rapid rate: a paradox which caused such alarm to the leaders of industry, and prompted writers abroad to announce triumphantly 'the breakdown of NEP.'"[25]

The question of how to help the industrial sector recover sparked the first economic policy debate during NEP. To alleviate the plight of industry, the Supreme Economic Council announced that the output program of several industries was to be reduced in April and May of 1922.[26] Reducing the output of certain industries, coupled with a good harvest in 1922, led to a shifting of the terms of trade. By the end of the year the terms would shift again, in the opposite direction, causing policymakers to wonder again how to balance the terms of trade between the town and country.

Because of the relative recovery of agriculture over industry in the post-May 1922 period, agricultural prices fell in relation to the prices for industrial goods. The scissors crisis was announced at the party congress in spring of 1923. Trotsky argued that if further lagging of industry continued to open the "scissors" it would inevitably lead to a break between city and country.[27]

In response, the Bolsheviks introduced measures of price controls to force the prices of state industrial products down and to prevent further price increases without proper authorization. The Supreme Economic Council, concerned over the scissors, continued to intervene to close the gap between the two sectors.[28] But this interference with prices had its perverse effects.

As would be expected, the interaction of strong market pressure for increased prices with a governmental policy that stubbornly maintained price ceilings (and pursued additional price cuts) resulted in an excess demand for industrial products. The resulting shortage of industrial goods, referred to as the goods famine, produced a situation where, as the Soviet economist V. Novozhilov described it, "Commodities no longer [sought] buyers, the buyers [sought] commodities."[29] Long queues developed. Free-market prices ran as much as 100 to 200 percent higher than the selling prices set by the state trusts. And even though the original intent of the price policy was to close the scissors and maintain the alliance between town and country, the goods famine threatened that alliance.

Urban workers were closer to the industrial sector, and therefore were the first to receive the artificially lower priced industrial goods. Peasants, on the other hand, were isolated from established industrial markets and had to go through the Nepmen to purchase industrial products. The policy not only failed to lower prices of industrial goods in the country, but, quite to the contrary, also lowered prices in the city at the expense of higher prices in the country. As a result, peasants did not have any incentive to market their surplus (the grain crisis). In the Ukraine, for example, it is estimated that the marketed share of grain between 1923 and 1926 was only 26 percent for 1923-1924; 15 percent for 1924-1925; and 21 percent for 1925-1926.[30] Net marketings of grain in 1926-1927 were only 50 and 57 percent of their pre-war level, although grain output for that period was almost equivalent to the pre-war level of output.[31]

Economic policy proved to be more difficult and confusing than had been expected. The Industrialization Debate was the attempt to come to grips with the serious task of economic policy formulation. The public ideology of Bolshevism died with Lenin, and the complexity of economic planning (even the modified mixed planning of NEP) produced a fundamental rethinking of the economic policy of socialist construction.[32] Against this ideological and historical backdrop the various industrialization strategies were devised and hotly debated.

The Debate

All the participants in the debate believed that industrialization was necessary for the development and maintenance of socialism.[33] They differed, however, on the proper methods by which to achieve industrialization. The differences that divided participants, Alec Nove comments, "lay in tempos, methods, the assessment of dangers, the strategy to be followed in pursuit of aims very largely held in common."[34]

The left wing of the party argued that the Russian backwardness was due to an underdeveloped industrial sector. This called for the adoption of an industrialization program to support heavy industry. The right wing argued, on the other hand, that Russian backwardness was a result of the cultural underdevelopment of the peasantry. In addition, the right wing argued that the alliance with the peasantry was essential for the maintenance of political power. This assessment led to a prescription of balanced growth to assure the stability of the alliance between the peasantry and the proletariat. Leon Trotsky and Evgeny Preobrazhensky are the most celebrated exponents of the left wing, while Lev Shanin and Nikolai Bukharin were the theoreticians of the right" In all four cases, the theorists were reacting to the policies of war communism and NEP, and they offered arguments in response to the ideological and economic challenges of the period that they felt were consistent with the Marxian dynamics of economic development.

Leon Trotsky and Industrialization

In many ways Leon Trotsky offered the first argument of the Industrialization Debate. Trotsky was a devotee of strict hierarchical economic planning, and he urged the Soviet government to use it to develop the industrial sector. He argued that the dictatorship of the proletariat was not enough to ensure the victory of the working class. "The working class," he argued, "can maintain and strengthen its guiding position not through the apparatus of government, not through the army, but through industry, which reproduces the proletariat itself....Only the development of industry," he concluded, "creates an unshakable foundation for the proletarian dictatorship."[35]

Trotsky did not argue (at least during the 1920s) that war communism had produced economic irrationality because it brought too much on itself in principle.[36] Rather, Trotsky argued that its failure was due to lack of administrative ability.[37] As he stated at the 11th Party Congress in March 1922:

> How did we start? We began...in economic policy by breaking with the bourgeois past firmly and without compromise. Earlier there was a market—we liquidate it, free trade—we liquidate it, competition—we abolish it, commercial calculation—we abolish it. What to have instead? The central, solemn, sacred, Supreme Economic Council for National Economy that allocates everything, organizes everything, cares for everything: where should machines go to, where raw materials, where the finished products—this all will be decided and allocated from a single centre, through its authorized organs. This plan of ours has failed. Why? Because it did not prove to be sufficiently prepared, or—as put by Comrade Lenin—because of our low cultural level.[38]

NEP did not differ substantially from war communism with regard to the planning principle, Trotsky argued. The difference lay in the method of planning. "Arbitrary administration by bureaucratic agencies is replaced by economic maneuvering. In their administrative application, methods of planning must be extended with extraordinary caution, by way of carefully feeling out the ground."[39]

Though he offered such a caution, Trotsky's plan for economic industrialization demanded the implementation of one-man management throughout industry from top to bottom.[40] The State Planning Commission must stand over the organization of industry and develop its interlocking with state finance and transportation. It was essential, in Trotsky's model, that the leading economic organs "have authority over the selection of functionaries and their transfer and removal." The failure of the industrial sector to develop was due to "the inadequate selection of business executives, in their lack of experience, in their lack of incentives to succeed in their own work. We need correct systematic measures in all these directions." One of Trotsky's proposals was to tie the wages of enterprise directors to balance sheets.[41]

The extension of the planning principle would not just lead to the modification of the market, but to its eventual overcoming. "In the final analysis," Trotsky said at the 12th Party Congress in 1923, "we will spread the planning principle to the entire market, thus swallowing and eliminating it. In other words, our successes on the basis of the New Economic Policy automatically move towards its liquidation, to its replacement by a newer economic policy, which will be a socialist policy."[42]

But Trotsky was also convinced that in the absence of world revolution, socialist construction in Russia would be tentative at best. In 1922 he wrote:

> So long as the bourgeoisie remains in power in other European states we are forced, in the struggle against economic isolation to look for agreements with the capitalist world; at the same time it can be said with certainty that these agreements in the best instance can help us to heal one or another economic wound, to make this or that step forward, but a genuine upsurge of the socialist economy in Russia will become possible only after the victory of the proletariat in the most important countries of Europe.[43]

Because of the uneasy balance of the Russian communist political and economic situation, Trotsky was very concerned with the maintenance of political power. He feared that concession to capital, both internal and external, could threaten the delicate balance. As he argued in 1922:

> If our concessions policy were to grow boundlessly, multiplying and accumulating; if we began leasing ever newer and newer groups of nationalized industrial enterprises; if we began creating concessions in the most important branches of the mining industry or railway transport; if our policy were to continue sliding downwards on the gravity chute of concessions for a number of years, then a time would inevitably arrive, when the degeneration of the economic foundation would bring with it the collapse of the political superstructure.[44]

Not through more concessions to capital would socialism be advanced, but through a continued focus on administration of the socialized sector and on industrial development.

In the face of the goods famine and grain crisis, Trotsky argued in 1926 for the levy of an increased tax on the kulaks. "Face to the village," he argued, "does not mean turn your back to industry; it means industry to the village. For the 'face' of the state, if it does not include industry, is of no use to the village."[45] The solution to economic problems was not to be found in either foreign loans or increased market reforms in the village. To allow for the importation of manufactured goods in exchange for the exportation of agricultural goods would have meant the development not of a connection between the peasant economy and socialist industries, "but between the kulak and world capitalism. It was not worth while to make the October revolution for that."[46]

But Trotsky did not offer a coherent strategy for economic growth and industrialization. He feared concessions to foreign capital, yet he wanted to import capital resources to build up industry.[47] He maintained a siege mentality and argued that foreign capitalists would not deal with Soviet Russia, yet he supported foreign trade. He supported Nepist reforms, yet argued that the market must be liquidated.

Trotsky's own ambiguity and lack of formulating a coherent strategy contributed to his downfall as much as the political maneuvering of his adversaries.[48]

Preobrazhensky and Unbalanced Growth in Industry

Evgeny Preobrazhensky's views on economic development have been the subject of discussion among economists since Alexander Erlich presented an extended treatment of his ideas to an English audience.[49] Preobrazhensky's views in the debate are particularly interesting, Erlich argues, because "no other viewpoint developed during these years was so violently repudiated at the beginning only to be implemented ultimately on a scale surpassing anything its author had ever thought possible."[50]

Erlich's interpretation of Preobrazhensky, however, has come under increasing criticism because of his tendency to read Keynesian theoretical arguments unto Preobrazhensky's arguments for industrialization.[51] This habit of viewing the debate as one over marginal propensities to save on the part of the peasants and marginal efficiency of capital in industry plagues standard treatments of not only Preobrazhensky's views but also of the issues of the Industrialization Debate in general. This unfortunate habit was the result of economic scholars' treating issues of economic development as if they were synonymous with the issues of Keynesian growth theory.[52] Perhaps the most undesirable aspect of this interpretation was that little or no attention has been given a primary issue of the debate: the existence of an integrated capital structure and the capital proportionality between the producer and consumer sectors of the economy.[53]

Key to understanding the thought of Preobrazhensky is the concept of "primitive socialist accumulation."[54] This concept, which was supposedly analogous to Marx's theory of capitalist accumulation, states that the first act of socialist accumulation was the nationalization of large-scale industry. "The nationalization of large-scale industry is," Preobrazhensky argued, "the first act of socialist accumulation, that is, the act which concentrates in the hands of the state the minimum resources needed for the organization of socialist leadership of industry."[55] Whereas in the transition from feudalism to capitalism, primitive accumulation "bore an unorganized, spontaneous character," accumulation in the transition from capitalism to socialism would be planned and follow a rational strategy.

The period of accumulation does not end with nationalization of industry, but only begins with it and the conquest of political power. Unlike capitalism's ability to build on the foundation of petty-bourgeois social relations through the use of foreign capital, the socialist organization of production could not be built on partial or insignificant amounts of socialist accumulation. To solve the problems of socialist organization of production in the Soviet Union, the Bolsheviks must accumulate enough to: (1) enable the state economy to achieve the present-day (1920s) level of capitalist production; (2) enable the whole state economy to be organized rationally according to a scientific plan (something impossible without a large accumulation of stocks and reserves); and (3) guarantee the advancement of the whole economy (and not just particular parts), because an uncoordinated advance (because of the interdependency) would be vulnerable to a capitalist counterrevolution.[56]

Primitive socialist accumulation, Preobrazhensky wrote, would be accomplished by relying on sources outside the socialized sector of the economy. In a backward country such as Russia, this meant building socialism on the backs of the peasants.[57] During the period of primitive socialist accumulation "the state economy cannot get by without alienating part of the surplus product of the peasantry and handicraftsmen, without making deductions from capitalist accumulation for the benefit of socialist accumulation."[58] By drawing liberally on presocialist forms of enterprise, the Soviet state could acquire the resources required for socialist construction.[59] Since this was a matter of the life and death of proletarian rule in Russia, Preobrazhensky argued, it was the obligation of the socialist state to take more, not less, from the petty-bourgeois than capitalism took. And, owing to the rationalization of the whole economy (including petty production), this would lead, under primitive socialist accumulation, to the state's taking more from still larger incomes.

One of the primary tools to accomplish the transfer of funds from the presocialist sector (agriculture) to the socialist sector (industry) was the nationalized banks.[60] Through the emission of bank notes the state could transfer resources from the peasants to industry. "When the state is at the same time an organ which rules the country and the master of a huge economic complex, issue of paper money directly serves as a channel for socialist accumulation. This accumulation is carried out at the expense either of the incomes of the petty-bourgeois and capitalist elements or of reduced wages of the state's workers and office employees."[61] And since the peasants were farthest removed from organized markets, they would always be last in line in the inflation process and therefore hardest hit.

The use of inflation for primitive socialist accumulation would be accomplished through credit expansion to the state enterprises. This would concentrate benefits on the state industrial sector by diffusing the costs, largely unseen, on the petty-bourgeois sector of the Soviet economy. "This explains the fact," Preobrazhensky pointed out, "that at the present moment [that is, 1924-1926] the State Bank hardly grants any credits to private trade and industry, in spite of their readiness to pay more than state enterprises, but grants them almost exclusively to the latter. *From the standpoint of the tasks of socialist accumulation this policy is the only correct one.*"[62]

Besides the redistribution of resources as a result of the printing press, Preobrazhensky argued that other methods of primitive socialist accumulation would include tariffs, foreign trade monopolies, direct taxation, concentration of industry, and monopoly pricing. Successful socialist construction depended upon the ability to accumulate the necessary resource base. As Preobrazhensky wrote:

> The fundamental law of primitive socialist accumulation is the mainspring of the entire Soviet state economy. But it is probable that this law is of universal significance, except perhaps for those countries which will be the last to go over to the socialist form of economy. Proceeding from what we have said above, we can formulate this law, or at least that part of it which relates to the redistribution of the material resources of production, in this way. The more backward economically, petty-bourgeois, peasant, a particular country is which has gone over [to] the socialist organization of production, and the smaller the inheritance received by the socialist accumulation fund of the proletariat of this country when the social revolution takes place, by so much the more, in proportion, will socialist accumulation be obliged to rely on alienating part of the surplus product of pre-socialist forms of economy and the smaller will be the relative weight of accumulation on its own production basis, that is, the less will it be nourished by the surplus product of the workers in socialist industry.[63]

And Russia was perceived to be industrially backward. The peasants would have to be relied upon. On their backs Russia would build socialism.[64]

Donald Filtzer, though, has argued that traditional, as well as Marxist, treatments of Preobrazhensky's views unnaturally divorce his economic theories "from his general methodology and from the goals to which he applied them."[65] It should be remembered that Preobrazhensky was engaged in a political debate. Moreover, interpreters should never forget that he was a revolutionary Marxist. The policies he advocated, Filtzer argues, were not descriptive of socialism, but rather strategies suggested for building socialism. "Any society," Filtzer points out, "in which the division of labor, commodity fetishism or reified production and social relations exist cannot be called socialist.... Those who describe Preobrazhensky, Trotsky or other members of the Left as 'super industrialisers' are themselves victims of the most banal Stalinist propaganda. Industrialization offered only the prerequisite for building socialism."[66]

Thus Preobrazhensky should be understood at all times as an ideological Marxist who was advocating a path toward the complete socialization of the Russian economy. Just like the organization and maintenance of the socialist economy, the transition to socialism would not depend on anarchistic and spontaneous forces, but should be planned each step along the way.

Preobrazhensky argued that the Bolsheviks needed to move away from NEP and nonsocialist social relations of production, and toward socialism.[67] He realized, however (after the collapse of war communism), that socialization was not immediately possible because of economic backwardness. Russia was a backward peasant economy infested with a petty-bourgeois false consciousness; socialism could not be constructed on such a basis. As Filtzer points out, socialism to a Marxist "cannot be conceived as consisting of the development of the means of production alone, but only in terms of the development of the productive forces as a whole: that is, the development of human and extra-human resources simultaneously."[68]

The development of the productive forces as a whole, though, depend on the establishment of complete and comprehensive centralized economic planning. The rationalization of economic life would achieve the development of the industrial means of production. The rationalization of politics, on the other hand, would provide for a general system of proletarian education and the breakdown of the division of knowledge in society.[69] But the political rationalization depended on the development of the forces of industrial production reaching an advanced level. This was the reason underlying Preobrazhensky's argument for unbalanced growth in industry supported by primitive socialist accumulation.

The motive for his strategy of economic growth was ideological. But it was also utopian—the utopianism of a Marxist-Leninist system of social organization that was (is) unattainable. Fundamental to Preobrazhensky's understanding of proletarian emancipation was the elimination of the division of labor, and thus the division of knowledge in society. But the very increases in the forces of production, which Preobrazhensky saw as providing the foundation for the political project, depend on increasing the division of knowledge in society. The assumption of generalizable knowledge was (is) inconsistent with advanced economic development and renders Preobrazhensky's views of an advanced industrialized socialist economy untenable.

Against these "extreme" views of the "Left Opposition," Lev Shanin and Nikolai Bukharin countered. Both maintained a vision of a future Marxist world, but they argued that it would be accomplished in a fashion different from that suggested by Preobrazhensky. Both rejected the notion of primitive socialist accumulation as an explicit policy, though they probably did hold the position that Alec Nove has attributed to all who reacted against Preobrazhensky: "Of course we will have to exploit the peasants in due time, but for goodness' sake let us keep quiet about it now."[70] But despite their similarities in reaction against Trotsky and Preobrazhensky, there were differences within the right wing of the Bolshevik party over the proper path to socialism.

Lev Shanin and Unbalanced Growth in Agriculture

Lev Shanin, a representative of the extreme right wing of the Bolshevik party, argued that to alleviate Russia's economic woes the government should pursue unbalanced growth in agriculture.[71] The scissors crisis of 1923 and the goods famine of 1924 and 1925, he argued, suggested that agriculture was the more efficient and least cost-productive sector in Soviet Russia. Accordingly, Shanin called for increased investment in agricultural production, leading to industrialization through the use of agricultural exports.

Shanin's argument relied on a demonstration of the maintenance of capital proportionality through agricultural and opposed to industrial investment. The current problems facing the Soviet economy were a result of disproportionality, not backwardness. As Shanin stated:

> The disparity between the development of agriculture and the development of industry by no means signifies that our industry is not developing vigorously enough, for our industry is not parasitic upon agriculture; the disproportion lies on another plane and consists in the fact that industry's fixed capital is developing too fast and that the industrial branches which are developing are not those which could satisfy the consumer goods demand that the development of industry is creating. This is the essence of the phenomenon currently observable in our country.[72]

The Soviet economy was malcoordinated due to the government's continually committing capital resources to higher order (producer) goods. This malcoordination produced recurring crises, that is, the sales crisis, the scissors crisis, the goods famine, and so on. Within a communist society, as understood by Marx, the strict proportionality between producer goods and consumer goods sectors would be maintained because of the rationalization of economic life. Quoting Marx, Shanin states that the communist "society must calculate beforehand how much labor, means of production, and means of subsistence it can, without difficulty, invest in branches of production such as railroad building, for example, which for a long time, a year or more, furnish neither means of production nor means of subsistence and in general produce no useful effect, while they withdraw labor, means of production, and means of subsistence from the total annual production."[73]

The Soviet government had failed to maintain a strict proportionality. Almost twice as much capital had been invested in heavy industry, Shanin points out, as in light industry. Associated with this structural disproportionality were the recurring crises. "A precondition for crisis-free expansion of fixed capital," he argued, "is a certain prior saturation of the market with both agricultural and industrial goods."[74] This was necessary because the restriction in current consumption required to build up capital investment would only be forthcoming after immediate consumer demand had been satisfied. Investments in fixed capital are only crisis-free if individuals have enough consumer goods to make them willing to wait calmly. There must be a commodity reserve, Shanin argued, before investments in fixed capital can be coordinated. "When there is a deficiency of commodity reserves, however, investment in fixed capital initially becomes, on the contrary, the source of an acute commodity shortage crisis, and only later can it bring some relief."[75]

By following a policy of investment in agricultural production, and open international trade, that is, exportation of agricultural surplus and importation of capital resources, industrialization would be achieved faster and more efficiently. Russia was a low-cost producer of agricultural goods, and, under existing conditions, a high-cost producer of industrial goods. Following a least-cost strategy in production, Shanin argued, the Soviet economy could advance toward industrialization.[76]

His policy can be summarized as an agriculture-first strategy to economic growth. Shanin did not abandon his belief in economic administration; his argument was just that economic planners should follow economic strategies that exploit Russia's comparative advantage. "Our economic strategy," he stated, "should involve, first, export of agricultural commodities, and, second, investment of capital in the branches which serve that export."[77] By channeling resources first through agriculture, the Bolsheviks would maximize their industrial capacity. "It is clear," Shanin concluded, "that by taking the resources intended for diversion to industry and passing them first through agriculture, we enable them to advance industrial development more tellingly than if we pour them immediately and directly into industry."[78]

Bukharin and Balanced Growth

Nikolai Bukharin represented the official position of the Bolshevik party throughout most of the 1920s. A revolutionary hero and close associate of Lenin, "he was undoubtedly the best-educated economist not only of his group, but of the whole party as well, with a truly outstanding facility for the rationalization, in terms of theory, of any political viewpoints he happened to embrace, and for pushing them toward the furthest logical consequences."[79] His books *The ABC of Communism* and *The Economics of the Transition Period* were regarded as the theoretical manifestos of war communism. They defended the extreme centralization policies, as well as the use of noneconomic coercion, that the Bolsheviks had implemented from 1918 to 1921. Although many readers are shocked by the conclusions and justifications contained in these books, it is even more shocking to witness Bukharin's swing to the right. Not only was Bukharin one of the premier theorists of war communism, he was also the premier theorist of NEP.[80]

The failure of war communism in many ways affected Bukharin's thinking more profoundly than perhaps any other Bolshevik besides Lenin. The collapse of their illusions would change forever his ideas toward the construction of socialism.[81] The tentativeness of the political alliance between the workers and the peasantry and the economic annihilation of industry and agriculture conflicted with Bukharin's original expectations of socialist construction. But Bukharin had a paradigm to interpret the failure: economic theory.

In 1925, for example, he refers to Ludwig von Mises as "one of the most learned critics of communism" and admits that Mises was right on the feasibility of socialism, at least given the current stage of cultural development.[82] Bukharin's admission, however, was confused. On the one hand, he referred to the change in economic course toward NEP, that is, the reintroduction of market methods of allocation, as a shift to "rational economic policy," and he admitted that these concessions were necessary to provide proper economic incentives for both workers and peasants. But he argued in the final analysis that "we can say our opponents were the ones who lost in this debate. In the course of the struggle, we *upheld what was most important and had to be upheld, namely, the dictatorship of the proletariat*."[83]

To Bukharin, the Bolsheviks could make all the economic concessions to capital deemed necessary; as long as they maintained the proletarian dictatorship and possessed power over the commanding heights of industry, they would be building the road to socialism, however far off success may be. The market and the incentives of commerce were necessary, Bukharin argued, for economic coordination. He also recognized as vital to his incentives argument the importance of the stability of rules.[84]

Bukharin's policies for economic growth were derived from his understanding of economic interdependence. During the transition period it was of the utmost importance to maintain a balance between the industrial and agricultural sectors in the economy. As he wrote in 1928:

> In order to attain the most favorable (or most crisis-free) course of social reproduction possible, together with systematic growth of socialism and, therefore, the most advantageous possible relation of class forces within the country for the proletariat, it is necessary to attain the best possible combination of the basic elements of the national economy (to "balance" them, to arrange them in the most useful manner, actively influencing the course of economic life and the class struggle).[85]

Bukharin criticized both the Trotskyists (Preobrazhensky included) and the "petty-bourgeois knights" (Shanin) for not understanding this fundamental point of economic interdependence. Both wings, Bukharin argued, must be dismissed.[86] "To think," he wrote against Preobrazhensky, "that the growth of a planned economy makes it possible for the left leg to do whatever it wants (simply because the law of value withers away) is to misunderstand even the ABCs of economic science."[87]

Bukharin adopted a balanced-growth strategy for both agriculture and industry. Through such a policy, he believed, Russia could slowly grow into a socialist economy.[88] Socialism in one country could be achieved.[89] If the policies of either the left (Trotsky and Preobrazhensky) or the right (Shanin) were adopted, political and economic crises would result.

Bukharin's policies, on the other hand, were calculated for building the economic base on which the socialist future could be constructed. To build the appropriate base he argued that the Bolsheviks should pursue policies that allowed and in fact encouraged private profit-seeking on the part of peasants. It was Bukharin's belief that by allowing the peasants to pursue their own economic interest, while the proletarian dictatorship maintained power over the banking system and other commanding heights of industry, the peasants would be eventually brought into cooperation with the socialist government through regard for their own self-interest. A peasant, for example, who deposits money in a state bank would be less likely to revolt against the state. Through cooperation and interdependence, Bukharin argued, political stability and economic growth could be maintained.[90]

Stalin's Rise to Power

Stalin's program of industrialization derives its importance from "his regime's decisive and unparalleled impact on development patterns in the USSR East Asia and 1950s Eastern Europe, on the political culture of communist parties everywhere, on the fortunes of socialist movements in the West, on widely held conceptions of forced industrialization and development planning, and on the course of world history since the 1930s."[91] But Stalin's own theoretical articulations of this program are not widely discussed.

The usual interpretation, however, portrays Stalin as a dullard who borrowed Bukharin's ideas from 1924 to 1927 during the factional struggle with Trotsky and the left opposition, and then adopted the Trotskyite platform to outmaneuver Bukharin and the right wing.[92] But this position is basically untenable.

For one thing, it distorts the positions of the major protagonists in the debate—Preobrazhensky and Bukharin—and for another, it does little to explain Stalin's rise to power. Alexander Erlich, in his survey of Stalin's views on economic development, points out, "The assertion that Stalin's interventions in the debate of 1924-1927 did not break the impasse would be an understatement." Even if Stalin's "pronouncements on controversial issues of economic policy in these years exhibit such a definite tendency against sin and in favor of eating one's cake and having it too that it appears at first almost hopeless to distill out of them a clear view not only of the nature of the problems, but also of the attitude of the man," it must be admitted that his strategic pronouncements were of great political import.[93] His statement at the 14th Congress, for example, that "we back Bukharin" revealed Stalin's basic position in the 1920s, and served to defeat the left opposition.[94]

But there were differences between Stalin and Bukharin. Stalin, by 1925, was already developing a theory of socialism in one country.[95] Complete victory of socialism would be possible only with international revolution because complete and final victory required a guarantee against future attempts at intervention and the restoration of capital. And as long as the Soviet Union existed within capitalist encirclement, this problem would persist. But this did not mean that socialism could not be constructed. Stalin, to the contrary, argued:

> For if the possibility and necessity of building a complete

> socialist society is precluded for some reason or other, the October Revolution becomes meaningless. Anyone who denies the possibility of building socialism in one country must necessarily deny that the October Revolution was justified; and vice versa, anyone who has no faith in the October Revolution cannot admit the possibility of the victory of socialism in the conditions of capitalist encirclement.[96]

At the Party Congress in 1925 Stalin announced that "we must make every effort to make our country an economically self-reliant, independent country...a centre of attraction for all other countries which gradually drop out of capitalism and enter the channel of socialist economy." To accomplish this, Stalin went on, "the utmost expansion of our industry" would be required. Priority must be given to the development of large-scale state industry.[97]

By 1927 Stalin was arguing for increased acceleration of the rate of growth of nationalized industry and, to maintain a balance, the conversion of small peasant farms into collective farms using the most technologically advanced techniques.[98] It was time to eliminate the capitalist influence within the countryside, that is, the kulaks. The grain-procurement crisis of 1927-1928 provided the final justification for Stalin to begin his assault from above. Stalin, "ignoring the proposals of Bukharin and others to increase grain prices,...decided to launch a direct attack which revived memories of the excesses of war communism."[99]

With the left wing no longer a serious threat, Stalin turned his political sword to the right wing in 1928. Only "if we disregarded the external and internal situation," Stalin wrote in his attack on the right-deviation, could we "conduct the work at a slower pace." But first, Stalin argued, the Bolsheviks could not ignore the external and internal situation, and second, "if we take the surrounding situation as our starting point, it has to be admitted that it is precisely this situation that dictates a fast rate of development of our industry."[100]

Fear of foreign intervention and the uncomfortable ideology of NEP led to Stalin's revolution from above.[101] Stalin, with political power firmly in hand, began a military siege over the economy.[102] As Stephen Cohen points out, Stalin's political and economic strategy was:

> Military rather than traditionally Marxist in inspiration, Stalin's intensification theory was perhaps his only original contribution to Bolshevik thought; it became the sine qua non of his twenty-five year rule. In 1928, applied to the kulaks, "Shakhtyites," and anonymous "counter-revolutionaries," it rationalized his vision of powerful enemies within and his "extraordinary," civil war politics. By the thirties, he had translated it into a conspiratorial theory of "enemies of the people," and the ideology of mass terror.[103]

The decision to collectivize was not justified on economic grounds, but based on political ones.[104] Erlich concluded his analysis of the industrialization debate by arguing that Stalin's decision was more a matter of protecting the ruling elite than a conscious decision to pursue a path toward economic growth. As Erlich argues:

> The conclusions were obvious. A policy of moderate growth tempos which would strengthen the position of the upper strata of the villages and would make the adroit balancing between them and the unruly radicals of the cities a necessity could be adopted only as a temporary expedient. Had such a course been pursued over a long period of time, the regime would have stood to lose not only from its possible failures but also from its successes. The alternative to such retreats and maneuvers leading to the gradual erosion of the dictatorial system was clearly a massive counter-attack which would have broken once and for all the peasants' veto power over the basic decisions on economic policy.[105]

Total war required crushing the enemy with a degree of finality. "The rapid-fire industrialization and the sweeping collectivization," Erlich concluded, "were not merely devices of economic policy, but means of extending the direct control of the totalitarian state over the largest possible number within the shortest time."[106]

This was not just a problem of Stalin's "cult of personality" but a problem of social institutions. The Stalinist regime was merely the manifestation of a more serious disease inherent in economic planning institutions in general. As Don Lavoie argues, "Planning does not accidentally deteriorate into the militarization of the economy; it is the militarization of the economy."[107]

Conclusion

The implications of the Soviet Industrialization Debate are vast and important. The debate should shed light on what economists mean by economic development, growth, and well-being. Certainly the concentration on per-capita income, gross national product, or rates of growth within economic development does not provide the answer. Such aggregate measures do not reveal the condition of economic life of the people.[108] The Soviet experience, for example, reveals the fallacy of this approach. As Erlich pointed out in 1960: "Soviet society, after a quarter century of unparalleled industrial and urban development, had to live on a lower-quality per capita diet than at the time when it was, to a very large extent, a society of wretchedly poor peasants—a fact, which, for obvious reasons, was deeply disturbing not merely from the viewpoint of consumers' welfare."[109]

Yet there are still those who wish to argue that the Soviet experience of collectivization and industrialization was a success.[110] But by what criterion are these economists judging success? The industrialization drive was not successful from the point of view of increasing consumer well-being. Economic welfare and development were not enhanced. It was, however, very successful in establishing and maintaining a ruling elite. Is that what we mean by economic development?

Current development theory, under the influence of the belief in the success of Soviet forced industrialization strategy, continues to emphasize the planning of industrial growth in underdeveloped countries.[111] Economic development and human welfare, however, are fundamentally problems of mobilizing knowledge, only part of which is held by any given member of society.

Bukharin and Shanin understood, at least to some degree, this coordination problem; this understanding underlies their demand for capital proportionality within a strategy for economic growth. Bukharin, especially, seemed to grasp the meaning of economic coordination. It was the basis for his acceptance of an essentially market-oriented model of economic development and industrialization. But in the ideal Marxian world, where production would be for direct use as opposed to exchange, this proportionality would be maintained by the planning board's calculating the appropriate use of capital resources *in advance*.

The Austrian challenge to economic planning was directly aimed at this assertion of economic rationalization. The competitive capitalist process of exchange and production relies on the market system of prices, profit, and loss to discover and disseminate the knowledge necessary for the coordination of plans.[112] In advanced capitalist production, that is, a complex economy with higher or more remote stages of production, the coordination between the consumer-goods sector and the producer-goods sector depends crucially upon the ability of the price system to convey knowledge to the various market participants.

Economic growth concerns the growth of knowledge in society. It is about the discovery and use of new knowledge of existing or previously unknown opportunities. As Israel Kirzner writes: "The great neglected question in development economics concerns the existence of a social apparatus for ensuring that available opportunities are exploited."[113] Or, as he writes elsewhere:

> Treating growth simply as a phenomenon best achieved through deliberate planning inevitably clamps economic growth into a framework from which open-ended discovery is excluded. To plan is not to discover; in fact, to plan presumes that the framework within which planning takes place is already fully discovered. In contrast, I see the unfolding development of a nation's economy over time as a process made up, to a major extent, of the interaction of innumerable individual acts of mutual discovery. An understanding of the institutional climate within which such spontaneous processes of unpredictable mutual discovery can best flourish is central.[114]

It is a recognition of the knowledge-conveyance role of markets that underlies the case for freedom of exchange and production in economic development. The political and economic institutions of a truly free society are flexible enough to allow for human creativity and innovation, yet at the same time are "rigid" enough to establish the mutually reinforcing sets of expectations necessary for economic coordination. As F.A. Hayek states: "Liberty is essential in order to leave room for the unforeseeable and unpredictable; we want it because we have learned to expect from it the opportunity of realizing many of our aims. It is because every individual knows so little, and, in particular, because we rarely know which of us knows best that we trust the independent and competitive efforts of many to induce the emergence of what we shall want when we see it."[115]

Notes

[1] Alec Nove, *An Economic History of the U.S.S.R.* (New York: Penguin Books, 1984[1969]), 129.

[2] See Robert M. Solow, "Growth Theory and After," *American Economic Review*, Vol. 78, n. 3 (June 1988), 307-317.

[3] Domar, *Essays in the Theory of Economic Growth* (New York: Oxford University Press, 1957), 10.

[4] See H. W. Arndt, "Economic Development: A Semantic History," *Economic Development and Cultural Change*, Vol. 29 (April 1981), 457-466. "In the immediate postwar years," Arndt points out, "'economic development' became virtually synonymous with growth in per capita income in the less developed countries" (465). Sukhamoy Chakravarty, "The State of Development Economics," *The Manchester School of Economics and Social Studies*, Vol. 55, n. 2 (June 1987), 125-143, also documents this preoccupation of development theory with economic growth and offers suggestions for a "new agenda." In the final analysis Chakravarty argues that economic development must be closely connected to the theory of economic evolution as advanced by Marx and Schumpeter, but without Marx's linear determinism and Schumpeter's open-ended analysis of innovation. What is needed in development economics is not more advanced theoretical models of "growth," but more detailed historical studies of particular countries' economic development. What is needed is "a much closer integration of history and theory" (139).

This equating of economic development with neo-classical growth theory had severe consequences for the theoretical foundations of development economics. Domar, for example, in describing his original interest in G.A. Fel'dman's article, "A Soviet Model of Growth" (published in 1928), states: "I have always felt that the Marxists, concerned as they were with the process of accumulation, should have developed some theory of growth." See Domar, *Essays in the Theory of Economic Growth*, 10. But in developing Fel'dman's model Domar was unimpressed with specifically *the* unique character of Marxism, that is, the structural proportionality between consumer and producer goods industries. As a result, growth theory developed in a direction opposite that of capital theory. But capital theory, properly understood, provides the basis for the microfoundations of macroeconomic analysis without which the theorist is left either with a world in which there are no market problems (the Walrasian world) or one where there are no market solutions (the Keynesian world). Neither theoretical world does much to advance our understanding of intertemporal coordination. See Roger Garrison, "Time and Money: The Universals of Macroeconomic Theorizing," *Journal of Macroeconomics*, Vol. 6, n.

2 (Spring 1984), 197-213.

[5] See, for example, the standard account in Alexander Erlich, *The Soviet Industrialization Debate, 1924-1928* (Cambridge: Harvard University Press, 1960). A somewhat similar argument against the standard interpretation is offered by James Millar, "A Note on Primitive Accumulation in Marx and Preobrazhensky," *Soviet Studies*, Vol. 30, n. 3 (July 1978), 385, where he states that "both Preobrazhensky's and Marx's concepts [of primitive accumulation] are much richer analytically than has been generally presumed.... Alexander Erlich's famous article [later expanded into the book] infused more consistency and *contemporary economics* into Preobrazhensky's theoretics than was there in the first place" (emphasis added). Also see Millar, "What's Wrong with the 'Standard Story,'" *Problems of Communism* (July-August 1976), 51, where he states that "The first problem with the standard story is that Alexander Erlich's famous article on Preobrazhensky contains more of Erlich (and of John Maynard Keynes) than it does of Preobrazhensky."

[6] Consider the following statement of Keynes: "I expect to see the State, which is in a position to calculate the marginal efficiency of capital-goods on long views and on the basis of the general social advantage, taking an ever greater responsibility for directly organising investment." See Keynes, *The General Theory of Employment, Interest and Money* (New York: Harcourt Brace Jovanovich, 1964[1936]), 164. Also see Saul Estrin and Peter Holmes, "Uncertainty, Efficiency and Economic Planning in Keynesian Economics," *Journal of Post-Keynesian Economics*, Vol. VII, n. 4 (Summer 1985), 463-473, for an example of Keynesian arguments for economic planning. This social engineering aspect of both systems of thought is responsible for the unity of Hayek's criticism of both socialist constructions and Keynesian fine-tuning. See Hayek, "The Pretense of Knowledge," *New Studies in Philosophy, Politics, Economics and the History of Ideas* (Chicago: University of Chicago Press, 1978), 23-34. This was Hayek's Nobel Lecture in December 1974. Also see the critique of neo-Keynesian theories of economic growth in Ludwig M. Lachmann, *Macro-economic Thinking and the Market Economy* (Menlo Park, CA: Institute for Humane Studies, 1978[1973]).

[7] This was the last great political and economic debate in the Soviet Union until perhaps today when debate is encouraged. The Industrialization Debate was the closest thing to an open political and economic forum that has ever been witnessed in the history of that government. Unfortunately, the debates of the twenties were ended not by the force of superior argument, but rather with the introduction of the bullet as a conversation stopper.

[8] Gregory and Stuart, *Soviet Economic Structure and Performance*, 2nd ed. (New York: Harper and Row, 1981), 81-82.

[9] See Deutscher and King, *The Great Purges* (New York: Basil Blackwell, 1984). This is also the theme of George Orwell's *Animal Farm* (New York: Harcourt Brace Jovanovich, 1946), where the character Snowball is analogous to Trotsky and Napoleon represents Stalin. Arthur Koestler's *Darkness at Noon* (New York: Macmillan, 1941) also captures the psychological and physical horror of Stalin's bloody purges.

[10] Dobb, "The discussion of the 'twenties on planning and economic growth'," in *Papers on Capitalism, Development and Planning* (London: Routledge and Kegan Paul, 1967), 127.

[11] Robert Bideleux, *Communism and Development* (New York: Meuthuen, 1985), 84.

[12] Lenin, "Notes of a Publicist: On Ascending a High Mountain; The Harm of Despondency, The Utility of Trade; Attitude Towards the Mensheviks, etc.," *CW* (33: 207).

[13] See "Declaration of Twenty-Two Members of the Russian Communist Party to the International Conference of the Communist International," in *A Documentary History of Communism*, ed. Robert V. Daniels, 2 vols. (New York: Vintage, 1962), I: 219.

[14] Prokopovitch, *The Economic Conditions of Soviet Russia* (London: P.S. King and Sons, 1924), 230.

[15] For an interesting discussion of the tension between Marx's theory of praxis and command planning see David L. Prychitko, "The Political Economy of Workers' Self-Management: A Market Process Critique" (unpublished PhD thesis, George Mason University, 1989), 28-80. Also see Radoslav Selucky, *Marxism, Socialism, Freedom* (New York: St. Martin's Press, 1979) for a discussion of Marx's contradictory economic and political projects. It should be kept in mind, however, that the tension between Marx's political and economic project is a problem of the transition period. But its existence suggests that neither Marx nor Lenin addressed seriously enough the question of how to get from here to there—a serious problem for philosophers who were concerned not only with interpreting the world but also with changing it.

[16] See Karl Marx and Frederick Engels, "The German Ideology," *Selected Works*, 3 vols. (Moscow: Progress Publishers, 1969), I: 35-36. Also see Lenin, *The State and Revolution*, *CW* (25: 473), where he states that: "The economic basis for the complete withering away of the state is such a high stage of development of communism at which the antithesis between mental and physical labour disap-

pears...."

[17] Marx had no love for the machinery of the state. For example, consider his description of the state in "The Eighteenth Brumaire of Louis Bonaparte," *Selected Works*, I: 477: "This executive power with its enormous bureaucratic and military organization, with its ingenious state machinery, embracing wide strata, with a host of officials numbering half a million, besides an army of another half million, this appalling parasitic body, which enmeshes the body of French society like a net and chokes all its pores, sprang up in the days of the absolute monarchy, with the decay of the feudal system, which it helped to hasten." This leads Marx to view taxes as "the source of life for the bureaucracy, the army, the priests and the court, in short, for the whole apparatus of the executive power. Strong government and heavy taxes are identical" (482). The basis of this parasitic state was small-holding property. These problems would disappear under the dictatorship of the proletariat and communal ownership of property.

Also see Marx's discussion of the state in *Critique of Hegel's Philosophy of Right* (New York: Cambridge University Press, 1970), where he states: "The opposition between state and civil society is thus fixed; the state does not reside within but outside of civil society; it affects civil society merely through office holders to whom is entrusted the management of the state within this sphere. The opposition is not overcome by means of these office holders but has become a legal and fixed opposition. The state becomes something alien to the nature of civil society; it becomes this nature's overworldly realm of deputies which makes claims against civil society. The police, the judiciary, and the administration are not deputies of civil society itself, which manages its own general interest in and through them. Rather, they are office holders of the state whose purpose is to manage the state in opposition to civil society" (49-50). But this opposition is due, according to Marx, to an unnatural separation of man from his communal existence. "In order to behave as an actual citizen of the state, to acquire political significance and efficacy, he must abandon his civil actuality, abstract from it, and retire from this entire organization into his individuality....existence as a citizen is an existence lying outside the realm of his communal existences." Marx continues: "The separation of civil society and the political state appears necessarily to be a separation of the political citizen, the citizen of the state, from civil society, i.e., from his own actual, empirical reality" (78). Political alienation was as serious a problem to Marx as estranged labor. Both, however, would be overcome by proletarian revolution. It never occurred to Marx, nor Lenin, that political estrangement could worsen for the proletariat under the dictatorship in its name. It was a surprise—an unintended and undesirable consequence of the Marxian project.

[18] Bukharin and Preobrazhensky, *The ABC of Communism* (Ann Arbor: University of Michigan Press, 1969[1919]), 74.

[19] Bukharin and Preobrazhensky, *The ABC of Communism*, 74; 282. This is the participatory planning advocated by the Bolsheviks. The trade unions would participate in the work of the commissariats, the economic councils, and the Supreme Economic Council until the whole economy, from top to bottom, was rationalized, constituting a unified economic plan.

[20] Schapiro, *The Communist Party of the Soviet Union* (New York: Vintage, 1971[1960]), 334.

[21] See "Appeal of the 'Workers' Truth' Group," *A Documentary History*, 220-222.

[22] Thus, Bukharin's criticism of the irrationality of the Soviet system of economic bureaucracy under war communism would continue throughout the NEP period. This problem of bureaucracy would become Bukharin's major source of criticism of the left opposition and the later Stalinist regime in the 1920s and 1930s. It underlies his total rethinking of the economics of socialism as he tried to steer clear of what he referred to as the "Genghis Khan plan" toward socialist construction.

[23] An excellent account of Lenin's decline in health and the turmoil of political leadership is found in Moshe Lewin, *Lenin's Last Struggle* (New York: Monthly Review Press, 1968). Also see Richard Day, *Leon Trotsky and the Economics of Isolation* (New York: Cambridge University Press, 1973), 69, where he argues that: "The party's age of innocence ended in the spring of 1922. Shortly thereafter, Lenin's terminal illness initiated a vicious and protracted contest among his potential successors for total political power. Economic policy emerged almost immediately as one of the main issues in dispute. Lenin had led his followers into the wilderness only to die before he could lead them out. The road to socialism had still to be defined. Confusion bred the desire first for certainty and ultimately for a faith supplemented by force."

[24] Cohen, *Bukharin and the Bolshevik Revolution*, 184.

[25] Maurice Dobb, *Soviet Economic Development Since 1917* (New York: International Publishers, 1948), 156-157. Even though prevailing market prices were high for agricultural goods this did not signal a betterment of the peasants; the higher prices were due to the shortage of agricultural goods. The famine of 1921 had left the peasants at a level of mere subsistence. Industrial workers, on the other hand, faced a reduction in their real income as a result of the higher food prices. The economic situation in the town and the country was bleak.

[26] Many argued that this was not the proper policy. A report of the Economic Planning Commission, for example, argued that the problem would not be solved by a reduction of output, but by the introduction of a more liberal grant policy on

the part of the state budget to industry. Cut off in 1921 from state credit and required to meet the harsh reality of profit and loss accounting, many firms were already selling their products well below operating costs just to liquidate their stock pile of products. (This was the so-called *razbazarovania* or squandering crisis of 1921.) Cutting output figures and curtailing state credit even further, it was argued, would just increase the misery of the industrial sector and demonstrate a "tuning of the face" of the government toward the peasantry and away from the worker. But the policy of output reduction and the combining of state enterprises into "trusts" proved to be a temporary expedient. It lead to an easing of the fuel situation through the summer of 1922, which benefited light industry, and to a recovery of the terms of trade between town and country. See Dobb, *Soviet Economic Development*, 158.

[27] See Trotsky, *The Revolution Betrayed* (New York: Pathfinder Press, 1972[1937]), 25. Trotsky's argument also contained a class character. In particular, Trotsky was concerned over the growing kulak (well-off peasants) influence in the village.

[28] Industrial selling prices fell an estimated 23.3 percent in 1923-1924. The Soviet state established a Commissariat for Trade to market manufactured goods in rural areas below the prices charged by the Nepmen. "By April 1924," Alec Nove points out, "the agricultural price index had risen to 92 (1913=100) and the industrial index had fallen to 131." See Nove, *An Economic History of the U.S.S.R*, 96.

[29] Novozhilov, *Vestnik Finansov*, No. 2, 1926, as quoted in Nove, *An Economic History of the U.S.S.R.*, 139.

[30] See Gregory and Stuart, *Soviet Economic Structure and Performance*, 56, fn. 47. The *tovarnost* or marketing problem took the Bolsheviks by surprise. Whereas before the war the kulaks and large agricultural estates produced more than 50 percent of the total grain and supplied more than 70 percent of the marketable grain, now grain was mainly produced by small peasant farms. Moshe Lewin argues that the peasants consumed rather than marketed their surplus and thus explains why marketed surplus in 1927 was half that of the pre-war level: 13 percent as against 26 percent of the harvest. The procurement for the year 1926-1927 was only 428 million poods of grain, and in 1927 the state only collected 630 million poods of grain, as compared to 1,300 million poods in 1913. And the Soviet state possessed no reserves in case of war or famine. And this is the crux of the problem: grain production was smaller than it was before the war, and the peasants marketed less, but the requirements were greater. See Moshe Lewin, "The Immediate Background of Soviet Collectivization," *The Making of the Soviet System* (New York: Pantheon, 1985), 91 ff. Also see Lewin, *Russian Peasants and Soviet Power* (New York: Norton, 1975[1968]), 214 ff.

[31] In response to the grain-procurement problem the *dekulakization* began. The

Bolsheviks enacted article 107 of the penal code (a law against speculation that was introduced in 1926 and provided for prison sentences and confiscation of property for persons found guilty of causing a rise in the price of good by repurchase or hoarding) directly against the kulak. By February 1928 Stalin, feeling the need for a scapegoat, argued that the kulaks in Siberia had reserves of about 50,000-60,000 poods per farm and were waiting for the price to go up. Even though these figures were considered to be highly unreliable, it was accepted that any kulak who refused to sell his surplus grain at state prices was a speculator and his surplus was to be confiscated. Stalin's tactic was to explain the procurement crisis as a general kulak strike. "This enabled him," as Moshe Lewin points out, "to use coercive measures not only against the kulaks, but also against the majority of the peasants and against those elements within the Party who had doubts about the operation. In fact, the danger of being labeled as an ally of the kulaks was such that no communist could afford to incur it." See Lewin, *Russian Peasants*, 219.

[32] I contend that how the different theorists interpreted the debacle of war communism was extremely influential on their positions in the twenties. The fact that neither Trotsky nor Preobrazhensky never quite understood the problem with either the militarization model nor the strict-unity-of-plan model explains why they adopted the industrialization strategy they did. Any other strategy would concede that socialism was not feasible. On the other hand, Bukharin's recognition of some of the fundamental problems of socialist planning (at least at the current stage of development) led him to his position of pro-market growth to support the development of state capitalist industry (guided by the proletarian dictatorship) until the Soviets developed the proper industrial foundation for socialist construction.

[33] Within the debate over general industrialization strategy another debate took place. This was the debate over the proper role of economic planning within economic policy. Thinkers such as Kondratiev, Bazarov, and Groman argued that consumer demand should signal what the economic planners should do and in what direction the economy should be changed. In other words, they advocated a sort of indicative planning model that would concentrate on alleviating short-run market problems. To do otherwise and expand the industrial sector without paying attention to the effects on the other sectors in the economy would produce economic disproportionality and thus economic crises. The basic model of economic coordination, therefore, should be the market methods of allocation that existed under NEP. These theorists became known as the "geneticists" and were associated with the right wing of the party. Advocates of more long-term planning models, such as Strumlin, Pyatakov, Kuibyshev, and Fel'dman, were known as "teleologists." In dealing with problems of development, these economists argued that the planner should not be concerned with current market conditions, but rather, should pursue policies that would maximize long-run economic growth. The planner should not subject the growth of the economy to the spontaneous and anarchistic forces of the

market, but instead rationally control the economy's growth and supersede the market. To do otherwise was to submit to the "genetical inheritance" of tsarism. These issues will not be directly addressed within my discussion, since I am limiting my discussion to industrialization strategy. See Gregory and Stuart, *Soviet Structure and Performance*, 93 ff., for a discussion of the debate between the geneticists and teleologists. Also see Alec Nove, *An Economic History of the U.S.S.R.*, 132 ff. In addition, many translations of the original articles are contained in Nicolas Spulber, ed., *Foundations of Soviet Strategy for Economic Growth* (Bloomington: Indiana University Press, 1964).

[34] Nove, *An Economic History of the U.S.S.R.*, 128.

[35] Trotsky, "Theses on Industry," March 6, 1923, in *A Documentary History*, 235.

[36] During the 1920s Trotsky's emphasis was on the backwardness of the Russian industrial sector and the failure of world revolution. Trotsky would later argue for a sort of market socialism in the transition period and maybe even beyond. In *Revolution Betrayed*, 23, he argued that even if the German revolution had been successful it would have still "been necessary to renounce the direct state distribution of products in favor of the methods of commerce." Yet, within the same text he argued that "Socialism is a structure of planned production to the end of the best satisfaction of human needs; otherwise it does not deserve the name of socialism" (61). Trotsky may well have been a Nepist, as Stephen Cohen suggests, but he accepts market principles only tentatively—as sort of the rules for socialist competition. The superiority of industrial planning will eliminate the anarchy of market discipline. See Stephen Cohen, *Rethinking the Soviet Experience* (New York: Oxford University Press, 1985), 38-70. Also see Alec Nove, "New Light on Trotskii's Economic Views," *Slavic Review*, Vol. 40, n. 1 (Spring 1981), 84-97, who, while supporting Cohen's thesis, points out that Trotsky was especially concerned with the "market devil" and argued for an expanded socialist sector. Nove argues that Trotsky "learned fast from the poor performance of centralized planning under war communism" and that "the market mechanism is needed." He learned that while "one day a socialism would arise in which there could be the kind of planning envisaged by Marx—that is, an end to commodity production—but there would be a long transition period" (88). NEP, again, was viewed as a retreat from the proper model of comprehensive planning. Trotsky did clearly change his mind from his early war communism period to a position that was conciliatory toward markets—but is the change with the introduction of NEP or only after the left opposition is defeated? His thesis on industry seems to suggest that he did not learn the lesson of war communism—bureaucracy, not economic irrationality, eventually convinced him.

[37] This is the essence of his complaint of bureaucracy. The Declaration of the Forty-

Six of October 1923, for example, argues: "The economic and financial crisis which began at the end of July of this year, together with all the political (including intra-party) consequences which have stemmed from it, has unmercifully uncovered the unsatisfactoriness of the party leadership, in the area of the economy and especially in the area of intra-party relations." The bureaucracy had choked off the "party's social mind," and unless something was done to introduce democratic measures within the workers' dictatorship in Russia, the Russian Communist Party would suffer a serious set-back. But the democracy Trotsky envisaged was a democratic centralism within the party, because as he argued in his open letter to the party of December 8, 1923, "the party must subordinate to itself its own apparatus without for a moment ceasing to be a centralized organization." See "The Declaration of the Forty-Six" (secret document to the Central Committee of the Russian Communist Party, October 15, 1923), *A Documentary History*, 239-242, and "The New Course" (open letter to a party meeting, December 8, 1923), *A Documentary History*, 243-246. The response from the party came in January 1924 and was contained in the resolution of the Thirteenth Party Conference ("On the Results of the Controversy and on the Petty-Bourgeois Deviation in the Party"). The party responded by denouncing Trotsky for "intellectual anarchism" on questions of party discipline, and Trotsky was eliminated as a serious threat to the party leadership (even before Lenin's death).

[38] As quoted in Laszlo Szamuely, *First Models of the Socialist Economic System* (Budapest: Akademia Kiado, 1974), 94.

[39] Trotsky, "Theses on Industry," 236.

[40] Trotsky argued that "in contrast to capitalist countries, the area of the planning principle is not limited here to the framework of individual trusts or syndicates, but extends to all industry as a whole. Not only that: the state must embrace the interrelationship of industry on the one hand and of agriculture, finance, transport, domestic and foreign trade, on the other." See Trotsky, "Theses on Industry," 236.

[41] Trotsky, "Theses on Industry," 237. It seems here that Trotsky recognized an incentive problem within state industrial organization, but he did not recognize the inherent administrative difficulty in mobilizing enough economic knowledge to coordinate advanced industrial production.

[42] As quoted in Richard Day, *Leon Trotsky*, 82.

[43] As quoted by Richard Day, *Leon Trotsky*, 99.

[44] Trotsky, *The First Five Years*, II: 253, as quoted in Day, *Leon Trotsky*, 58.

[45] Trotsky quoting himself in *Revolution Betrayed*, 30.

[46] *Revolution Betrayed*, 30. Richard Day, however, provides evidence that Trotsky, faced with the failure of the world revolution, supported importation of capital resources to build industry. See *Leon Trotsky*, 69 ff. Day also argues that this is the major difference between Trotsky and Preobrazhensky. See "Trotsky and Preobrazhensky: The Troubled Unity of the Left Opposition," *Studies in Comparative Communism*, Vol. X, n. 1 and 2 (Spring/Summer 1977), 69-86. Robert Bideleux, *Communism and Development*, 102-110, also argues that Trotsky advocated a "least-cost" strategy for economic development. The theory of "Trotskyism" was a fabrication, Bideleux argues; Trotsky was just not the "super-industrializer" he was made out to be. But Trotsky was ambiguous himself, and in many ways contributed to his own defeat.

[47] Day's argument about Trotsky's intellectual commitment to the world division of labor is subject to some questions from a Marxist point of view. Marx was especially concerned with the problems of the division of labor. The social division of labor, in particular, confronted man as an anarchistic and alien will and was an expression of man's estranged and alienated state under commodity production. On the other hand, the division of labor within a capitalist firm was more rational, but despotic within bourgeois society. The goal of Marxist-Leninism, at least in some sense, was to transform the economic life of society from the anarchistic and alien organization of the social division of labor to the more rational division of labor with a consciously regulated, though not despotic, social organization within the proletarian society. This is what underlies, at least intellectually, Zinoviev's criticism of Trotsky and the British loan negotiations at the beginning of 1924. Submitting to the international division of labor would, from a Marxist-Leninist point of view, represent surrendering the "socialist fatherland" to the anarchy and despotism of international capitalism.

[48] Trotsky was forced into exile at the beginning of 1928. In exile he published, along with the aid of his son Leon Sedov, the journal *Byulleten' Oppozitsii*. Trotsky argued that the Soviet socialism had been perverted by centrism. "Centrism," he argued, was "a midpoint between reformism and communism. It does not and cannot have its own line....It zigzags from one extreme to the other....It is wholly bureaucratised and wholly subordinate to the commands of the top of the Stalinist faction." Trotsky's arguments against the Soviet industrialization drive were not that it was wrong—in fact, he argued that the government had been forced to adopt many of his targets. His criticism from the scissors crisis on was that the Soviet leaders were going too slow in building up industry. Throughout the 1920s he criticized Bukharin for his theory of socialism at a snail's pace. The kulaks must be taxed to support industrialization, Trotsky argued. And the grain crisis of 1927-1928 was a result of the kulaks' power—earlier concessions to the kulaks (a position of the right) had

strengthened their power. He thus agreed in principle with some of the Stalinist program against the kulak; disagreement was with the Stalinist bureaucracy. But Trotsky did not oppose some of the most obnoxious manifestations of that bureaucracy unless they were turned against him. During the so-called trial of the Mensheviks in 1931, for example, Trotsky's journal endorsed all the accusations. The "incontrovertible evidence" was that it was not possible to advocate "pure democracy" without advancing towards capitalism and "one cannot move towards capitalism without becoming agents of the international bourgeoisie." See Alec Nove, "A Note on Trotsky and the 'Left' Opposition," *Political Economy and Soviet Socialism* (Boston: George Allen and Unwin, 1979), 44 ff., for an analysis of the articles in the *Byulleten*.

[49] See Erlich, "Preobrazhensky and the Economics of Soviet Industrialization," *Quarterly Journal of Economics* (February 1950) and *The Soviet Industrialization Debate, 1924-1928*. Preobrazhensky's principle writings have been translated into English. See Preobrazhensky's books, *The New Economics* (Oxford: Clarendon Press, 1965[1926]), *From the New Economic Policy to Socialism* (London: New Park Publications, 1973[1922]) and the selection of his principle essays of the twenties in *The Crisis of Soviet Industrialization*, ed. Donald Filtzer (New York: M.E. Sharpe, Inc., 1979).

[50] Erlich, "Preobrazhensky," 58. This is also the thesis implied in Robert Bideleux, *Communism and Development*, 111-127, where he discusses the "socialist forced industrialization strategies" of Preobrazhensky and Stalin.

[51] See James Millar, "A Note on Primitive Accumulation," and Donald Filtzer, "Preobrazhensky and the Problem of Soviet Transition," *Critique*, n. 9 (Spring-Summer 1978), 63-84.

[52] Economists in general, it is now asserted, agree that mathematical growth theory "is a separate subject overlapping rather little with Development Economics." See W.A. Lewis, "The State of Development Economics," *American Economic Review*, Vol. 74, n. 1 (March 1984), 9.

[53] Erlich in *The Soviet Industrialization Debate*, 158, does mention the importance of an integrated capital structure for economic coordination, but he does not go any further in demonstrating this point. Ironically, this view of capital coordination and economic crises is a point of commonality, at least to a substantial degree, between Marxian and Austrian economists. Marx's theory of economic crises, as well as that of Mises or Hayek, depends on the occurrence of disproportionality in the capital structure. The underlying difference in the respective theories lies in what generates the disproportionality. Both theories advocate a nonneutrality view of money, and both emphasize the disequilibrium characteristics of a monetary exchange and

production economy. What causes disproportionality for the Marxist, however, is the very unplanned nature of capitalist production. For the Austrian, on the other hand, the disproportionality results from monetary intervention in the economy. See Peter Rosner, "A Note on the Theories of the Business Cycle by Hilferding and by Hayek," *History of Political Economy*, Vol. 20, n. 2 (Summer 1988), 309-319. Also see Paul Craig Roberts and Matthew A. Stephenson, *Marx's Theory of Exchange, Alienation and Crisis* (New York: Praeger Publishers, 1983[1973]), 48-63, 95-104, and Don Lavoie, "Some Strengths in Marx's Disequilibrium Theory of Money," *Cambridge Journal of Economics*, Vol. 7 (1983), 55-68.

[54] See *The New Economics*, 77 ff. The term, as Preobrazhensky points out, was not his own but employed instead by several other Bolshevik theorists, in particular, V. M. Smirnov (83, fn. 1).

[55] Preobrazhensky, *The New Economics*, 80.

[56] Preobrazhensky, *The New Economics*, 82-83. Thus, the importance of primitive socialist accumulation. "By socialist accumulation," Preobrazhensky argued, "we mean the addition to the functioning means of production of a surplus product which has been created within the constituted socialist economy and which does not find its way into supplementary distribution among the agents of socialist production and the socialist state, but serves for expanded reproduction." On the other hand, primitive socialist accumulation "means accumulation in the hands of the state of material resources mainly lying or partly from sources lying outside the complex of state economy." The concept was of such importance in Preobrazhensky's scheme of socialist construction that he argued that "we can understand nothing of the essence of Soviet economy if we do not discover the central role which is played in this economy by the law of primitive socialist accumulation" (84).

[57] It is this idea that led Bukharin to charge Preobrazhensky with "internal imperialism."

[58] *The New Economics*, 88.

[59] At the beginning of NEP Preobrazhensky offered an interesting analysis of the world situation and socialist construction. By supporting industrial development within Russia the Soviet state (the proletariat dictatorship) would prepare the way for world revolution. "As a result of the rapid recovery of large-scale industry and the creation of favorable material conditions for the proletariat, and with the prospects of an industrial crisis or crises abroad, unemployment, and persecution by bourgeois governments, masses of foreign workers will stream into Russia; this proletarian colonization of Russia will provide support to our developing industry to compensate for Russia's own lack of skilled labor. Not only will the proletariat

as a class grow continuously in number, but its qualitative composition will also improve." See Preobrazhensky, "The Outlook for the New Economic Policy," *The Crisis of Soviet Industrialization* (1921), 10.

[60] Other sources of socialist accumulation would be various taxes on capitalist profits in industry or on kulaks and other traders. Preobrazhensky also, rightfully, viewed inflation as a tax. The difference between the period of primitive capitalist accumulation and primitive socialist accumulation was that socialist accumulation was based not only on the surplus product of petty production but also on the surplus value of capitalist production. The proletarian state arises from out of the monopoly capitalist system, and as such, has within its means the ability to regulate the whole economy rationally—something that capitalism does not possess. One of the principle means for regulating the whole economy was the concentration of banking in the epoch of finance capital and the later nationalization of banks following the proletarian revolution.

[61] Preobrazhensky, *New Economics*, 91.

[62] *The New Economics*, 97; emphasis added.

[63] *New Economics*, 123-124.

[64] This, of course, was the aspect of Preobrazhensky's thought that Stalin used to justify the collectivization.

[65] Filtzer, "Preobrazhensky and the Problem of Soviet Transition," 65.

[66] Filtzer, "Preobrazhensky and the Problem of Soviet Transition," 66.

[67] This, in fact, was the subject of Preobrazhensky's futuristic account, *From the New Economic Policy to Socialism*. In *From the New Economic Policy to Socialism*, 116, Preobrazhensky describes Soviet Europe, that is, the future socialist world, as a combination of German industrial technique and Russian agriculture.

[68] Filtzer, "Preobrazhensky and the Problem of Soviet Transition," 75.

[69] The elimination of the division of knowledge in society rests on the fundamental assumption that "knowledge is potentially accessible to every member of the working class....Without this assumption both the proletarian revolution and socialism are unthinkable, and the struggle of the left against Stalin is reduced to a debate over economic policy." See Filtzer, "Preobrazhensky," 77.

[70] Nove, *An Economic History of the U.S.S.R.*, 126. Evidence that this was, indeed

the case was provided by the debate between Preobrazhensky and Bukharin. As Preobrazhensky states: "Comrade Bukharin agreed that the state economy cannot but utilize the surplus resources of petty production. We have taken these resources up to now, we continue to take them, and inevitably we shall go on taking them. How astonished we are when reference to this completely indubitable fact is seen by Comrade Bukharin as an arrow shot at the 'petty-bourgeois policy of our party.' It is astonishing that Comrade Bukharin has not noticed this contradiction within his own article. Generally speaking, all that I have done is to describe what has happened up to now in our country." See *The New Economics*, 249.

[71] See Shanin, "The Economic Nature of Our Commodity Shortage," (November 1925), and "Questions of the Economic Course," (January 1926), in Spulber, ed., *Foundations of Soviet Strategy for Economic Growth*, 205-220.

[72] Shanin, "Economic Nature of Our Commodity Shortage," 206.

[73] Shanin, "The Economic Nature of Our Commodity Shortage," 207. The quote is from chapter 16 of the second volume of *Capital*. This problem of managing capital investment is the crux of Mises's challenge to the Marxian system. In the absence of a market for the means of production, and thus money prices for capital resources, Mises asked, how is society (the planners) going to decide which economic projects are feasible and which are not.

[74] Shanin, "Questions of the Economic Course," 212.

[75] Shanin, "Questions of the Economic Course," 213.

[76] Shanin's case for international trade was right out of the Ricardian textbook case for comparative advantage. There is a tension here between Marx's condemnation of the social division of labor and Shanin's argument for free trade. There was also a class character, as pointed out in my discussion of Trotsky, associated with the agriculture first argument—one did not want to be seen as a friend of the kulak. It is for these reasons that Shanin's advice fell mainly on deaf ears.

[77] Shanin, "The Economic Nature of Our Commodity Shortage," 210.

[78] "Questions of the Economic Course," 219.

[79] Erlich, *Soviet Industrialization*, 9. It is interesting to keep in mind that during Bukharin's exile from Russia in 1914, he studied economics in Vienna and attended Böhm-Bawerk's famous seminar on economic theory. He later embarked on a serious study of the theories of Leon Walras and Vilfredo Pareto. His economic studies produced the book *The Economic Theory of the Leisure Class* (New York:

Augustus M. Kelley, 1970[1919]), which is a criticism of the Austrian school of economics and other non-Marxian neo-classical schools of economics. Bukharin was well aware of both Böhm-Bawerk's and later Mises's criticism of Marxian economics.

[80] Bukharin's ideas toward NEP are contained in such writings as *Building Up Socialism* (London: Communist Party of Great Britain, 1926) and *Selected Writings on the State and the Transition to Socialism*, Richard Day, ed. (New York: M.E. Sharpe, 1982).

[81] See Nove, "Some Observations on Bukharin and His Ideas," *Political Economy and Soviet Socialism.*

[82] See Bukharin, "Concerning the New Economic Policy and Our Tasks," *Selected Writings*, 188.

[83] Bukharin, "Concerning the New Economic Policy," 189; emphasis added. Bukharin's emphasis on establishing the appropriate incentives can be found throughout his writings during the twenties. Consider the following statement made at the beginning of NEP in 1921 concerning the fall in industrial output during war communism: "the picture in industry came to resemble that in agriculture; the absence of a direct material interest in production, for both individuals and groups, led to a fall in production." See, "The New Course in Economic Policy," *Selected Writings*, 106.

[84] This is what underlies his famous slogan about the peasants enriching themselves. Ambiguity in rules would produce nothing but contradictory expectations, which would deter economic progress. "Consider the fact that the well-to-do upper stratum of the peasantry, along with the middle peasant, who is also striving to join the well-to-do, are both afraid at present to accumulate. A situation has been created in which the peasant is afraid to buy an iron roof and apprehensive that he will be declared a kulak; if he buys a machine, he makes certain that the communists are not watching. Advanced technology has become a conspiracy....The result is that the middle peasant is afraid to improve his farm and lay himself open to forceful administrative pressure; and the poor peasant complains that we are preventing him from selling his labor power to the wealthy peasants, etc." In response, Bukharin argued, "In general and on the whole, we must say to the entire peasantry, to all its different strata: enrich yourselves, accumulate, develop your farms. Only an idiot can say that the poor will always be with us. We must now implement a policy whose result will be the disappearance of the poor." See Bukharin, "Concerning the New Economic Policy," 196-197.

[85] Bukharin, "Notes of an Economist (At the Beginning of a New Economic Year),"

Selected Writings, 308.

[86] Bukharin argued: "If the Trotskyists do not understand that the development of industry depends on the development of agriculture, then the ideologists of petit bourgeois conservatism do not understand that *the development of agriculture depends on industry*, that agriculture, without the tractor, chemical fertilizers, and electrification, is condemned to mark time. They do not understand that it is precisely industry that represents the lever of radical change in agriculture, that without the *leading role* of industry it will be impossible to eliminate rural narrowness, backwardness, barbarism, and poverty." See Bukharin, "Notes of an Economist," 310-311, emphasis in original.

[87] Bukharin, "Notes of an Economist," 316-317.

[88] This was Bukharin's idea of socialism at a "snail's pace" or creeping socialism. See Robert Bideleux, *Communism and Development*, 86-94, for a discussion of Bukharin's theory of creeping socialism. Bukharin basically, after war communism, adopted a Fabian strategy toward socialist construction. The Fabians, as opposed to Marxists, had always argued that socialism would be achieved by small victories, rather than a radical transformation, because of the inherent efficiencies of socialism, that is, socialism would win on economic grounds by outcompeting the capitalists. The shift from the war communism strategy of revolutionary implementation of the Marxian program to the interventionism of NEP explains why Bukharin could argue that "we see that rationalization is a *process*, that the 'planning principle' grows. In a certain sense every state intervention in the spontaneous course of economic life represents a penetration of this rational principle of a 'plan.'" See "Toward of Critique of the Economic Platform of the Opposition (The Lessons of October 1923)," *Selected Writings*, 125.

[89] See Bukharin, *Building Up Socialism*, 52-53, for a criticism of the opposition to the theory of socialism in one country (Trotsky and Zinoviev) and Bukharin's defense of the concept.

[90] It is important to keep in mind, in contrast to Stephen Cohen or Moshe Lewin, that Bukharin's model of market-based socialist construction was a model of the transition, not of socialism. Through the use of the market, Bukharin argued, socialism could be constructed. The ideal of full rationalization of economic life did not collapse with war communism; it was just postponed until the appropriate economic base was established.

[91] Bideleux, *Communism and Development*, 115.

[92] Stalin could not have adopted the Trotsky platform because, as I have argued

above, there was no platform to speak of. What Stalin adopted from Trotsky was an arbitrary and ambiguous strategy toward economic development.

[93] Erlich, "Stalin's Views on Soviet Economic Development," *Continuity and Change in Russian and Soviet Thought*, ed. Ernest Simmons (Cambridge: Harvard University Press, 1955), 85-86. Stalin's economic views during the industrialization debate can be found in J.V. Stalin, *On the Opposition* (Peking: Foreign Language Press, 1974) and *The Foundations of Leninism* (Peking: Foreign Language Press, 1975).

[94] See Stalin, "The Fourteenth Congress of the C.P.S.U.(B.): Reply to the discussion on the Political Report of the Central Committee," (December 23, 1925), *On the Opposition*, 242. Also see Stalin's defense of Bukharin against the left opposition over his "mistake" of telling the peasants to "enrich" themselves, 255 ff.

[95] See Stalin's discussion in "The Results of the Work of the Fourteenth Conference of the R.C.P.(B.)," (May 9, 1925), and "Concerning Questions of Leninism," (January 25, 1926), *On the Opposition*, 206 ff., 317 ff. For a discussion of some of the criticisms raised against Stalin's formulation of socialism in one country, see William Korey, "Zinoviev's Critique of Stalin's Theory of Socialism in One Country, December, 1925 - December, 1926," *American Slavic and East European Review*, Vol. 9 (1950), 255-267.

[96] "The Results of the Work of the Fourteenth Conference of the R.C.P.(B.)," *On the Opposition*, 215.

[97] See Bideleux, *Communism and Development*, 117, where he discusses Stalin's speech at the 1925 Party Congress. Also see Stalin, "Results of the Work of the Fourteenth Congress," *On the Opposition*, 225, where he discusses the importance of the development of the metal industry. "At the present time," Stalin pointed out, "we have an industrial proletariat of about 4,000,000. A small number, of course, but it is something to go with in building socialism and in building up the defense of our country to the terror of the enemies of the proletariat. But we cannot and must not stop here. We need 15-20 million industrial proletarians, we need electrification of the principal regions of our country, the organisation of agriculture on co-operative lines, and a highly developed metal industry. And then we need fear no danger. And then we shall triumph on an international scale" (229).

[98] That Stalin adopted Preobrazhensky's view toward socialist accumulation is questionable. The problem with Preobrazhensky's scheme was that if carried out, it would have destroyed the very town-country relations on which the accumulation was to take place. In this regard, the solution was to collectivize, that is, colonize the peasantry. But Preobrazhensky did not see this "solution" in his work. Erlich, *Soviet*

Industrialization Debate, 177, quotes Preobrazhensky as stating: "Collectivization—this is the crux of the matter! Did I have this prognosis of the collectivization? I did not." Erlich continues by pointing out that Preobrazhensky "was careful not to add that neither did Stalin at the time when the industrialization debate was in full swing. And he was wise not to point out that the decision to collectivize hinged not on superior intellectual perspicacity but on the incomparably higher degree of resolve to crush the opponent with utter disregard of the staggering human costs of the operation."

[99] Nove, *An Economic History of the U.S.S.R.*, 151.

[100] Stalin, "Industrialization of the Country and the Right Deviation," Spulber, ed. *Foundations for Soviet Strategy for Economic Growth*, 266-267. Bukharin, "exposed" as a right deviationist was expelled from the politburo in November 1929.

[101] Many observers argue in the final analysis that the decision to collectivize was justified on military grounds. But as Robert Bideleux, *Communism and Development*, 127, argues, "[T]he Stalinist strategy increased military vulnerability of the U.S.S.R. by squandering manpower on an unprecedented scale and by antagonizing, disrupting and demoralizing large sections of Soviet society."

[102] Isaac Deutscher, *Stalin: A Political Biography*, 2nd ed. (New York: Oxford University Press, 1967[1949]), 228, points out:

> Few important developments in history are so inconspicuous and seem so inconsequential to their contemporaries as did the amazing accumulation of power in the hands of Stalin, which took place while Lenin was still alive. Two years after the end of the civil war Russian society already lived under Stalin's virtual rule, without being aware of the ruler's name. More strangely still, he was voted and moved into all his positions of power by his rivals. There was to be an abundance of somber drama in his later fight against these rivals. But the fight began only after he had firmly gripped all the levers of power and after his opponents, awakening to his role, had tried to move him from his dominant position. But then they found him immovable.

Stalin's rise to power and the fact that none of his rivals seemed to notice what they had done until it was too late reveals one of the two fundamental flaws of Marxist-Leninism, a complete disregard of organizational checks against totalitarian problems associated with the concentration of power in the hands of a few or one person.

[103] Cohen, *Bukharin and the Bolshevik Revolution*, 314-315.

[104] See the debate between Nove and Millar on the "necessity" of Stalin, "A Debate on Collectivization: Was Stalin Really Necessary?," *Problems of Communism* (July-August 1976), 49-62. While Millar makes some cogent points about grain procurement *before* and agricultural production *after* collectivization, I do not believe he understands the political and logical continuity between Lenin and Stalin. The rise of Stalin was "necessary" neither economically (to industrialize the Soviet economy) nor historically (determined), but he was the logical outcome of the Marxian rationalization project—though Stalinism is the unintended and undesirable outcome of that project. Nove, on the other hand, does not seem to understand either the economic issues (that collectivization did not increase productive capacity of the Soviet Union) or the political problems of economic planning and totalitarianism.

[105] Erlich, *Soviet Industrialization Debate*, 174-175.

[106] Erlich, *Soviet Industrialization Debate*, 180. The militaristic attitude also serves to mobilize individuals under the unified power of the state. See James Buchanan, "Markets, States, and the Extent of Morals," *What Should Economists Do?* (Indianapolis: Liberty Press, 1979), 219-229, for a discussion of how the perception of a common enemy can be used by a political regime in the attempt to extend our morals. This, of course, was also the theme of Orwell's constant "wars" in *1984*.

[107] Lavoie, *National Economic Planning: What Is Left?* (Cambridge: Ballinger Publishing, 1985), 230. As Lavoie goes on to say: "The theory of planning was, from its inception, modeled after feudal and militaristic organizations. Elements of the Left tried to transform it into a radical program, to fit into a progressive revolutionary vision. But it doesn't fit. Attempts to implement this theory invariably reveal its true nature. The practice of planning is nothing but the militarization of the economy."

[108] As Alain Besançon writes in discussing the differences in Soviet studies between those who approach the subject from an economic perspective and those who approach it from history, literature, or travel, "There seems to be an unbridgeable gap between this system, conceived through measurement and figures, and the other system, without measurements or figures, which they have come to know through intuition and their own actual experience." See Besancon, "Anatomy of a Spectre," *Survey*, Vol. 25, n. 4 (Autumn 1980), 143.

[109] Erlich, *Soviet Industrialization Debate*, 183.

[110] See Michael Ellman, "Did the Agricultural Surplus Provide the Resources for the Increase in Investment in the U.S.S.R. During the First Five Year Plan?" *Economic Journal*, Vol. 85 (December 1975), 844-864. Ellman argues that the

collectivization did, indeed, work in providing the basis for tremendous industrialization. "Agriculture," he concludes, "made an essential contribution to the development of the Soviet economy during the First Five Year Plan." It (1) provided the industrial sphere with a greatly increased supply of bread, cabbage, and potatoes; (2) supplied industry with a large addition to its labor force; (3) provided exports; (4) contributed to import substitution; and (5) provided a residual economic sector to absorb economic shocks such as bad harvests. Therefore, Ellman concludes calmly that "in this period collectivization appears as a process which enabled the state to increase its inflow of grain, potatoes and vegetables and its stock of urban labour, at the expense of livestock and the rural and urban human population" (858-859). But see the argument contained in Bideleux, *Communism and Development*, 123 ff., where he discusses the betrayal of the peasants. Also see Micha Gisser and Paul Jonas, "Soviet Growth in Absence of Centralized Planning: A Hypothetical Alternative," *Journal of Political Economy*, Vol. 82 (1974), 333-347, who argue that industrialization without 'super-industrializers' would have achieved at least the same growth rates if not more than what actually did happen.

[111] For a criticism of standard development theory see P.T. Bauer, *Dissent on Development* (Cambridge: Harvard University Press, 1976). As Bauer states: "Comprehensive planning has thus not served to raise general living standards anywhere. There is no analytical reason or empirical evidence for expecting it to do so. And in fact both analytical reasoning and empirical evidence point to the opposite conclusion. But the failure of comprehensive planning to raise general living standards has not affected its appeal for politicians, administrators, and intellectuals, that is for actual or potential wielders of power" (92).

[112] An excellent discussion of a capital-using economy is provided by Roger Garrison, "A Subjectivist Theory of a Capital-Using Economy," in Gerald P. O'Driscoll and Mario J. Rizzo, *The Economics of Time and Ignorance* (New York: Basil Blackwell, 1985), 160-187.

[113] Kirzner, *Perception, Opportunity and Profit* (Chicago: University of Chicago Press, 1979), 118.

[114] Kirzner, *Discovery and the Capitalist Process* (Chicago: University of Chicago, 1985), 71-72.

[115] Hayek, *The Constitution of Liberty* (Chicago: University of Chicago Press, 1960), 29.

6

CONCLUSION

Ideas, good and bad, have consequences. Madmen, as well as saints, in authority rely upon the academic scribbler to justify their actions. The momentous history of the Soviet experience with socialism is living proof of the power of ideas to shape human intercourse.

Yet I have argued that traditional accounts of this experience have misunderstood its meaning. In my attempt to understand this experience, I have relied on evidence from the Old Bolsheviks, and have documented their purposes and plans for socioeconomic construction. I then attempted to trace out the consequences, intended and unintended, of the political and economic policy initiatives instituted by the Old Bolsheviks and render them intelligible in light of the economic coordination problem that all societies confront and the problems of political organization. The result of my endeavor, I hope, is not only a better intellectual and economic history of the first decade of Soviet socialism but also a contribution to our understanding of social cooperation.

The lesson of the Soviet experience with socialism should teach us more than we are perhaps willing to learn. The failure of the Marxian experiment in social engineering suggests that attempts to supersede market methods of exchange and production are problematic.[1] The utopian aspiration of a fully emancipated world came into conflict with the political and economic reality of the knowledge and totalitarian problems. The result was an atrocity.

Yet the values of the revolution—the elimination of exploitation by a ruling elite, full participatory democracy, and the flourishing of the human spirit—are all worthy ideals. The paradox of Soviet history is how a revolution in the name of these values could lead to the renunciation of these very same values. To those who hold the virtues of human freedom in reverence, understanding this paradox is more than a mere academic interest. It is of supreme importance to the betterment of the human condition.

Understanding it is not a matter of finding the error or the perversion in application. Human understanding will not improve by looking for a condemnation *in advance* of the Gulag in the texts of either Marx or Lenin. It is rather, as Michael Foucault suggests, "a matter of asking what in those texts could have made the Gulag possible, what might even now continue to justify it, and what makes its intolerable truth still accepted today."[2]

Marxism and Market Processes

Modern socialists may run from the Soviet experience, but they can not hide if they wish to advance the human condition.[3] They must address the Soviet experience head on, and provide an answer to both the knowledge problem and the totalitarian problem. The current crisis on the left is a result of the despair over the totalitarian problem associated with socialist politics and economics.

Marx's *Economic and Philosophic Manuscripts of 1844* may suggest a socialist humanism and his *Critique of Hegel's 'Philosophy of Right'* might supply a potent criticism of the political alienation of bureaucracy, but no convincing answer has come forth to explain why socialism has so consistently succumbed to bureaucratic organization and been so inhumane in its practice. All socialist theorists, be they Marxist, market socialists, or participatory planners, must analyze these problems and offer solutions if they hope to retain their intellectual case for man's emancipation.

The answer, however, may lie in a totally different direction from that which socialist writers have traditionally been willing to accept.[4] Just as Marx's criticism of capitalism implied a positive view of socialism, the critique of socialism offered throughout this study suggests a positive view of a completely free society, one that handles both the knowledge problem and the totalitarian problem.[5]

This is not just idle reflection of pure theory, but a fundamental problem of political and economic praxis. The political economy of Marxism possesses two fundamental errors. It fails to understand the communicative role of the market system and specifically the function of money prices, and second, it relies on a naive understanding of political organization under socialism.

Soviet History and Soviet Reform

Throughout this study I have referred to the current reform movement in Russia. I contend that by understanding the Soviet past we can better understand the possibility of reform and its meaning.[6] Not since war communism have the Soviets sought to realize the Marxian dream of a completely rational economic society so persistently, because that vision is a hopeless and unachievable utopia. The choice of development strategy was certainly shaped by ideology, but the consistent quest to abolish, posthaste, market methods of allocation was abandoned. Instead, a state capitalist system of economic management was instituted.[7] Even at the height of the Stalin regime, no attempt was made to achieve the Marxian utopia of a moneyless, comprehensively planned economic order.

Thus, *perestroika* does not represent a move away from the ideal form of central planning—that move was made over 60 years ago. Rather, it is a movement away from the bureaucratic system of economic management.[8] But is it really? Do Gorbachev or his economic advisers plan to correct the fundamental flaws in the political economy of Marxist-Leninism?

This question has rightfully caught the imagination of Western intellectuals. But their enthusiasm also betrays a certain innocence toward political economy. Neither Gorbachev nor his economic adviser Abel Aganbegyan in any of his written work recognizes the fundamental economic role of market prices. Their reform measures are limited to providing better incentives for workers and planners to accomplish the task of economic management. There may be talk of "radical price reform," but there is no discussion about freely fluctuating prices subject only to the conditions of supply and demand.[9]

The problem, according to the Soviets (as well as many Western observers), with the Soviet system is one of economic incentives, not a problem of generating the knowledge necessary for the coordination of plans. There is no recognition of the fundamental economic problem of mobilizing the bits and pieces of knowledge scattered throughout society in the manner necessary for the coordination of economic activities. And thus their proposals for economic reform do not address the first fundamental problem of Marxist-Leninism.

Politically, Gorbachev has generated tremendous excitement with *glasnost* (public frankness). But he has also engaged in a series of political maneuvers that must startle any political commentator. Within such a short span of time Gorbachev advanced through the politburo to become the general secretary, and then moved to consolidate his power by becoming the president of the government.[10]

Along the way he has purged all opposition. The problem, politically, with the Soviet system is said to have been the vested interests of the old bureaucracy. So Gorbachev had to replace the old guard with a new generation of leaders: capable leaders, public-spirited leaders, good communist comrades. But the problem is not one of good people; it is the structure of the system.

Perhaps Gorbachev's intent is to scrap the entire administrative economic system, and he needs to concentrate his power in order to accomplish that goal.[11] In that case he would perhaps be the most dynamic liberal political figure since Thomas Jefferson. But there does not yet appear to be any evidence to suggest that this is his intention. The planning bureaucracy, though streamlined, is intact. And when a system is *designed* to turn discretionary economic power over to the hands of a few (the bureaucracy), the theory of political economy suggests that we can expect those who have a comparative advantage in exercising discretionary power to rise to the top of the organization. The problem with the Soviet bureaucracy is not one of putting better, more cultured people in power; it is a problem inherent in the operation of the bureaucratic management of economic life.[12] The knowledge problem associated with economic planning leads directly to the totalitarian problem of political control.

Conclusion

If, as Voltaire argued, history is philosophy that teaches us by example, then the lesson of the Soviet experience with socialism should challenge all our preconceptions about economic policy. We must rethink not only the political economy of socialism but also the political economy of interventionism and its attempts at promoting economic development, macroeconomic stability, or microeconomic efficiency. The system of state capitalism (or state socialism) confronts the same fundamental problems of political economy as the Marxian utopia of comprehensive central planning. By forgetting that the Russian Revolution set out to abolish the market system of exchange and production, and to substitute for it a scientific plan, we have failed to grasp the lesson that this experiment offers us. As long as scholars believe that central planning originated not in the effort to abolish market relations during war communism, but with the collectivization and industrialization drive under Stalin, this lesson will lie beyond their grasp.

Our hope today for real improvement in the human condition lies in ideas. It rests in our ability to persuade others of these truths of political economy. The political and economic violence of this century is the result of a false conception of the ability of the human mind to control rationally the entire span of economic life. "The enemies of liberty," states F.A. Hayek, "have always based their arguments on the contention that order in human affairs requires that some should give orders and others obey. Much of the opposition to a system of freedom under general laws arises from the inability to conceive of an effective coordination of human activities without deliberate organization by a commanding intelligence."[13] The *fatal conceit* that captured man's mind and spirit in the socialist movement was a result of falsely priding ourselves on having built the world as if we had designed it, and then blaming ourselves for not having designed it better.[14] But as Zbigniew Brzezinski concludes in *The Grand Failure*:

> The communist phenomenon represents a historical tragedy. Born out of an impatient idealism that rejected the injustice of the status quo, it sought a better and more humane society—but produced mass oppression. It optimistically reflected faith in the power of reason to construct a perfect community. It mobilized the most powerful emotions of love for humanity and of hatred for oppression on behalf of morally motivated social engineering. It thus captivated some of the brightest minds and some of the most idealistic hearts—yet it prompted some of the worst crimes

> of this or any century....No experiment in social reconstruction in all of human history has entailed a higher price in human terms—or has been as wasteful—as humanity's encounter with communism during the twentieth century.[15]

Even now as the failure of communism is generally recognized throughout the world, it is not understood that the nature of the failure does not lie in any lack of humanity to live up to the moral demands of communism. The problem lies in the intellectual failure of an overzealous rationalism that argued for the conscious and planned regulation of economic and social processes. This idea still permeates our thinking concerning economic and social policy and manifests itself in the social ills that continue to haunt civilization. This is not yet understood because we have failed to grasp the full meaning of the political economy of Soviet socialism. As Michael Polanyi, commenting on the state of Soviet studies on the fortieth anniversary of the revolution, said: "So foolish is history."[16]

Notes

[1] As the chapters on NEP and the Industrialization Debate attempted to demonstrate, the political and economic problems of planning are not limited to the complete Marxian experiment of superseding the market. They also plague interventionist economic policies in either their micro- or macro-variant. Thus, the consistency of the Austrian criticism of economic planning from Marxism to Keynesianism to antitrust policy represents sound economic logic rather than "mere" ideology. For a contrasting view point see Geoff Hodgson, *Economics and Institutions* (Philadelphia: University of Pennsylvania Press, 1988). Hodgson argues that while the Austrian argument against central planning represents a devastating critique, the argument does not hold for "mixed systems." The Austrians, Hodgson argues, merely assert dogmatically that such mixed systems face the same problems. But see Israel Kirzner, "The Perils of Regulation," in *Discovery and the Capitalist Process* (University of Chicago Press, 1985), 119 ff., for a discussion of the economic problems that even a benevolent regulator would have to overcome in coordinating economic decisions. Kirzner's argument is, of course, enhanced when public-choice problems are introduced into the analysis.

[2] Foucault, *Power/Knowledge* (New York: Pantheon, 1980), 135.

[3] The running began in many ways with the Western Marxists' rejection of Soviet Marxism. But it also includes the anarcho-socialist critics of the Russian Revolution, such as Emma Goldman and Peter Kropotkin, as well as Marxist critics such as Rosa Luxemburg. See Luxemburg, "The Problem of Dictatorship," from *The Russian Revolution* (1919) reprinted in *Essential Works of Socialism*, ed. Irving Howe (New York: Bantam Books, 1970), 254-257.

Western Marxism usually dates its origins with Georg Lukas's *History and Class Consciousness*. For a general history of Western Marxism see Martin Jay, *Marxism and Totality* (Berkeley: University of California Press, 1984), and for a Western Marxist critique of Soviet Marxism see Herbert Marcuse, *Soviet Marxism* (New York: Columbia University Press, 1958). But although several theorists have come to recognize the manifestation of the totalitarian problem in the Soviet experience, there does not yet appear to be any appreciation of the knowledge problem, and as a result, the totalitarian problem is not really understood.

[4] Jürgen Habermas, perhaps the leading representative of Western Marxism today, has advanced an alternative system of politics in *The Theory of Communicative Action*, Vol. 1 (Boston: Beacon Press, 1984). His vision is that of an ideal speech community model characterized by uncoerced discourse. The openness of such a system of social interaction would, of course, be the opposite of the totalitarian

politics that has traditionally characterized socialist regimes in practice. But the economic model of openness may actually be the opposite of that envisaged by the traditional socialist also. Consider the following statement from Habermas:

> If we assume that the human species maintains itself through the socially coordinated activities of its various members and that this coordination has to be established through communication—and in certain central spheres through communication aimed at reaching agreement—then the reproduction of the species also requires satisfying the conditions of a rationality that is inherent in communicative action. These conditions have become perceptible in the modern period with the *decentration of our understanding* of the world and the differentiation of various universal validity claims (397; emphasis added).

But if the "decentration" of our understanding, that is, the movement of scholarship away from the central control of the state church or state propaganda, has improved our social existence, then perhaps the decentration of economic life, which surely exists within the social world, may also have desirable consequences. Namely, in order to mobilize the knowledge that is necessary to coordinate economic activity beyond the simple relations of a face-to-face society one may have to rely upon decentralized social relations of production that exist in a market. The truly free market may be the only system capable of sustaining advanced industrial production and at the same time maintain man's human dignity and support the flourishing of his human potential.

Along similar lines to Habermas, Hans-Georg Gadamer argues that the philosophical project of phenomenological-hermeneutics demands an openness in human relations that fits well with liberal social philosophy. We cannot, and must not, treat others as mere things. In scholarship, as well as in life, we must be open to the other, respect their claim, and listen to what they say. In other words, we must respect their fundamental humanity, that is, the individual right to their personhood. As Gadamer says, "Openness is necessary. But this openness exists ultimately not only for the person to whom one listens, but rather anyone who listens is fundamentally open. Without this kind of openness to one another there is no genuine human relationship. Belonging together always means being able to listen to one another. When two people understand each other, this does not mean that one person 'understands' the other, in the sense of surveying him. Similarly, to hear and obey someone does not mean that we do blindly what the other desires. We call such a person a slave." See Gadamer, *Truth and Method* (New York: Crossroad, 1985[1965]), 324. Also see Tom G. Palmer, "Gadamer's Hermeneutics and Social Theory," *Critical Review*, Vol. 1, n. 3 (Summer 1987), 91-108, for a discussion of the implications for social theory of Gadamer's philosophy.

[5] See Don Lavoie, *National Economic Planning: What Is Left?* (Cambridge: Ballinger Publishing, 1985b), 211 ff. Lavoie argues: "What was wrong with the Russian revolution was the very direction in which it was trying to go, while all that was wrong with the American one was that its leaders did not carry it far enough in the right direction in which it pointed them. Our task now, therefore, is to complete the American revolution. Unlike the failed Marxist utopia of Planning, the Jeffersonian Market-guided society is a workable ideal, an ideal that when properly understood is far more consistent with the humanitarian and internationalistic values of the Left" (238). Also see Randy Barnett, "Pursuing Justice in a Free Society—Part I: Power vs. Liberty," *Criminal Justice Ethics* (Summer/Fall 1985) and "Pursuing Justice in a Free Society—Part II: Crime Prevention and the Legal Order," *Criminal Justice Ethics* (Winter/Spring 1986).

[6] Moshe Lewin makes a similar argument with reference to reform in any Marxist countries that treat their history as a state secret. "The leaders seem to believe that knowledge of an often tragic past acts as a discouragement for those whose duty it is to build the future; *whereas in fact ignorance of history destroys any forward-looking attitude far more surely than its divulgence and analysis.*" See Lewin, *Lenin's Last Struggle* (New York: Monthly Review Press, 1968), x; emphasis added.

[7] Or state socialist system, whatever term one wants to employ. Both systems are fundamentally the same, the differences lying in degree, not kind. Both substitute political rationales for economic ones in the final coordination of economic activities, though both systems fundamentally rely on the market as the primary coordinating device. For example, within the Soviet planning system managers must rely on the "secondary" market to obtain the minimum resources necessary to even meet the planned targets. Under political capitalism, as in the United States, businessmen use the government to gain and protect their profits (rent-seeking). For example, the long history of antitrust policy in the United States has been one of political intervention to aid political friends. This problem in the antitrust system in the United States has been recognized by economists across the ideological spectrum. See Dominick T. Armentano, *Antitrust and Monopoly: Anatomy of a Policy Failure* (New York: John Wiley and Sons, 1982), and William J. Baumol and Janusz A. Ordover, "The Use of Antitrust to Subvert Competition," *Journal of Law and Economics*, Vol. 28, n. 2 (May 1985), 247-265. Monetary policy in the United States has a similar history. See Gabriel Kolko, *The Triumph of Conservatism* (New York: The Free Press, 1963), 217-254, and Murray N. Rothbard, "The Federal Reserve System as a Cartelization Devise: The Early Years, 1913-1930," in *Money in Crisis*, ed. Barry Siegel (Cambridge: Ballinger Publishing, 1984), 89-136.

[8] This is also the impetus for the reform movement in China. The interventionist

system breaks down, that is, suffers a legitimation crisis, and cannot supply its people with the minimum of economic subsistence. Something must give, and economic liberalization provides a means for the ruling regime to deliver the economic goods. But unless structural reform of the system (political and economic) is instituted, arbitrary intervention will again soon return. In the United States the legitimation crisis of the welfare-warfare state of the 1960s reached its peak during the Carter administration. The "conservative" counterreaction was the so-called Reagan revolution in 1980. But *no* structural changes were instituted, so by 1982, the revolution was dead—trapped by the tyranny of the status quo. Gorbachev faces a similar problem. The problem is not reform, but restructuring a rent-seeking society.

[9] See Gertrude Schroeder, "Anatomy of Gorbachev's Economic Reform," *Soviet Economy*, Vol. 3, n. 3 (July-September 1987), 219-241.

[10] Gorbachev only came to Moscow in 1978, after 20 years of service as a local politician in Stavropol, to assume the post as the party secretary for agriculture. In 1980 he became a full member of the politburo, and by 1984 he was second secretary to Konstantin Chernenko. On March 11, 1985, he became the general secretary. See Ed Hewett, *Reforming the Soviet Economy* (Washington, DC: Brookings Institution, 1988), 303 ff., for a general discussion of Gorbachev's rise to power and the reforms he has proposed.

In a series of adroit political moves, Gorbachev consolidated his leadership of the Soviet Union in late September and early October of 1988. His maneuvering was reminiscent of the "cold political rituals of the past." On September 30 Andrei Gromyko stepped down from the presidency and on October 1, 1988, Gorbachev assumed that post. In addition, Yegor K. Ligachev, the number two man in the Soviet Union, but an opponent of Gorbachev's, was "demoted" to the head of the party's commission on agriculture. See *The New York Times* (Sunday, October 2, 1988), 1, 10, for various reports on these events and excerpts from Gorbachev's speech accepting the presidency.

[11] It may also be that he wishes to decentralize political control, and to do that he had first to *centralize* political control. This, of course, is the great paradox in the Soviet reform effort. See Zbigniew Brzezinski, *The Grand Failure* (New York: Scribner's, 1989) and William Odom, "How Far Can Economic and Social Change Go in the Soviet Union?" in *Gorbachev's New Thinking*, ed. Ronald Liebowitz (Cambridge: Ballinger Publishing, 1988), 69-95.

[12] For an analysis of economic bureaucracy see Ludwig von Mises, *Bureaucracy* (New York: Arlington House, 1969[1944]) and Gordon Tullock, *The Politics of Bureaucracy* (Lantham, MD: University Publications of America, 1987[1965]).

[13] Hayek, *The Constitution of Liberty* (Chicago: University of Chicago Press, 1960), 159.

[14] Hayek, *The Fatal Conceit*, ed. W. W. Bartley, III (Chicago: University of Chicago Press, 1988), 67.

[15] Brzezinski, *The Grand Failure*, 231, 238.

[16] Polanyi, "The Foolishness of History," *Encounter*, Vol. IX, n. 5 (November 1957), 37.

References

Primary and Secondary Sources on the Soviet Union

Abalkin, Leonid. *The Strategy of Economic Development in the USSR*. Moscow: Progress Publishers, 1987.

"A Day in the Life of the Soviet Union," *Time*, 26 October 1987.

Aganbegyan, Abel. *The Economic Challenge of Perestroika*, Bloomington: University of Indiana Press, 1988.

Anderson, Gary. "Profits from Power: The Soviet Economy as a Mercantilist State." *The Freeman*, December 1988.

Avrich, Paul. *Kronstadt 1921*. New York: W.W. Norton & Co., 1970.

Bandera, V.N., "Market Orientation of State Enterprises During NEP." *Soviet Studies* 22, n. 1 (July 1970).

Barfield, Rodney. "Lenin's Utopianism: *State and Revolution*." *Slavic Review* 30, n. 1 (March 1971).

Baron, Samuel. "Between Marx and Lenin: George Plekhanov." In *Revisionism: Essays on the History of Marxist Ideas*, edited by Leopold Labedz. New York: Praeger Publishers, 1962.

Baron, Samuel. *Plekhanov: The Father of Russian Marxism*. Stanford, CA: Stanford University Press, 1963.

Baykov, Alexander. *The Development of the Soviet Economic System*. New York: Macmillan, 1948.

Berdyaev, Nicolas. *The Origin of Russia Communism*. 1937. Ann Arbor: University of Michigan Press, 1972.

Bergson, Abram. "Perestroika Before and After." *The New York Times Book Review*, May 1988.

Berliner, Joseph. "Marxism and the Soviet Economy." *Problems of Communism* 12, n. 5 (September/October 1964).

Besançon, Alain "Anatomy of a Spectre." *Survey* 25, n. 4 (Autumn 1980).

_____. *The Rise of the Gulag: Intellectual Origins of Leninism* . New York: Continuum, 1981.

Bettelheim, Charles. *Class Struggles in the USSR, 1917-1923*. New York: Monthly Review Press, 1976.

Bideleux, Robert. *Communism and Development*. New York: Methuen, 1985.

Bohlen, Celestine. "The Soviet Economy." *The Economist*, 9 April 1988.

Boettke, Peter J. "The Political and Economic Challenges of Perestroika." *Market Process* 8 (1990).

_____. "Soviet Admissions." *The Freeman*, February 1990.

_____. "The Russian Experiment with Pure Communism." *Critical Review* 2, n. 4 (Fall 1988).

Bonnell, Victoria E. "Moscow: A View from Below." *Dissent*, Summer 1989.

Brutzkus, Boris. *Economic Planning in Soviet Russia.* 1935. Westport, CT: Hyperion Press, 1982.

Bukharin, Nikolai I. *The Economic Theory of The Leisure Class.* 1919. New York: Augustus M. Kelley, 1970.

_____. "The Economics of the Transition Period." 1920. In *The Politics and Economics of the Transition Period*, edited by Kenneth J. Tarbuck. Boston: Routledge & Kegan Paul, 1979.

_____. *Building Up Socialism.* London: Communist Party of Great Britain, 1926.

_____. "Organized Mismanagement in Modern Society." *Pravda*, 30 June 1929. In *Essential Works of Socialism*, edited by Irving Howe. New York: Bantam Book, 1970.

Bukharin, Nikolai I. *Selected Writings on the State and the Transition to Socialism.* Edited by Richard Day. New York: M.E. Sharpe, 1982.

Bukharin, Nikolai I., and Preobrazhensky E. *The ABC of Communism.* 1919. Ann Arbor: University of Michigan Press, 1966.

Carr, E. H. *The Soviet Impact on the Western World.* New York: Macmillan, 1947.

_____. *The Bolshevik Revolution 1917-1923*, 3 vols. 1951-1953. New York: W. W. Norton, 1980.

Chamberlin, William Henry. *The Russian Revolution.* 2 vols. 1935. Princeton: Princeton University Press, 1987.

Cohen, Stephen. *Bukharin and the Bolshevik Revolution: A Political Biography, 1888-1938.* 1971. New York: Oxford University Press, 1980.

_____. "In Praise of War Communism." In *Revolution and Politics in Russia*, edited by Alexander and Janet Rabinowitch. Bloomington: Indiana University Press, 1972.

_____. *Rethinking the Soviet Experience.* New York: Oxford University Press, 1985.

Conquest, Robert. *The Harvest of Sorrow.* New York: Oxford University Press, 1986.

The Current Digest of the Soviet Press

Daniels, Robert V. *The Conscience of Revolution.* Cambridge, MA: Harvard University Press, 1960.

Daniels, Robert V., ed. *A Documentary History of Communism.* 2 vols. New York: Vintage Books, 1960.

Day, Richard. *Leon Trotsky and the Politics of Economic Isolation.* New York: Cambridge University Press, 1973.

_____. "Trotsky and Preobrazhensky: The Troubled Unity of the Left Opposition." *Studies in Comparative Communism* 10, n. 1 and 2 (Spring/Summer

1977).
Deutscher, Issac. *Stalin: A Political Biography*. 2d ed. 1949. New York: Oxford University Press, 1967.
Deutscher, Issac, and King, David. *The Great Purges*. New York: Basil Blackwell, 1984.
Djilas, Miloran. *The New Class*. New York: Praeger, 1957.
Dobb, Maurice. *Soviet Economic Development Since 1917*. New York: International Publishers, 1948.
_____. "The Discussion of the 'Twenties on Planning and Economic Growth.'" In *Papers on Capitalism, Development and Planning*. London: Routledge and Kegan Paul, 1967.
Dolot, Miron. *Execution by Hunger*. New York: W.W. Norton and Co., 1985.
Domar, Evsey. *Essays in the Theory of Economic Growth*. New York: Oxford University Press, 1957.
Draper, Theodore. "Soviet Reformers: From Lenin to Gorbachev." *Dissent*, Summer 1987.
Ellman, Michael. "Did the Agricultural Surplus Provide the Resources for the Increase in Investment in the USSR During the First Five Year Plan?" *Economic Journal* 85 (December 1975).
Erlich, Alexander. "Preobrazhensky and the Economics of Soviet Industrialization." *Quarterly Journal of Economics*, February 1950.
_____. "Stalin's Views on Soviet Economic Development." In *Continuity and Change in Russian and Soviet Thought*, edited by Ernest Simmons. Cambridge, MA: Harvard University Press, 1955.
_____. *The Soviet Industrialization Debate, 1924-1928*. Cambridge, MA: Harvard University Press, 1960.
Evans, Alfred. "Rereading Lenin's *State and Revolution*." *Slavic Review* 46, n. 1 (Spring 1987).
Filtzer, Donald. "Preobrazhensky and the Problem of Soviet Transition." *Critique*, no. 9 (Spring/Summer 1978).
Gerschenkron, Alexander. *Economic Backwardness in Historical Perspective*. Cambridge, MA: Harvard University Press, 1962.
_____. "History of Economic Doctrines and Economic History." *American Economic Review* 59, n. 2 (May 1969).
Gisser, Micha, and Jonas, Paul. "Soviet Growth in Absence of Centralized Planning: A Hypothetical Alternative." *Journal of Political Economy* 82 (1974).
Goldman, Emma. *My Disillusionment in Russia*. New York: Doubleday, Page and Co., 1923.
_____. *My Further Disillusionment in Russia*. New York: Doubleday, Page and Co., 1924.
Goldman, Marshall. *Gorbachev's Challenge*. New York: Norton, 1987.
Goldman, Marshall, and Goldman, Merle. "Soviet and Chinese Economic Reform."

Foreign Affairs 66, n. 3 (1988).
Gorbachev's Economic Plans. 2 vols. Washington DC: Joint Economic Committee, 1987.
Gorbachev, Mikhail. *Perestroika: New Thinking for Our Country and the World*. New York: Harper and Row, 1987.
_____. "Revolution's Road from 1917 to Now." *The New York Times*, 3 November 1987.
Gregory, Paul, and Stuart, Robert. *Soviet Economic Structure and Performance*. 2d ed. New York: Harper and Row, 1981.
Gubsky, N. "Economic Law in Soviet Russia." *Economic Journal* 37 (June 1927).
Heller, Mikhail, and Neckrich, Aleksandr. *Utopia in Power: The History of the Soviet Union from 1917 to the Present*. New York: Summit Books, 1986.
Hewett, Ed. *Reforming the Soviet Economy*. Washington, DC: Brookings Institution, 1988.
History of the Communist Party of the Soviet Union. 1939. San Francisco: Proletarian Publishers, 1976.
Holman, Paul. "'War Communism,' or the Besieger Besieged: A Study of Lenin's Social and Political Objectives from 1918 to 1921." Ph.D. dissertation, Georgetown University, 1973.
Jasny, Naum. *Soviet Economists of the Twenties*. New York: Cambridge University Press, 1972.
Kaufman, Adam. "The Origin of 'The Political Economy of Socialism.'" *Soviet Studies* 4, n. 3 (January 1953).
Kennedy, Paul. "What Gorbachev is Up Against: The Problem Isn't in the System—It is the System." *The Atlantic Monthly*, June 1987.
Koestler, Arthur. *Darkness At Noon*. New York: Macmillan, 1941.
Korey, William. "Zinoviev's Critique of Stalin's Theory of Socialism in One Country, December 1925-December 1926." *American Slavic and East European Review* 9 (1950).
Laquer, Walter. *The Fate of the Revolution*.1967. New York: Macmillan, 1987.
Lawton, Lancelot. *An Economic History of Soviet Russia*. 2 vols. London: Macmillan, 1932.
Leites, K. *Recent Economic Developments in Russia*. New York: Oxford University Press, 1922.
Lenin, V.I. *Collected Works*. 45 vols. Moscow: Progress Publishers, 1977.
Lenin, V.I.; Bukharin, Nikolai; and Rutgers, S. J. *The New Policies of Soviet Russia*. Chicago: Charles H. Kerr, 1921.
Lewin, Moshe. *Lenin's Last Struggle*. New York: Monthly Review Press, 1968.
_____. *Political Undercurrents in Soviet Economic Debates*. Princeton: Princeton University Press, 1974.
_____. *Russian Peasants and Soviet Power*. 1968. New York: Norton, 1975.
_____. *The Making of the Soviet System*. New York: Pantheon Books, 1985.

Lih, Lars. "Bolshevik *Razverstka* and War Communism." *Slavic Review* 45, n. 4 (Winter 1986).

Linz, Susan. "Reorganization and Reform in the Soviet Economy." *Comparative Economic Studies* 29, n. 4 (Winter 1987).

Lovell, David. *From Marx to Lenin: An Evaluation of Marx's Responsibility for Soviet Authoritarianism.* New York: Cambridge University Press, 1984.

Luxemburg, Rosa. "The Problem of Dictatorship." In *The Russian Revolution.* 1919. *Essential Works of Socialism,* edited by Irving Howe. New York: Bantam Books, 1970.

Malle, Silvana. *The Economic Organization of War Communism, 1918-1921.* New York: Cambridge University Press, 1985.

Marcuse, Herbert. *Soviet Marxism.* New York: Columbia University Press, 1958.

Medvedev, Roy. *Let History Judge: The Origins and Consequences of Stalinism.* Rev. and exp. ed. New York: Columbia University Press, 1989.

Millar, James. "A Note on Primitive Accumulation in Marx and Preobrazhensky." *Soviet Studies* 30, n. 3 (July 1978).

Nove, Alec, and Millar, J. "A Debate on Collectivization: Was Stalin Really Necessary?" *Problems of Communism,* July-August 1976.

Nove, Alec. *An Economic History of the U.S.S.R.* 1969. New York: Penguin Books, 1984.

_____. "A Note on Trotsky and the 'Left' Opposition." In *Political Economy and Soviet Socialism.* Boston: George Allen and Unwin, 1979.

_____. Introduction to *The Economic Challenge of Perestroika,* by Abel Aganbegyan. Bloomington: Indiana University Press, 1988.

_____. "New Light on Trotsky's Economic Views." *Slavic Review* 40, n. 1 Spring 1981.

_____. "Some Observations on Bukharin and His Ideas." In *Political Economy and Soviet Socialism.* Boston: George Allen & Unwin, 1979.

_____. *The Economics of Feasible Socialism.* London: George Allen and Unwin, 1983.

Nutter, G. Warren. *The Growth of Industrial Production in the Soviet Union.* Princeton: Princeton University Press, 1962.

Ofer, Gur. "Soviet Economic Growth: 1928-1985." *Journal of Economic Literature* 25 (December 1987).

Pasternak, Boris. *Doctor Zhivago.* New York: Signet Books, 1958.

Pasvolsky, Leo. *The Economics of Communism: With Special Reference to Russia's Experiment.* New York: Macmillan Co., 1921.

Polan, A.J. *Lenin and the End of Politics.* Berkeley: University of California Press, 1984.

Polanyi, Michael. *The Contempt of Freedom: The Russian Experiment and After.* London: Watts & Co., 1940.

_____. "The Foolishness of History." *Encounter* 9, n. 5 (November 1957).

_____. "Toward a Theory of Conspicuous Production." *Soviet Survey,* October/December, 1960.

Preobrazhensky, E. *From the New Economic Policy to Socialism*. 1922. London: New Park Publications, 1973.

_____. *The New Economics*. 1926. Oxford: Clarendon Press, 1965.

_____. "The Outlook for the New Economic Policy." In *The Crisis of Soviet Industrialization*, edited by Donald Filtzer. New York: M.E. Sharpe, Inc. 1979.

Prokopovitch, S.N. *The Economic Conditions of Soviet Russia*. London: P.S. King and Sons, 1924.

Rabinowitch, Alexander. *The Bolsheviks Come to Power*. New York: Norton, 1978.

Raleigh, Donald., ed. "The Soviet Union in the 1920s: A Roundtable." *Soviet Studies in History* 28, n. 2 (Fall 1989).

_____, ed. "Glasnost and the October Revolution." *Soviet Studies in History* 27, n. 2 (Fall 1988).

_____, ed. "Glasnost and Soviet Historians." *Soviet Studies in History* 27, n. 1 (Spring 1988).

Ransome, Arthur. *Russia in 1919*. New York: B.W. Huebsch, 1919.

Reed, John. *Ten Days That Shook the World*. 1919. New York: Penguin Books, 1985.

Remington, Thomas. *Building Socialism in Bolshevik Russia: Ideology and Industrial Organization, 1917-1921*. Pittsburgh: University of Pittsburgh Press, 1984.

Rizzi, Bruno. *The Bureaucratization of the World*. 1939. New York: The Free Press, 1985.

Roberts, Paul Craig. "The Soviet Economy: A Hopeless Cause?" *Reason*, July 1988.

_____. *Alienation and the Soviet Economy*. Albuquerque: University of New Mexico Press, 1971.

Roberts, Paul Craig, and Stephenson, Matthew. *Marx's Theory of Exchange, Alienation and Crisis*. 1973. New York: Praeger, 1983.

Sakwa, Richard. *Soviet Communists in Power: A Study of Moscow During the Civil War, 1918-21*. New York: St. Martin's Press, 1988.

_____. "The Commune State in Moscow in 1918." *Slavic Review*, Fall/Winter 1987.

Schroeder, Gertrude. "Anatomy of Gorbachev's Economic Reform." *Soviet Economy* 3, n. 3 (July-September 1987).

Selyunin, Vasil. "Sources." *Novy Mir*, n. 5 (May 1988). In *The Current Digest of the Soviet Press* 40, n. 40 (1988).

Serge, Victor. *Memoirs of a Revolutionary, 1901-1941*. New York: Oxford University Press, 1963.

Shadwell, Arthur. *The Breakdown of Socialism*. Boston: Little, Brown and Company, 1927.

Shenin, Lev. "Questions of the Economic Course." 1926. In *Foundations of Soviet*

Strategy for Economic Growth, edited by Nicolas Spulber. Bloomington, Indiana University Press, 1964.

_____. "The Economic Nature of Our Commodity Shortage." 1925. In *Foundations of Soviet Strategy for Economic Growth.* Bloomington: Indiana University Press, 1964.

Shapiro, Leonard. *The Communist Party of the Soviet Union.* 1960. New York: Vintage, 1971.

Shmelev, Nikolai. "Advances and Debts." *Novy Mir*, n. 6 (1987). In *Problems of Economics*, February 1988.

Shmelev, Nikolai, and Popov, Vladimir. *The Turning Point: Revitalizing the Soviet Economy.* New York: Doubleday, 1989.

Smith, Keith, ed. *Soviet Industrialization and Soviet Maturity.* New York: Routledge & Kegan Paul, 1986.

Smolinsky, Leon. "Planning Without Theory, 1917-1967." *Survey*, July 1967.

Solzhenitsyn, Aleksandr I. *The Gulag Archipelago.* 3 vols. New York: Harper and Row, 1974.

Spulber, Nicolas, ed. *Foundations of Soviet Strategy for Economic Growth.* Bloomington: Indiana University Press, 1964.

Stalin, J.V. *On the Opposition.* Peking: Foreign Language Press, 1974.

_____. *The Foundations of Leninism.* Peking: Foreign Language Press, 1975.

Stojanovic, Svetozar. "Marx and the Bolshevization of Marxism." *Praxis International* 6, n. 4 (January 1987).

Szamuely, Laszalo. *First Models of the Socialist Economic Systems: Principles and Theories.* Budapest: Akademiai Kiado, 1974.

Treml, Vladimir. "Interaction of Economic Thought and Economic Policy in the Soviet Union." *History of Political Economy* 1, n. 1 (Spring 1969).

Trotsky, Leon. *Our Revolution.* 1906. In *Extracts in Marxism: Key Documents (1879-1906)*, edited by Neil Harding. New York: Cambridge University Press, 1983.

_____. *Permanent Revolution.* Edited by Neil Harding. Calcutta: Atawar Rahman, 1947.

_____. *The History of the Russian Revolution.* 3 vols. Edited by Neil Harding. Calcutta: Atawar Rahman, 1947.

_____. *The Revolution Betrayed: What is the Soviet Union and Where is it Going?* 1937. New York: Pathfinder Press, 1972.

_____. *The Trotsky Papers.* London: Mouton and Co., 1964.

Webb, Sidney and Beatrice. *Soviet Communism: A New Civilisation?* New York: Scribner's, 1938.

Wells, H.G. *Russia in the Shadows.* New York: George H. Doran, 1921.

Wilson, Edmund. *To The Finland Station.* New York: Doubleday and Co., 1940.

Zaleski, Eugene. *Planning for Economic Growth in the Soviet Union, 1918-1932.*

1962. Chapel Hill: University of North Carolina Press, 1971.
_____. *Stalinist Planning for Economic Growth*. London: Macmillan, 1980.

Politics, Philosophy, Economics, and the History of Ideas

Armentano, Dominick T. *Antitrust and Monopoly: Anatomy of a Policy Failure*. New York: John Wiley and Sons, 1982.
_____. "A Critique of Neoclassical and Austrian Monopoly Theory." In *New Directions in Austrian Economics*, edited by Louis M. Spadaro. Kansas City: Sheed, Andrews and McMeel, 1978.
Arndt, H.W. "Economic Development: A Semantic History." *Economic Development and Cultural Change* 29 (April 1981).
Arnold, N. Scott. "Marx and Disequilibrium in Market Socialist Relations of Production." *Economics and Philosophy* 3 (1987).
Baker, John. *Science and the Planned State*. New York: Macmillan, 1945.
Bakunin, Michael. *Bakunin on Anarchism*. Edited by Sam Dolgoff. Montreal: Black Rose Books, 1980.
Balabkins, Nicholas. "*Der Zukunftsstaat*: Carl Ballod's Vision of a Leisure Oriented Socialism." *History of Political Economy* 10, n. 2 (Summer 1978).
Barnett, Randy. "Pursuing Justice in a Free Society—Part I: Power vs. Liberty." *Criminal Justice Ethics*, Summer-Fall 1985.
_____. "Pursing Justice in a Free Society—Part II: Crime Prevention and the Legal Order." *Criminal Justice Ethics*, Winter-Spring 1986.
Barry, Norman, and others. *Hayek's "Serfdom" Revisited*. London: Institute for Economic Affairs, 1984.
Bauer, P.T. *Dissent on Development*. Cambridge: Harvard University Press, 1976.
Baumol, William J., and Ordover, Janusz A. "The Use of Antitrust to Subvert Competition." *Journal of Law and Economics* 28, n. 2 (May 1985).
Bergson, Abram. "Socialist Economics." In *A Survey of Contemporary Economics*, edited by Howard Ellis. Philadelphia: Blakiston Company, 1948.
Bernstein, Richard. *Beyond Objectivism and Relativism*. Philadelphia: University of Pennsylvania Press, 1983.
Böhm-Bawerk, Eugen V. "The Historical vs. The Deductive Method in Political Economy." *Annals of the American Academy of Political Science* 1 (July 1890).
Boettke, Peter J. "Evolution and Economics: Austrians as Institutionalists." *Research in the History of Economic Thought and Methodology* 6 (1989).
_____. "Austrian Institutionalism: A Reply." *Research in the History of Economic Thought and Methodology* 6 (1989).
_____. "Comment on 'Information and the Coase Theorems.'" *Journal of Economic Perspectives* 3, n. 2 (Spring 1989).
_____. "Story-Telling and the Human Sciences." *Market Process* 6, n. 2 (Fall 1988).
_____."Virginia Political Economy: A View from Vienna." *Market Process* 5, n.

2 (Fall 1987).

Boettke, Peter; Horwitz, Steve; and Prychitko, David. "Beyond Equilibrium Economics: Reflections on the Uniqueness of the Austrian Tradition." *Market Process* 4, n. 2 (Fall 1986).

Bottomore, Tom. "Is Rivalry Rational?" *Critical Review* 1, n. 1 (Winter 1986-87).

Brennan, Geoffrey, and Buchanan, James. *The Reason of Rules*. New York: Cambridge University Press, 1985.

Buchanan, James. *Freedom in Constitutional Contract*. College Station: Texas A&M Press, 1977.

_____. *Liberty, Market and State*. New York: New York University Press, 1985.

_____. "Markets, States, and the Extent of Morals." In *What Should Economists Do?* Indianapolis: Liberty Press, 1979.

_____. "The Constitution of Economic Policy." *American Economic Review* 77, n. 3 (June 1987).

_____. "The Economic Theory of Politics." *Challenge*, March/April 1988.

_____. *The Limits of Liberty: Between Anarchy and Leviathan*. Chicago: University of Chicago Press, 1975.

_____. "The Relevance of Constitutional Strategy." *The Cato Journal* 6, n. 2 (Fall 1986).

Buchanan, James, and Brennan, Geoffrey. "Is Public Choice Immoral?" *Virginia Law Review* 74, n. 2 (March 1988).

Buchanan, James, and Tullock, Gordon. *The Calculus of Consent*. Ann Arbor: University of Michigan Press, 1962.

Caldwell, Bruce. "Austrians and Institutionalists: The Historical Origins of their Shared Characteristics." *Research in the History of Economic Thought and Methodology* 6 (1989).

Chakravarty, Sukhamoy, "The State of Development Economics." *The Manchester School of Economics and Social Studies*, June 1987.

Coase, Ronald. "The Nature of the Firm." *Economica*, November 1937.

Demsetz, Harold. "Barriers to Entry." *American Economic Review* 72, n. 1 (March 1982).

Ebeling, Richard. "Expectations and Expectations Formation in Mises's Theory of the Market Process." *Market Process* 6, n. 1 (Spring 1988).

_____. "Cooperation in Anonymity." *Critical Review* 1, n. 4 (Fall 1987).

_____. "The Roots of Austrian Economics." *Market Process* 5, n. 2 (Fall 1987).

Ekelund, Robert, and Tollison, Robert. *Economics*. 2d ed. Boston: Scott, Foresman and Co., 1988.

Estrin, Saul, and Holmes, Peter. "Uncertainty, Efficiency and Economic Planning in Keynesian Economics." *Journal of Post-Keynesian Economics* 7, n. 4 (Summer 1985).

Finer, Herman. *Road to Reaction*. 1945. Chicago: Quadrangle Books, 1963.

Foucault, Michael. *Power/Knowledge*. New York: Pantheon, 1980.

Friedman, Milton. *Capitalism and Freedom*. 1962. Chicago: University of Chicago Press, 1982.

Gadamer, Hans-Georg. *Truth and Method*. 1960. New York: Crossroad, 1985.

Garrison, Roger. "A Subjectivist Theory of a Capital-Using Economy." In *The Economics of Time and Ignorance*, by Gerald P. O'Driscoll and Mario J. Rizzo. New York: Basil Blackwell, 1985.

_____"Time and Money: The Universals of Macroeconomic Theorizing." *Journal of Macroeconomics* 6, n. 2 (Spring 1984).

Habermas, Jürgen. "Ideologies and Society in the Post War World." In *Habermas: Autonomy & Solidarity*. Edited by Peter Dews. London: New Left Books, 1986.

_____. *The Theory of Communicative Action: Reason and the Rationalization of Society*. Translated by Thomas McCarthy. Boston: Beacon Press, 1984.

Hayek, F.A. *The Fatal Conceit*. Edited by W.W. Bartley, III. Chicago: University of Chicago Press, 1989.

_____. *Law, Legislation and Liberty*. 3 vols. Chicago: University of Chicago Press, 1973-1979.

_____. *New Studies in Philosophy, Politics, Economics and the History of Ideas*. Chicago: University of Chicago, 1978.

_____. *Studies in Philosophy, Politics and Economics*. 1967. Chicago: University of Chicago Press, 1980.

_____. *The Constitution of Liberty*. Chicago: University of Chicago Press, 1960.

_____. *The Counter-Revolution of Science: Studies on the Abuse of Reason*. 1952. Indianapolis: Liberty Press, 1979.

_____. *Individualism and Economic Order*. 1948. Chicago: University of Chicago Press, 1980.

_____. *The Road to Serfdom*. 1944. Chicago: University of Chicago Press, 1976.

_____. Foreword to *Economic Planning in Soviet Russia*, by Boris Brutzkus. 1935. Westport, CT: Hyperion Press, 1981.

_____, ed. *Collectivist Economic Planning*. 1920. New York: August M. Kelley, 1975.

Held, David. *An Introduction to Critical Theory*. Berkeley: University of California Press, 1980.

Higgs, Robert. *Crisis and Leviathan*. New York: Oxford University Press, 1987.

High, Jack. "Is Economics Independent of Ethics?" *Reason Papers* 10 (Spring 1985).

Hilferding, Rudolf. *Finance Capital: A Study of the Latest Phase of Capitalist Development*. 1910. London: Routledge & Kegan Paul, 1985.

Hodgson, Geoff. *Economics and Institutions*. Philadelphia: University of Pennsylvania Press, 1988.

Hoff, Trygve J.B. *Economic Calculation in the Socialist Society*. 1949. Indianapolis: Liberty Press, 1981.

Hunt, R.N. Carew. *The Theory and Practice of Communism*. 1950. Baltimore:

Penguin Books, 1969.

Husserl, Edmund. *The Crisis of European Sciences and Transcendental Phenomenology*. Evanston: Northwestern University Press, 1970.

Jay, Martin. *Marxism and Totality: The Adventures of a Concept from Lukacs to Habermas*. Berkeley: University of California, 1984.

Johnson, Paul. *Modern Times*. New York: Harper and Row, 1983.

Kalt, Joseph, and Zupan, Mark. "Capture and Ideology in the Economic Theory of Politics." *American Economic Review* 74, n. 3 (1984).

Keizer, William. "Two Forgotten Articles by Ludwig von Mises on the Rationality of Socialist Economic Calculation." *Review of Austrian Economics* 1 (1987).

Keynes, John M. *Collected Works*. New York: Cambridge University Press, 1980.

_____. *The General Theory of Employment, Interest and Money*. 1936. New York: Harcourt Brace Jovanovich, 1964.

Kirzner, Israel M. "The Economic Calculation Debate: Lessons for Austrians." *Review of Austrian Economics* 2 (1988).

_____. *Discovery and the Capitalist Process*. Chicago: University of Chicago Press, 1985.

_____. *Perception, Opportunity and Profit*. Chicago: University of Chicago Press, 1979.

_____. *Competition and Entrepreneurship*. Chicago: University of Chicago Press, 1973.

Kolakowski, Leszek. *Main Currents of Marxism*. 3 vols. 1978. New York: Oxford University Press, 1985.

Kolko, Gabriel. *The Triumph of Conservatism*. New York: The Free Press, 1963.

Konrad, George, and Szelenyi, Ivan. *The Intellectuals on the Road to Class Power*. New York: Harcourt Brace Jovanovich, 1979.

Kuhn, Thomas. *The Structure of Scientific Revolution*. 1962. Chicago: University of Chicago Press, 1970.

Lachmann, Ludwig. *The Market as an Economic Process*. New York: Basil Blackwell, 1986.

_____. *Capital, Expectations and the Market Process*. Edited and introduced by Walter E. Grinder. Kansas City: Sheed, Andrews and McMeel, 1977.

_____. *Macro-Economic Thinking and the Market Economy*. 1973. Menlo Park, CA: Institute for Humane Studies, 1978.

_____. *The Legacy of Max Weber*. Berkeley: Glendessary Press, 1971.

Lange, Oskar. *On the Economic Theory of Socialism*. Edited by Benjamin Lippincott. 1939. New York: Augustus M. Kelley, 1970.

Lavoie, Don. "A Political Philosophy for the Market Process." *Market Process* 6, n. 2 (Fall 1988).

_____. "The Accounting of Interpretations and the Interpretation of Accounts: The Communicative Function of 'The Language Business.'" *Accounting Organizations and Society* 12, n. 6 (1987).

_____. "Political and Economic Illusions of Socialism." *Critical Review* 1, n. 1, (Winter 1986-87).

_____. "The Market as a Procedure for Discovery and Conveyance of Inarticulate Knowledge." *Comparative Economic Studies*, Spring 1986.

_____. *National Economic Planning: What is Left?* Cambridge, MA: Ballinger Press, 1985.

_____. *Rivalry and Central Planning: The Socialist Calculation Debate Reconsidered.* New York: Cambridge University Press, 1985.

_____. "Some Strengths in Marx's Disequilibrium Theory of Money." *Cambridge Journal of Economics* 7 (1983).

Lerner, Abba. *The Economics of Control.* New York: Macmillan, 1944.

Lewis, W.A. "The State of Development Economics." *American Economic Review* 74, n. 1 (March 1984).

Lutz, Mark A., and Lux, Kenneth. *Humanistic Economics: The New Challenge.* New York: The Bootstrap Press, 1988.

Madison, G.B. "Hayek and the Interpretive Turn." *Critical Review* 3, n. 2 (Spring 1989).

_____. "Hermeneutical Integrity: A Guide for the Perplexed." *Market Process* 6, n. 1 (Spring 1988).

Marx, Karl. *Capital: A Critique of Political Economy.* Vol. 1. 1867. New York: The Modern Library, 1906.

_____. *Capital: A Critique of Political Economy.* Vol. 3. 1894. New York: Vintage Books, 1981.

_____. *Critique of Hegel's 'Philosophy of Right.'* New York: Cambridge University Press, 1970.

_____. *Economic and Philosophical Manuscripts of 1844.* Moscow: Progress Publishers, 1977.

_____. *Grundisse.* New York: Vintage Books, 1973.

_____. *The Poverty of Philosophy.* Moscow: Progress Publishers, 1978.

Marx, Karl, and Engels, Frederick. *Selected Works.* 3 vols. Moscow: Progress Publishers, 1969.

McCarthy, Thomas. *The Critical Theory of Jürgen Habermas.* Cambridge. MA: The MIT Press, 1985.

McCloskey, Donald. *The Rhetoric of Economics.* Madison: University of Wisconsin Press, 1985.

Menger, Carl. *Principles of Economics.* 1871. New York: New York University Press, 1981.

_____. *Investigations into the Method of the Social Sciences with Special Reference to Economics.* 1884. New York: New York University Press, 1985.

Merkle, Judith. *Management and Ideology.* Berkeley: University of California Press, 1980.

Mises, Ludwig von. *Theory and History: An Interpretation of Social and Economic Evolution.* 1957. Auburn, AL: Ludwig von Mises Institute, 1985.

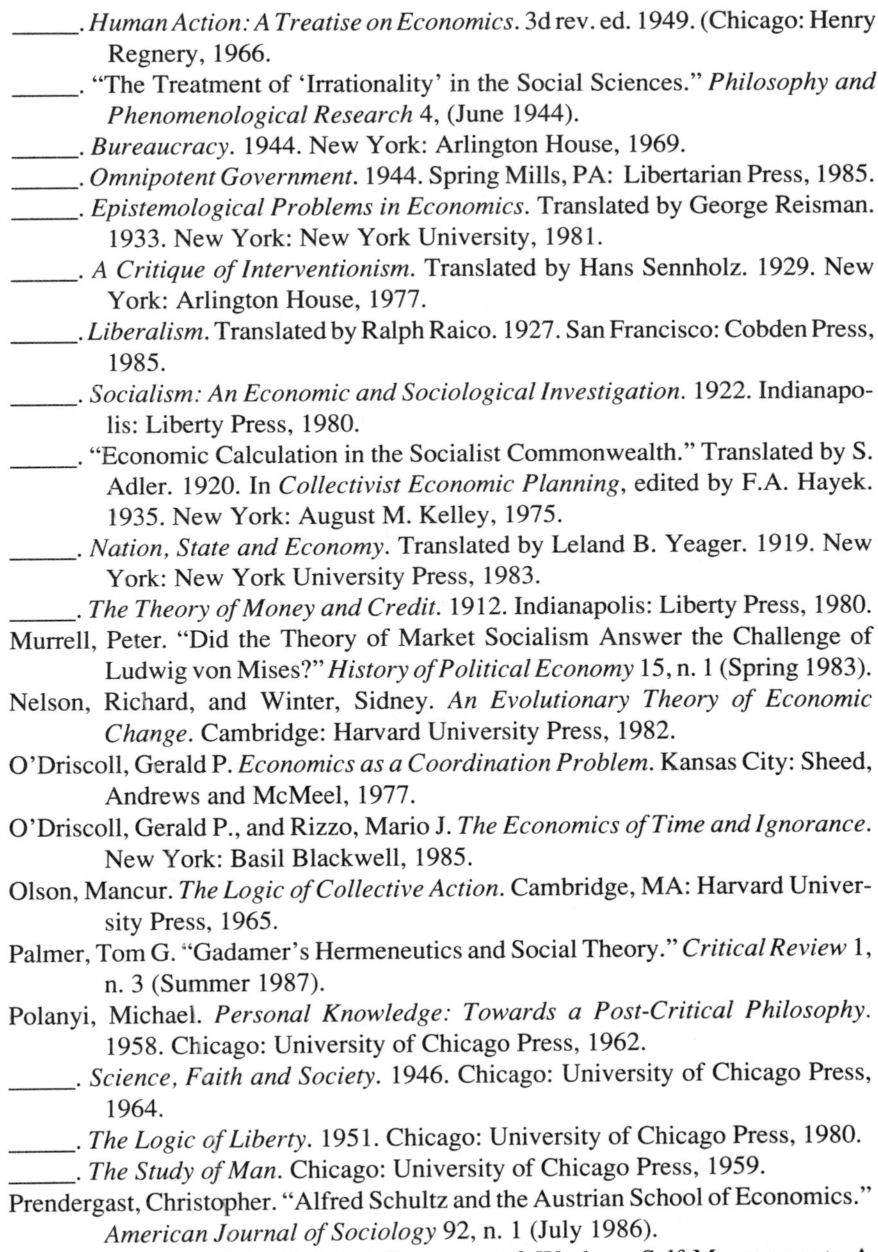

_____. *Human Action: A Treatise on Economics*. 3d rev. ed. 1949. (Chicago: Henry Regnery, 1966.

_____. "The Treatment of 'Irrationality' in the Social Sciences." *Philosophy and Phenomenological Research* 4, (June 1944).

_____. *Bureaucracy*. 1944. New York: Arlington House, 1969.

_____. *Omnipotent Government*. 1944. Spring Mills, PA: Libertarian Press, 1985.

_____. *Epistemological Problems in Economics*. Translated by George Reisman. 1933. New York: New York University, 1981.

_____. *A Critique of Interventionism*. Translated by Hans Sennholz. 1929. New York: Arlington House, 1977.

_____. *Liberalism*. Translated by Ralph Raico. 1927. San Francisco: Cobden Press, 1985.

_____. *Socialism: An Economic and Sociological Investigation*. 1922. Indianapolis: Liberty Press, 1980.

_____. "Economic Calculation in the Socialist Commonwealth." Translated by S. Adler. 1920. In *Collectivist Economic Planning*, edited by F.A. Hayek. 1935. New York: August M. Kelley, 1975.

_____. *Nation, State and Economy*. Translated by Leland B. Yeager. 1919. New York: New York University Press, 1983.

_____. *The Theory of Money and Credit*. 1912. Indianapolis: Liberty Press, 1980.

Murrell, Peter. "Did the Theory of Market Socialism Answer the Challenge of Ludwig von Mises?" *History of Political Economy* 15, n. 1 (Spring 1983).

Nelson, Richard, and Winter, Sidney. *An Evolutionary Theory of Economic Change*. Cambridge: Harvard University Press, 1982.

O'Driscoll, Gerald P. *Economics as a Coordination Problem*. Kansas City: Sheed, Andrews and McMeel, 1977.

O'Driscoll, Gerald P., and Rizzo, Mario J. *The Economics of Time and Ignorance*. New York: Basil Blackwell, 1985.

Olson, Mancur. *The Logic of Collective Action*. Cambridge, MA: Harvard University Press, 1965.

Palmer, Tom G. "Gadamer's Hermeneutics and Social Theory." *Critical Review* 1, n. 3 (Summer 1987).

Polanyi, Michael. *Personal Knowledge: Towards a Post-Critical Philosophy*. 1958. Chicago: University of Chicago Press, 1962.

_____. *Science, Faith and Society*. 1946. Chicago: University of Chicago Press, 1964.

_____. *The Logic of Liberty*. 1951. Chicago: University of Chicago Press, 1980.

_____. *The Study of Man*. Chicago: University of Chicago Press, 1959.

Prendergast, Christopher. "Alfred Schultz and the Austrian School of Economics." *American Journal of Sociology* 92, n. 1 (July 1986).

Prychitko, David. "The Political Economy of Workers Self-Management: A Market Process Critique." Ph.D. dissertation, George Mason University, 1989.

_____. "Marxism and Decentralized Socialism." *Critical Review* 2, n. 4 (Fall 1988).
Rathenau, Walter. *In Days to Come*. New York: Alfred A. Knopf, 1921.
Reese, David. "Alienation, Exchange and Economic Calculation: An Inquiry into the Nature and Possibility of Marxian Socialism." 2d rev. ed. 1985. Ph.D. dissertation, Virginia Polytechnic Institute, 1980.
Rosner, Peter. "A Note on the Theories of the Business Cycle by Hilferding and by Hayek." *History of Political Economy* 20, n. 2 (Summer 1988).
Rothbard, Murray N. "The Federal Reserve as a Cartelization Device: The Early Years, 1913-1930." In *Money in Crisis*, edited by Barry N. Siegel. Cambridge, MA: Ballinger Publishing, 1984.
_____. "Ludwig von Mises and Economic Calculation Under Socialism." In *The Economics of Ludwig von Mises*, edited by Lawrence Moss. Kansas City: Sheed and Ward, Inc., 1976.
_____. *Power and Market*. 1970. Kansas City: Sheed, Andrews and McMeel, 1977.
_____. *Man, Economy and State: A Treatise on Economic Principles*. 2 vols. 1962. Los Angeles: Nash Publishing, 1970.
Rüstow, Alexander. *Freedom and Domination: A Historical Critique of Civilization*. 1950-1957. Princeton, NJ: Princeton University Press, 1980.
Rutland, Peter. *The Myth of the Plan*. LaSalle, IL: Open Court, 1985.
Selgin, George. *The Theory of Free Banking*. Totawa, NJ: Rowman and Littlefield, 1988.
Selucky, Radoslav. *Marxism, Socialism, Freedom*. New York: St. Martin's Press, 1979.
Smith, Barry, and Grassl, Wolfgang, eds. *Austrian Economics: Historical and Philosophical Background*. New York: New York University Press, 1986.
Solow, Robert M. "Growth Theory and After." *American Economic Review* 78, n. 3 (June 1988).
Sowell, Thomas. *Knowledge and Decisions*. New York: Basic Books, 1980.
Tamedly, Elisabeth. *Socialism and International Economic Order*. Caldwell, Idaho: Caxton, Printers, 1969.
Taylor, Michael. *Anarchy and Cooperation*. New York: John Wiley and Sons, 1976.
Tullock, Gordon. *The Politics of Bureaucracy*. 1965. Lantham, MD: University Publications of America, 1987.
_____. *The Social Dilemma*. Blacksburg, VA: Center for the Study of Public Choice, 1974.
Vanberg, Viktor. "Individual Choice and Institutional Constraints." *Analyse & Kritik* 8 (1986).
Vaughn, Karen. "Economic Calculation Under Socialism: The Austrian Contribution." *Economic Inquiry* 18 (1980).
Vorhies, W. Francis. "Marx and Mises on Money: The Monetary Theories of Two Opposing Political Economies." Ph.D. dissertation, University of Colorado, 1982.

Wagner, Richard. "James M. Buchanan: Constitutional Political Economist," *Regulation*, n. 1 (1987).

Walicki, Andrzej. "Karl Marx as Philosopher of Freedom." *Critical Review* 2, n. 4 (Fall 1988).

Wanless, P.T. "The Efficiency of Central Planning: A Perspective from 'Markets vs Hierarchies.'" *Scottish Journal of Political Economy*, February 1987.

Weber, Max. *Economy and Society*. 2 vols. Edited by Guenther Roth and Claus Wittich. 1922. Berkeley: University of California Press, 1978.

Weinscheimer, Joel. *Gadamer's Hermeneutics*. New Haven: Yale University Press, 1985.

Weinstein, James. *The Corporate Ideal in the Liberal State, 1900-1918*. Boston: Beacon Press, 1968.

Wieser, Friedrich. *Social Economics*. 1927. New York: Augustus M. Kelley, 1967.

Williamson, Oliver E. *Markets and Hierarchies*. New York: The Free Press, 1975.

Wittfogel, Karl. *Oriental Despotism: A Comparative Study of Total Power*. 1957. New Haven: Yale University Press, 1964.

Wooton, Barbara. *Freedom under Planning*. Chapel Hill: University of North Carolina Press, 1945.

Index